BEIJING

YAN'AN

NSHUI

XI'AN

NANJING

WUHAN

DAO COUNTY

HONG KONG

DESERT

River

Han River

Yangtze River

REMEMBRANCE

記憶

DOMESTIC EDITION

MW00532876

SPARKS

SPARKS

CHINA'S UNDERGROUND HISTORIANS AND THEIR BATTLE FOR THE FUTURE

IAN JOHNSON

A COUNCIL ON FOREIGN RELATIONS BOOK

OXFORD
UNIVERSITY PRESS

Oxford University Press is a department of the University of Oxford. It furthers
the University's objective of excellence in research, scholarship, and education
by publishing worldwide. Oxford is a registered trade mark of Oxford University
Press in the UK and certain other countries.

Published in the United States of America by Oxford University Press
198 Madison Avenue, New York, NY 10016, United States of America.

© Ian Johnson 2023

CIP data is on file at the Library of Congress
ISBN 978–0–19–757550–5

Printed by Sheridan Books, Inc., United States of America

Even in the darkest of times we have the right to expect some illumination, and that such illumination may well come less from theories and concepts than from the uncertain, flickering, and often weak light that some men and women, in their lives and their works, will kindle under almost all circumstances and shed over the time span that was given them on earth—this conviction is the inarticulate background against which these profiles were drawn. Eyes so used to darkness as ours will hardly be able to tell whether their light was the light of a candle or that of the blazing sun.

—Hannah Arendt, Men in Dark Times

Contents

Preface

If one trend unites people around the world, it is how history has become a battleground for the present. Perhaps it has always been this way; humans have no sure way of predicting the future and so search the past for clues. Certainly if we look at our own countries today, whether in Africa, the Americas, Asia, or Europe, history remains contentious. Americans still debate the centrality of slavery to US history. Europeans grapple with the brutality of their colonial empires. Young Africans unearth buried memories of the Biafra War and the apartheid era. One could easily include Japan, Singapore, India, and dozens of other countries where events that occurred before most people were born have become crucial to shaping the future.

Nowhere is this idea more potent than in China, which for millennia has been obsessed with the interplay of past, present, and future. For modern Chinese leaders, history legitimizes their hold on power: history chose the Communist Party to save China; history has determined that it has succeeded; and history blesses its continued hold on power. This history is of course written by the party, which employs vast armies of scribes, filmmakers, videographers, and journalists to push its version of events, both recent and ancient. Through them, the party controls textbooks, movies, television documentaries, popular history magazines, and even video war games.

But a growing number of Chinese see the Party's monopoly of the past as the root of their country's current authoritarian malaise. In their eyes, too many people misunderstand the problems of the present because the Communist Party misrepresents the past. If people grow up thinking that the Chinese Communist Party played a key role in fighting the Japanese, took power thanks to popular support, and is led by a group of meritocratic patriots, then they will have a hard time understanding why China is prone to purges, corruption, and political violence.

This conviction of history's importance drives a movement of underground historians that has slowly gained momentum over the past twenty years. I call these people historians as a shorthand for a broad group of some of China's brightest minds: university professors, independent filmmakers, underground magazine publishers, novelists, artists, and journalists. Some are outsiders and might be thought of as dissidents, but most have one foot inside the system, where they continue to hold jobs, own property, and raise families. All of them risk their careers, their futures, and prison to publish samizdat journals, banned books, and independent documentary films. They seek to correct the Party's misrepresentation of the past and change their country's slide toward ever-stronger authoritarian control. And they do so by using new technologies to publicize the regime's failings, often linking current problems to debacles of the past.

Concern for the past has a long tradition in China. Just as today, emperors and kings employed official scribes to write authorized histories. But unofficial historians also existed. They wrote books known by the evocative name *yeshi*, which literally means "wild" history. Today, the more common term is *minjian lishi*, or grassroots history, something akin to what in other countries is called counter-history. I use all of these terms but gravitate toward "underground history," because it captures the asymmetrical battle between a few, often beleaguered citizens opposing an overwhelmingly strong state.

China's underground historians are inspired by another idea from traditional Chinese culture: the *jianghu*. The term literally means "rivers and lakes," and refers to the untamed world beyond the realm of courts and commercial centers. In ancient times, these areas served as hideouts for bandits, brigands, and others who lived outside the law but whose lives were governed by strict codes of honor. *Jianghu* can mean an anarchic free-for-all, but more often it evokes a world of sworn brother-and-sisterhoods committed to righteousness and justice.

Jianghu historians have existed since the start of the People's Republic but have taken on crucial importance in recent years. For the first fifty years of Communist rule, they were isolated individuals. Their articles, artworks, and books were quickly seized by the security apparatus. Few even knew they had existed.

But over the past two decades, underground historians have melded into a nation-wide network that has survived repeated crackdowns. Through digital technologies, such as PDF-style magazines and books, downloadable videos, and other creative ways of bypassing censorship, they have produced easily shared works that challenge the Communist Party's whitewashing of history. These technologies and stratagems have allowed China's counter-historians to withstand intense government pressure. Many work quietly and privately when faced with suppression but jump into the public fray when the government is overwhelmed by mass unrest, such as during the Covid lockdowns between 2020 and 2022.

Maybe just as important, digital technologies have allowed young Chinese to rediscover a lineage of like-minded people stretching back to the pre-history of the People's Republic. Books that were once available only in foreign research libraries are now easily shared. Stories of heroic resistance fighters are documented on films that are circulated on the sly. Taboo topics such as the murder of hundreds of thousands of small landowners in the early years of the People's Republic are explored in deeply researched historical fiction. Artworks fill in the visual gaps of heavily censored historical archives. Where critical thinkers in China once felt alone, they now share a powerful collective memory of Chinese people standing up to authoritarian rule. This, perhaps more than anything, inspires them to wave after wave of action, despite harsh lockdowns and lockups.

This book documents the rise of China's underground history movement over the past twenty years, its continued importance during the rule of Xi Jinping, and its implications for China's future.

After studying in China from 1984 to 1985 and working as a newspaper correspondent between 1994 and 2001, I returned to Beijing between 2008 and 2020, focusing on longer-form journalism and books. I visited underground historians at home and in the field. I read their books, watched their films, and followed their battles on social media. I saw their room for action shrink. Often it seemed they were simply able to endure, but when protests erupted, they were quick to join and influence public movements. I realized this was a story not just of survival but of active resistance.

It made the most sense to me to let this account unfold on three planes. One is China's geographic space. This allows us to trace the slowly shifting center of gravity of China's counter-history movement, from the cradle of the revolution in China's northwest to its cultural heartland, its arc southward to Hong Kong, and in recent years, its use of overseas allies and digital platforms.

This movement in space is matched by a shift in time: from past to present to future. These three eras that make up this book's three main sections. In the first, which takes place mainly in China's northwest, we focus on the Communist Party's founding and its early years of running China, a time of intense violence that left deep scars on the national psyche. In the second section, the present, we see efforts over the first decade of Xi Jinping's rule to challenge the Communist Party's domination of history. And in the third section, the future, we see events such as uprisings in Hong Kong and ethnic minority regions, and the Covid protests in the 2020s, that indicate future trends and potential for political change.

The third level, and the one that binds the sections together, are the personal stories and works of underground historians. The reader will encounter many people and stories throughout this book, but two accompany us from start to finish. One is the documentary filmmaker Ai Xiaoming, whom we meet in chapter 2 as she makes a film about a notorious labor camp in China's northwest. The other is the journalist Jiang Xue, who uncovers her family's tragedy and researches the story of a 1960 student-run journal called *Spark*—the inspiration for this book's title.

Ai and Jiang's stories are woven around half a dozen other important figures from today's counter-history movement, such as the filmmaker Hu Jie, the samizdat history journal editor Wu Di, and the historian Tan Hecheng. The context for these people and their work is centered in three chapters—5, 6, and 7—that focus on the role of history for the Communist Party before Xi, Xi's own use of history to cement his rule, and finally how digital technologies have allowed China's truth-tellers to challenge the party's misuse of history.

Separating these main chapters are a dozen vignettes that I have labeled "memories." These are based on the early 20th century concept of "places of memory," which are physical locations where history resonates—battlefields, museums, or execution grounds. In recent decades, new technologies have broadened this concept to "theaters of memory," which include movies, books, and the media. Based on this idea, I offer sketches of people, places, and iconic works of counter-memory that demonstrate the ambition of China's underground historians: to write a new history of contemporary China in order to change their country's future.

Some readers will immediately wonder what this means for China's trajectory. I venture some ideas in the conclusion, but let me mention two broad points worth keeping in mind as you start reading.

First, this book introduces us to people inside China who are worth knowing in their own right. They are making works of scope and ambition equal to the great writers or filmmakers of the Cold War—people like Solzhenitsyn, Kundera, or Forman. It is worth remembering that many of these giants of Eastern Bloc intellectual life had a limited impact on their countries at the time that they lived and worked there. It was only when these countries began sliding into economic stagnation that ordinary people began to seek out alternative ways of understanding the past as a way to assess the future.

Already, it is clear that China's boom years have passed. Many young people have responded with passivity. They talk of dropping out—"lying flat" or "running" away are two popular terms.

But this alienation can quickly flip to action. The Covid lockdowns are one especially relevant example, when many people in this book, such as Ai Xiaoming and Jiang Xue, were thrust back to public prominence after years of being marginalized. On New Year's Day 2023, for example, Jiang Xue published one of her most popular articles. It came a few weeks after a wave of protests across China helped convince the government to drop its draconian policy of pandemic lockdowns. She described the year of lockdowns and frustration, and the cry for freedom that young people had made, drawing on her wide reading of Eastern European intellectuals to make sense of China's ossified political system. The article was quickly posted and reposted on Telegram, WeChat, and other platforms. On WeChat it was blocked, but various versions of it were reposted repeatedly.

It is not difficult to construct similar scenarios that push her and others back to the fore, where their years of research and writing for smaller audiences help the broader public make sense of their world better than government propaganda. And when this happens, it would make sense for us to be familiar with these people, their history, and their network.

The second broad point is that these lives and works challenge conventional wisdom on how to view China.

After leaving China in 2020, I spent an academic year in Singapore at the Asia Research Institute and then started working at the Council on Foreign Relations in New York. From these perches, I could see firsthand the way that China has been written off by many of our opinion and political leaders. The dominant way of understanding

China is that nothing happens there except a string of dystopian horrors: surveillance, cultural genocide, mindless nationalism.

As someone who lived in China for more than twenty years and has written extensively about religious and political persecution, I know that these problems are real. But so, too, are Chinese people with other visions. Critical voices have not been silenced. This raises questions about how to engage with China, something I explore in the conclusion.

The persistence of China's counter-history movement also challenges assumptions about the Communist Party's ability to dominate society. As you will see in the coming pages, the party does not always win. Despite overwhelming odds, people inside China today still publish works and make films that challenge authority. Their ideas continue to spread, and when problems in society reach a critical point, people look to them for ways of thinking about their country. This is why Xi Jinping has made control of history one of his signature policies—because he recognizes counter-history as an existential threat.

The most important question that this book raises is whether amnesia really has triumphed. Change in any society usually comes through small numbers of people who start as outsiders. Sometimes, with dedication and persistence, their ideas become mainstream. Saying that "most people" don't know or care is a truism applicable to almost every society in every era: what matters is that many Chinese do know and continue to battle, today, to change their society.

This book is not a simple story about right triumphing over might. Just as China's surveillance state has not won, neither have its opponents. This is why I opened the book with Hannah Arendt's statement about people in dark times. We are so accustomed to the darkness of today's China that any sort of light blinds us. Perhaps by the end of this book you can decide if these people are flickering candles or blazing suns—or if they are both: flickering today but blazing tomorrow.

PART I

The Past

Nothing but earth is strong enough to withstand the burden of memory.

—Maaza Mengiste, *The Shadow King*

I

Introduction

The Landscape of Memory

The tectonic plates that form China have left it a checkerboard of mountains and rivers and memories. From the south, the Indian plate pushes up into the Eurasian, creating the Himalayas and the vast Tibetan plateau that almost cuts the country off from the rest of the continent. Rippling outward are smaller mountain ranges that ebb and flow toward the Pacific Ocean, like deep swells heaving through the land. Slicing through them are broad rivers that race down from the western highlands toward the coast. For travelers wandering among these ranges and rivers, it is hard to travel 200 miles in any direction without hitting a natural barrier. While many people think of China as remarkably homogenous—thousands of years of continuous history and more than 91 percent of the population ethnically Chinese—its geography has created another reality: a patchwork of distinct regions, each with its own climate, languages, and history.

As if to wrest control over this fierce land, Chinese people have turned it into a canvas. For thousands of years they have etched their thoughts on the rocks and cliffs that loom over them. In a country with such a long history, every hill and vale are home to myths, legends, battles, massacres, and acts of beauty. For millennia, travelers visited these sites and set down their thoughts, which were carved directly onto nearby rocks and cliffs—ancient graffiti that brings the past to life.

Some of it carried more than a note of boasting: I came here because I am a person of distinction who has read history, and I have a few ideas of my own. But a few choice words could also add to the site's meaning, helping future travelers think about history in a new way—a dialogue with the past, inscribed in stone. This might seem strange to modern sensibilities, where nature is seen as authentic only when it is pristine. And indeed, some Chinese writers have protested at the proliferation of inscriptions. But for most people this was rarely seen as a violation. Instead, this conversation with the past enhanced the present.

One of the most famous of these places is a red-colored cliff overlooking the Yangtze River upstream from the modern city of Wuhan. In the winter of 208 to 209 a decisive naval battle was fought there between the military dictator Cao Cao and an alliance of smaller states resisting his invasion. The underdogs won through ingenious tactics, making the Battle of Red Cliff similar to how many Westerners remember the Battle of Trafalgar: a brilliant victory that thwarted a tyrant's ambitions (even if these, like all stories, are more complex).

The location was immediately famous but only became a pilgrimage site after a visit there eight hundred years later, in 1082, by Su Dongpo. Su was one of China's most famous poets and an official in the emperor's court. He had been banished for opposing authoritarian-style reforms and was living in poverty on a farm near Red Cliff. Out on a boat one night with a friend, drinking wine and thinking of their fate, Su floated past the cliff. Back home, he wrote a poem about his impressions. Later that year he returned and wrote another.

The two works are among the best known in Chinese literature, not only for their language but because Su was also a famous calligrapher. Miraculously, one of the poems that Su himself wrote out with a brush on paper survived the centuries and is now one of the most precious pieces of art in the Chinese world. In the years that followed Su's visit, a shrine was built at the cliff to honor him, as well as a pavilion to house copies of his calligraphy.

The language and calligraphy made the poem famous, but it was the context that has inspired people over the past millennium. Su was commenting on what even then was an ancient battle. But his message was eternal: the righteous person's resistance to tyranny.

Readers would think of Cao Cao's defeat and how good had won, but also how Su himself was in exile for standing up for right. This universal idea—that in the end right triumphs over might—is central to the poem, as is the exile's sorrow, struggle, and loneliness. Without directly mentioning any of this, Su makes clear his tumultuous emotions—but also how he is unbroken.

In the first of the two odes, Su describes his unease: floating down the mighty Yangtze River "over ten thousand acres of dissolving surface which streamed to the horizon, as though we were leaning on the void with the winds for chariot, on a journey none knew where." He mentions the constellations in the night sky, making clear that he is facing the capital, his poem an entreaty to the emperor.

As they drift, Su's friend laments their fate. While towering figures like Cao Cao made history here, the two of them are nothing more than "infinitesimal grains in the vast sea, mourning the passing of our instant of life." Su disagrees.

> Do you really understand the water and the moon? Here, it flows by yet never leaves us; over there, it waxes and wanes without growing or shrinking. If you look at things as changing, then Heaven and Earth do not last for even the blink of an eye. If you look at them as unchanging, then I along with everything am eternal.

For people of Su's era, the political reading was clear. The court was pursuing gains that would not last—flowing away like the river's water, waning like the moon's vanishing light—while his values were permanent, just as the river never runs dry and the moon never really disappears. The critique was so obvious that when Su sent a copy of his "Ode to Red Cliff" to a friend, he added the warning: "With so many painful and dangerous matters . . . bury this away deeply and do not bring it forth."

Today, Red Cliff is one of China's most popular tourist attractions. Instead of floating on a skiff, people come on giant tour boats, some to gorge on all-you-can-eat buffets, others for no reason other than it is on every Chinese person's bucket list.

But many make the journey in order to commune with Su. They think of him in exile, of Cao Cao's arrogance, of the innumerable painters over the centuries who depicted Su against the cliff, seeing in his resistance their own struggles against authority. And all of this washes over these visitors: some grow silent, or nod to each other, or murmur a line from the poem when they see the promontory and gaze at two enormous characters that admirers of Su in the 15th century engraved on the sheer cliff face and painted in the brightest vermillion: *chi bi*, red cliff.

In China, history and morality are inseparable. The traditional task of historians was to judge dynasties and rulers, partly to set the record straight but also to comment on current affairs. That is why it was impossible for Su's allusion to Cao Cao to have been simply a memory of an ancient battle. The only possible reading was to see it as a critique of the current emperor—a tyrant who would be defeated just like Cao Cao.

This view of history makes it both judge and juror, collecting testimony and deciding a ruler's fate. If a dynasty was ruling correctly, then history viewed it well and its rule continued. But if the government ignored the people, if it neglected the affairs of state, if disasters accumulated, then history would judge it poorly and withdraw the "mandate of heaven." This led to two responses: rule justly in hopes that this would bring success and the benediction of history. Or crush dissent so no one would question your right to rule.

This made history a risky enterprise. Most famously, China's first great historian, Sima Qian, was castrated and then jailed by the emperor for sticking up for an official who was scapegoated at court. After his release, Sima Qian was expected to commit suicide rather than live with his mutilation and disgrace. Instead, he chose to live because he was determined to finish writing the first large-scale history of China. That set the template for writing history: it was a sacred calling worth any sacrifice.

One way to try to evade these dangers was to don the hat of the travel writer, visit a famous place, and describe it. The best of these works, like Su's poem, was not simply coded political criticism but explorations of the timelessness of nature, the folly of life, and the turmoil of the present.

Over the centuries, these places of memory have come to blanket China's physical and mental landscape. For all the invasions, foreign rulers, and divisions, it is still a land of memory stretching thousands of years. Part of this is because the physical past is so present in China. In Western terms, it would be as if the civilizations of ancient Greece, Rome, and Europe used the same script and cultural references and were transplanted into one geographic area about the size of the United States. Imagine if educated Americans could read ancient Greek, Latin, and most modern European languages, and that many key artifacts of these eras—the Acropolis, the Colosseum, Chartres, and Auschwitz—were located within the continental United States.

And that over the millennia famous writers—from Homer to Austen, Sappho to Hemingway—had lived on this same piece of land, visited these sites, and left their thoughts inscribed in stone.

This puts an unbearable burden on current-day events in China. Almost every site in the country is layered over something ancient. Bygones are never bygones. But this heavy past also empowers people. If the ancients dared to speak out, then how can I not? And if I face trials and tribulations, and if I am censored and humiliated, then wasn't this always the case? And isn't it also true that in the end people remember Sima Qian and Su Dongpo, and not the leaders who maimed and slandered them?

The difference between then and now is scale. The People's Republic of China is not just another chapter in China's long history. The modern bureaucratic state reaches deep into the recesses of the country in ways unimaginable in premodern times. This change occurred over the course of the 20th century, especially after the Communist Party took power in 1949. Founded in 1921, the party went through nearly three decades of purges, putsches, and campaigns to root out dissent before assuming power. By the time the Communists defeated the Kuomintang, or Nationalist, Party after four years of civil war, they were a highly disciplined force led by a core of battle-hardened veterans committed to violent revolution. They were able to push through policy with a singularity of focus that changed almost every aspect of Chinese society—some for the better but almost all of it ordered from above and based on coercion.

Central to the tumult was the character of Mao Zedong, the party's leader: enigmatic, mercurial, ruthless, and at times deluded first among equals. Under Mao's nearly thirty-year rule, China went through a series of political campaigns that led to the breakdown of normal social relations. State-led violence became part of everyday life. But even after Mao died in 1976 and relative moderates took over, the country has still been buffeted by unrest, crackdowns, harsh treatment of dissent, and brutalizing policies toward non-Chinese ethnic groups.

Just as in earlier times, China's contemporary leaders try to keep history on their side by telling myth-like stories: a popular uprising brought the Communist Party to power; famines were caused by natural disasters; minority areas like Xinjiang and Tibet have always been part of the country; Hong Kong's struggle for democracy is the work of foreign forces; the state dealt responsibly in handling the initial outbreak of the Covid-19 coronavirus. The not-so-subtle subtext is that only the Communist Party can save China from chaos and disintegration. Any alternative version of history is taboo. Every country has its foundational myths, but in China the lack of independent institutions—media, universities, or political parties—makes it difficult to challenge the official version of reality.

Communist Party myths dominate China's textbooks, museums, films, and tourist spots, and are a constant theme of China's top leaders. Since taking power in 2012, Xi Jinping has made control of history a top domestic priority. He has closed scores of unauthorized journals and museums and jailed those who oppose his version of the truth. These acts of disremembering warp the country's collective memory and have succeeded in convincing most Chinese people that even if the party is flawed, it is doing a good job and its opponents are at best unrealistic, and at worst traitors.

Countering this overwhelming state story, modern-day Sima Qians and Su Dongpos are engaged in an epic struggle to document the full picture of contemporary Chinese history. Even during a period that many outsiders see as a "perfect dictatorship," these independent writers, artists, and filmmakers still produce works about government-induced famines, political campaigns, massacres, and virus outbreaks. Their goal: to challenge, destabilize, and contest the state's version of reality. With success by no means certain, they carry on, believing that history vindicates the truth.

Many of these figures got their start in the 2000s, which was a period of unusual openness. It wasn't the most open time since the Communists took power—that title goes to the freewheeling 1980s, when leaders even talked of open elections. Those high-flying days crashed to an end with the 1989 Tiananmen massacre, when weeks of peaceful protests against corruption and for a more open political system ended with the massacre of hundreds by armed soldiers in Beijing and other cities. That set in motion a playbook that the government has followed until today: tight political control coupled with economic development.

But the 2000s were arguably more significant because new technologies allowed for a truly national conversation that involved far more people than the 1980s. Economic reforms had given people control over where they lived and put money in their pockets, allowing them to pursue their own interests. For some, that meant buying fancy cars or traveling abroad. For others, it meant exploring family histories or problems in society. The internet had begun to grow in popularity, but the government didn't yet know how to control it. Journalists and activists leaped into the void, publishing hundreds of blogs and journals that exposed official malfeasance.

Underground historians had been exploring the dark corners of the Communist Party's history since the 1940s, but digital technologies meant that their work could be republished and reach millions of people through social media, blogs, and some traditional media outlets. Documentary film festivals highlighted the work of people who were using new digital technologies, such as cheap handheld cameras, to interview survivors of the party's misrule—all of it raising questions about the validity of a political system of one-party rule with few checks and balances.

This period of relative freedom ended in the late 2000s. It's simplistic to say it was all due to Xi Jinping's taking power in 2012, because the tide had already turned against these critical citizen voices before he became the country's leader. In 2008, the party arrested future Nobel Peace Prize laureate Liu Xiaobo for helping to organize a petition calling for mild political reform. The following year, the government sentenced him to 11 years in prison. In 2010, it closed the social media accounts of many prominent government critics. In 2011, it shut down the most popular social media commentators.

Xi intensified this crackdown. One of his first moves was to end any possibility of questioning the Mao era, let alone later decades. In January 2013, he said that Communist rule can be divided into two periods: the first thirty years (roughly coinciding with Mao's rule from 1949 to 1976) and the next thirty years of economic and social reforms (from 1978 to 2012, a period when Deng Xiaoping and his handpicked successors ruled). It was not possible, Xi said, to accept one era but also criticize the other. In other words, you couldn't be for capitalist-style economic reforms and relative openness while also criticizing the Mao era, or the other way around. You had to accept both. They were two sides of the same coin.

Using logic that would have been familiar to Su Dongpo, Xi said that questioning any era of the People's Republic's history meant questioning the state's legitimacy. The Chinese Communist Party's rule, he said, is "the conclusion of history." To explain the importance of history, he cited a 19th-century Chinese poet, Gong Zizhen. Writing at the start of China's degradation at foreign hands, Gong wrote: "To destroy a country's people, start with destroying their history." That, Xi warned, happened to the Soviet Union a generation earlier but would not happen to the People's Republic of China. The Communist Party would make sure that its version of history was drilled into people's hearts and minds.

To accomplish these goals, Xi shuttered independent journals and film festivals and launched a barrage of counter-counter information. His government massively expanded history museums and tourist sites, underwrote epic history films, and revised textbooks. Capping it all was a 2021 document that rewrote the Communist Party's history, just the third such undertaking in the party's one hundred -year history.

One way to understand these efforts is to say they are simply superfluous—a piling on of ideological control that isn't really necessary. And yet this argument is hard to sustain. Even authoritarian leaders have limited political capital. They focus their attention on things that they perceive of as real problems. Most of Xi's other major policies have been based on actual threats to his power: his campaign against corruption was because corruption was indeed out of control and that he could leverage it to eliminate potential enemies; he cracked down on Hong Kong because it was a bastion of free speech where underground books and journals were published; and he targets the democratic state of Taiwan because it is a rebuttal to the Communist Party's myth that only an authoritarian state can effectively rule Chinese people. Likewise, he focuses on controlling history because he believes that losing control of history poses a grave threat to continued Communist Party rule.

Despite the government onslaught, independent voices continue to emerge. In 2016, I participated in a workshop on oral history and met dozens of people from across the country who wanted to know how to document their families and communities. (I write about this workshop in the vignette "Videoing China's Villages" at the end of this book's second section.) Even though many of them tread on dangerous ground, they are still active today. Most of the venues where they once showed their films have vanished, but that makes their efforts all the more remarkable. It raises the question of why they have kept at it, and why the government has a hard time suppressing them. Others, such as the editors of the underground history journal *Remembrance*, continue to publish. As of early 2023, *Remembrance* was 15 years old and had just published its 330th issue.

I see parallels in the religious communities that I also closely followed during my two decades in China. Faith-based groups and China's counter historians both seek to improve their country by addressing an inner problem—an unease or a pang of conscience that won't go away. For those who take the religious path, faith is a way to save the nation by first saving themselves—the idea being that China needs a moral revolution to construct a more just society. For the unofficial historians, it is the idea that a moral society cannot be based on lies and silence.

As I talked to more and more of these underground historians, I began to see that this wasn't the work of quixotic individuals but an organized effort—not in the sense of a political party or an association with bylaws and membership rolls. The party's security apparatus would easily crush anything that structured. Rather, it was unstructured and yet at the same time united by common ideas and beliefs that remain widespread across China, so much so that it is not an exaggeration to call this a movement. They share stories, heroes, and common beliefs. Many of them meet each other in person or virtually, and work on the same material. Cumulatively, they have created a collective memory about Chinese Communist Party misrule—something I explore in chapter 7.

Crucially, all these people share a mystical idea about the power of place. They know of Red Cliff and Su Dongpo, of course, but have created new places of memory, all of them based on events that took place after the Communists took power. Like the ancients, they leave physical markers at these sites of memory: tombstones, memorial tablets, or stones engraved with their names.

Many of these memorials have been erased by diligent government officials. But like Su, today's commentators make works of art—films, books, essays, poems—that can be suppressed but not erased. They circulate widely and many have gained mythic status. Even if banned, they are still accessible in virtual worlds and are known to many Chinese. They represent an open, humane China that has always existed and for which people have always struggled.

Time and again, people who hadn't met would tell me of one place where they thought the modern-day version of this movement began. They kept circling back to the far western reaches of China by the Tibetan Plateau. There, the geography led to some of the worst excesses of the Mao era but also to remarkably early efforts to understand

China's then-new authoritarian system. These people, long dead, and forgotten for decades, have been resurrected by Chinese filmmakers and underground historians, forming a lineage of counter-history that leads us to events today and suggests possible outcomes for China's future.

Memory: The Hexi Corridor

The Hexi Corridor is a narrow string of oases that links China with Central Asia. To its south looms the Tibetan plateau, while to its north is the Gobi Desert. It arches slowly across China like a bent bough, at times almost overwhelmed by the deserts and mountains, a small sliver of irrigated green amid the sands and rocks of China's far west. Some call it the throat of China: a narrow, fragile passageway essential to the country's survival.

In ancient times, caravans traveled along this route, forming part of the Silk Road that sent goods back and forth between China, India, Persia, the Middle East, and Europe. Its location meant that armies fought over it for centuries. When China was strong, it controlled the corridor and expanded into Mongolia, Tibet, and Central Asia. When weak, China couldn't defend the corridor, leaving the heartlandvulnerable to invasion.

The Hexi Corridor itself was never the prize. Its tiny rivers and oases could support only a small population of farmers and traders. Its value was always strategic, and its legacy reflects the interests of distant powers. Remote yet central, it was the site of some of China's greatest achievements and most grotesque failures, its dry, dusty climate preserving these places of memory from the erasure of nature and humans.

The corridor is best known as the home of Dunhuang and the nearby Mogao Caves. An oasis trading stop on the Silk Road, Dunhuang's location at the far western end of the corridor made it an inflection point of world culture. For nearly one thousand years, it was where Chinese, Western, and Central Asian cultures merged. Nobles and traders hired artisans to create elaborate Buddhist frescoes that rival the greatest artworks in the world, while a cache of tens of thousands of documents and paintings give a detailed look at life in medieval China and Central Asia. Today, it is a world heritage site, its caves attracting millions of tourists each year.

Heading east along the Hexi Corridor toward the heartland of China, other groups of Buddhist caves appear about every 50 miles. Like Dunhuang, they are always on the right-hand side of the road, the south, dug into the foothills of the Tibetan Plateau—way stations of civilization amid the bleak landscape. The monuments are something like cemeteries: inverted tombstones carved into the rock instead of out of it, but with the same function of honoring the dead.

Midway along the corridor lies one set of caves dedicated to the deity Manjusri. Built by traders starting in the 4th century, they are in remarkably good condition, works of piety that still speak to us. Fronted with colorfully painted wooden buildings, they call out boldly to the valley below: this is how we, your ancestors of more than a millennium ago, honored our dead; what will you do?

The valley offers three answers. One is Jiayuguan, home to the famous 14th-century Ming dynasty gate that marks the beginning of the Great Wall as we know it today. Lavishly renovated and maintained, it is postcard perfect, the walls high and broad, as if to say that the empire you are entering is mighty and strong: tremble and obey! Nearby is the Jiuquan Satellite Launch Center, off limits to most visitors but famous as China's most important space port. It, too, is a statement of authority and power: here, on the edges of the Gobi Desert the modern state will send humans to the stars.

In between the stone walls and the concrete launch pads is a stretch of desert encasing a more terrible monument. It was built in 1954, but within seven years it was closed, and immediately after that the state began to erase its existence. Its name is Jiabiangou, the Ditch, the most notorious labor camp in China, a place where thousands were worked and starved to death in the late 1950s and early 1960s. Improbably, this field of stone and sand, blown flat by the winds and patrolled by guards, has become a touchstone for Chinese people seeking to recover their past.

2

The Ditch

It is the Tomb Sweeping Festival, a day of commemoration for the dead. The university professor and documentary filmmaker Ai Xiaoming has traveled fifteen hundred miles from her hometown in Wuhan to Jiabiangou to document an effort by aging camp survivors to erect a tombstone. Years ago, the camp had been converted into a tree farm, but for decades survivors regularly traveled here to visit their lost friends. In the mid-2010s, however, the authorities declared it a military training area and posted guards during sensitive periods.

"Hello, can we get in? How about to the other side? No? Look, I am an artist. Is it okay if I read out a poem over there?"

Ai is in her early 60s, short, with a round face and persistent, penetrating eyes. She smiles and speaks in a friendly tone, but it's clear she is on a mission. The camera hangs off her shoulder, pointing toward the yellow sand. It swings back and forth, occasionally filming the cheap canvas shoes and camouflage trousers of local security—laborers who have been recruited by the state and given baggy uniforms. They give Ai no answer. They have probably just been deployed here, sent out to prevent her and the survivors from entering the area. They are silent.

"If you do have a problem with it, just come over and stop me because you haven't said yes or no. I have no idea otherwise. Because we want to commemorate these people . . . who should not have died." The camera swings back and forth in the spring sun. The yellow ground gyrates. The men's shoes come and go.

"An unnatural death. They are our ancestors."

She finds a location and sets the camera on her shoulder, then zooms into a faded sign that says "Jiuquan Jiabiangou Tree Farm."

She zooms past the sign up the road to two black sedans and more serious looking security people. Shot without a tripod, the camera work is jerky. It could be seen as amateurish but for Ai and other underground filmmakers it is a sign of authenticity. This is no slick film with a big budget. In fact, it has no budget; the travel money came out of Ai's pocket, while her assistants are volunteers. This is not a work of the state but something from the people: *minjian*, or grassroots. The state spends untold fortunes equipping its propagandists with the latest cameras and gear and hiring top talents from around the world. But this is purposefully low budget. The state is not involved.

Perhaps centuries down the road, someone will find Ai's movie on a hard drive or cloud databank and rediscover it; just as the Buddhist grottoes were rediscovered by the wider world in the 20th century. And that person will try to figure out what it was used for. Could it be to meditate on the landscape? To record a small fragment of history long forgotten? Could the film itself be a kind of cemetery that people in the 21st century built to commemorate their dead? If so, were these people really Ai's ancestors? Who were they and why did they die?

Understanding the world of Jiabiangou requires entering a violent era of endless political campaigns, famines, and persecution for tens of millions of Chinese people. It was a world all too familiar to Ai Xiaoming.

Ai grew up in Wuhan, the granddaughter of a famous general, Tang Shengzhi, who had fought for China against Japan in World War II. But he had served in the government's army, not the Communists' guerilla forces. That meant his family had a tumultuous time in the early years of the People's Republic, when people linked to the Kuomintang were viewed with suspicion. At first privileged, the family was later persecuted. In his 80s, General Tang was arrested, beaten by Maoist fanatics, and died in prison. His daughter, Ai's mother, went mad, while Ai's father was beaten, humiliated, and spent years cleaning toilets.

When all of this began in 1966, Ai was 12 years old. She tried her best to fit in. She took the authorities' advice and denounced her parents. She later joined the Communist Party. She got a university education and was the first woman to receive a PhD in literature after the Cultural Revolution. She taught at a university that trained future leaders. She kept her head down.

But the party made it hard for a person of conscience not to question its actions. The 1980s were a period when life went back to normal. Her parents were rehabilitated and settled down quietly in Wuhan while she lived with her husband and young son in Beijing. But it was still a period of campaigns against free thought, culminating in the 1989 Tiananmen student protests.

During this time Ai began to reflect on her upbringing. She began to try to understand China's authoritarian malaise by reading the works of Eastern European intellectuals, especially Milan Kundera, whose work *The Art of the Novel* she translated into Chinese. Later, when she thought of the Jiabiangou labor camp, she recalled these lines from Kundera:

> *The person punished does not know the reason for the punishment. The absurdity of the punishment is so unbearable that to find peace the accused needs to find a justification for his penalty: the punishment seeks the offense. Not only is the source of the verdict impossible to find, but the verdict itself does not exist! To appeal, to request a pardon, you have to be convicted first! The punished beg for recognition of their guilt!*

Ai spent the 1989 protests mainly on the sidelines, her experiences in the Cultural Revolution leaving her little doubt as to the likely outcome. In the 1990s, she moved out of the overly politicized capital to teach literature in the southern city of Guangzhou. There, her work became informed by feminism, especially after the United Nations' Fourth World Conference on Women was held in China in 1995. She studied abroad for a year at the University of the South in Sewanee, Tennessee, and began looking at the links between autocracy and patriarchy—why did the party opposefeminism, even though it officially supported women's rights?

She also sought other means to express herself. Academic books were important, but China had more pressing problems. When she returned to China, she took note of the documentary films of the

filmmaker Hu Jie, a crucial figure in the underground history movement and someone we will meet again in future chapters.

For Ai and scores of other filmmakers, digital cameras were a turning
point. In years past, the only way to make a film was to use expensive
cameras the size of cinder blocks that required strong shoulders and
unwieldy tripods. Film could only be developed at government-run
studios. And the product could only be shown at government-run
cinemas or on state television.

Digital technology made cameras small and affordable. Even cheap
cameras had image stabilization software that made it easy to shoot
a steady frame. The new equipment looked similar to something a
tourist might have. Files could be transferred directly onto a laptop
and edited there. And it could be shown on a computer, shared with
a flash drive, transferred via file-sharing software, or uploaded to foreign websites accessible with easily obtained virtual private network
(VPN) software. In 2004, Ai helped Hu film one of her classes per-
forming *The Vagina Monologues* and quickly got the hang of using a
camera. That same year she began making her own films.

Her other teachers were the giants of world cinema. During her
stint in the United States, she had regularly ransacked the university
library, watching two to three films a day until late into the night.
Now she was watching film with a purpose. For about a decade in the
2000s, Chinese street markets were flooded with cheap DVDs, often
featuring boxed sets of the work of the world's great filmmakers. She
watched Claus Lanzmann and his films on the Holocaust, French
New Wave directors such as Godard and Truffaut, and the Japanese
director Yasujiro Ozu. "I was crazy about classic films and learned
from all of them," she told me.

Unlike Hu, who is largely absent from his films, Ai inserted herself into her works. When filming about a murdered young woman
named Huang Jing, she invited the girl's mother to campus to speak
and joined lobby groups pushing for a government inquiry.

Soon she was making a film every six to twelve months, shooting
intensively in the field and editing back at her home in Guangzhou
or Wuhan, where she spent time caring for her aging parents. She

made films about the 2008 earthquake in Wenchuan that killed sixty thousand, the HIV epidemic in Henan province, and local efforts at grassroots democracy. By the time she arrived in the Hexi corridor in 2014 she had nearly two dozen films to her name.

For years she had heard about Jiabiangou and felt that the survivors must be recorded before they died. But she didn't focus on the past. The film documents historical events, many of them unknown to the broader public, but it centers on their legacy. The dramatic tension revolves around efforts to erect a monument to victims of the camp. So while she reveals startling information, some of it never recorded before, she is mostly interested in its relevance today.

"My film starts from the present, not the past," she told me. "Why do these people make monuments and why do they think they cannot be forgotten?"

In 1957, China's Communists had been in power eight years and had already made a profound mark on society. After defeating the ruling Kuomintang Party in a four-year civil war, they united the country for the first time in a generation. The party eliminated foreign enclaves, save for the colonies of Hong Kong and Macau. Under its leadership, China fought the United States to a standstill in the Korean War. It re-distributed land to farmers. It gave women the right to marry whom they chose. It initiated literacy programs. And it launched a Soviet-style industrialization policy, building steel works, railway lines, and bridges.

Underlying these accomplishments was one common denomin-ator: unbridled state power. Under Mao, the Communists saw every-thing in terms of violent struggle, partly a result of Marx's ideology but also their own history of endless battles, purges, and putsches. Mao needed enemies. One handy group was the landlords. Even though most were small-scale farmers with just a few acres of land, they were caricaturized as bloodthirsty capitalists. The state sent out work teams to foment anger against them. Many were denounced in show tri-als, beaten, tortured, humiliated, and killed—some buried alive in the ground that they were said to have unjustly owned.

The state also designated huge swaths of Chinese religious life as "superstitious." It banned fortune-tellers, itinerant monks, and others who for centuries had been part of the country's religious landscape. Along with prostitutes and drug addicts, religious officials were sent off to labor camps to be reborn as new Communist men and women. Businesses were nationalized, as was private property: all the farmland and fallow land, the mountains and rivers, the gorges and pasturelands, the deserts and forests—every square inch of China's vast landmass now belonged to the state. In this early phase of Communist rule, often seen as a golden age before the great violence that was about to unfold, state-sanctioned attacks had already claimed up to 2 million lives.

Mao's enemy list then expanded to include some of the staunchest members of the Communist Party itself. The economy was surging forward but not fast enough for Mao. He decided that China needed a jolt and declared that it was his own party that was holding things back. Mao had overseen purges before, but this time it wasn't aimed at a specific person, clique, or faction. Instead, Mao felt that the entire governing apparatus needed to be shaken to its foundation.

So in 1956 he launched a political movement called the Hundred Flowers Campaign. It was based on a saying from Confucius—"Let a hundred flowers bloom; let a hundred schools of thought contend"; in other words, allow people to speak and debate. Some people were cagey and had nothing but praise for the party, but many thousands did voice concerns. Overwhelmingly, their criticisms were constructive. Some said the government should consult with the people more often. Others said that officials were too bureaucratic. One person said that China shouldn't be run by a dictatorship of the proletariat but a dictatorship of all the people.

There are different interpretations of what happened next. Some argue that the call to speak out had always been a ruse to lure out enemies. Others say it was genuine but that the party was shocked at the volume of criticism. In any case, Mao struck back violently. Critics were now accused of being "Rightists" who threatened the leftist revolution. Universities, think tanks, and state companies were ordered to root out this menace. To make it clear that it meant business, the party declared that 5 percent of people were Rightists. Failure to find Rightists in a given organization meant that its leaders were themselves Rightists. Across the country began a giant, sweeping purge, largely of its intelligentsia.

This became known as the Anti-Rightist Campaign, launching what became twenty years of terror and turmoil. At least 550,000 people were labeled Rightists, with some figures as high as 1.8 million. In a country of 640 million this might not seem like a large percentage, but China had only a thin layer of educated people. Universities, high schools, research institutes, and government offices were gutted. Hundreds of thousands were sent to labor camps. Those who remained were cowed, trying to avoid the same fate by following the party's every whim to the letter. This began an era of denouncing, informing, obeying, parroting.

Liu Tianyou sits on a sofa in a simple, concrete-walled apartment adorned with calligraphy—the home of an educated person of modest means. He is dressed for his interview in a blue, Western-style dress shirt. He is 72 years old, his hair dyed and combed over to give the appearance of someone who is still trying. Professor Ai has come to film his father's story and he is ready.

"I had two brothers and a sister. I was the eldest at just 12 years of age. One night, my father was talking to my mother. I was woken up by it. I can still remember his words."

He begins to squint, blinking hard at the tears, controlling himself: this story has to be told properly. He forces his eyes open, looking up and rocking back and forth, modulating his voice. Later, when she edits the film, Ai will insert a scene shot from a car driving through the Hexi Corridor. The rolling hills, the desert, and the scrub give Liu privacy as he recounts what his father told his mother.

"He said, 'Now, there is no escape. I could be taken away. After I am taken away, go to your younger brother and ask him for help to raise the kids. If I can come back, we will see each other again.'"

"I was too young to know what he meant."

Ai cuts to Zhang Xihua, who was born in 1950. She has short hair, and her skin is tanned from years living in the bright, unyielding sun of the Hexi Corridor. She wears a pink and gray dress for the interview with a pearl necklace. Like the others, she lives in an old building of rattling windows and big silver radiators. Ai does not state it, but we understand that there has been no compensation paid to the families of the victims. Zhang tells us about her father's departure for Jiabiangou.

"I remember the day he left home. I was about eight or nine years old. I was playing outside."

She starts to tear up and forces a laugh as if to say, there I go again. She shakes her head to regain control. Not this time. Not in front of the camera. History has come to record us, finally. This is our turn. Someone will watch this someday and understand what happened to her dad. She rocks back and forth on the sofa to the rhythm of her family's disaster.

"When Papa came out, he was followed by a man. I remember it clearly. Papa was carrying a suitcase. And when he saw me playing with the neighborhood children he came over and picked me up, holding me real tight without a word before leaving."

Jiabiangou was as unimpressive as it was terrifying. It was made of wooden barracks that housed the inmates, a kitchen, and a camp headquarters. Located in the Gobi, it didn't have a fence—without a vehicle it was impossible to walk out of it. Some tried and died; their corpses found half-eaten by wolves. Others set out and returned a day or two later, begging for mercy. The camp also had satellite locations even farther out in the desert where inmates worked on pointless projects, such as digging canals between shriveled-up rivers. The men there lived in caves or dug pits in the sand and covered themselves with a tarp of branches of scrub. Only the very young and the very healthy survived.

The inmates were mostly local officials who up until a few weeks earlier had run their little corners of China, some from as far away as Shanghai. So many officials were housed at Jiabiangou that the head of one county joked in amazement after he arrived that "a meeting of county, town, and village-level officials could be called here without giving prior notice"—because they were all present. The party was self-destructing and taking Chinese society with it.

The elimination of outspoken officials became especially disastrous when Mao launched the Great Leap Forward in 1958. The events started in late 1957 when Mao visited Moscow for the grand celebration of the 40th anniversary of the October Revolution. Soviet leader Nikita Khrushchev had already annoyed Mao by attacking Stalin. Mao felt that Stalin was one of the greats of Communist history and shouldn't be knocked off his pedestal—not least because it made Mao himself vulnerable; if even the great Stalin could be purged, then Mao could be challenged too. On top of that, the Soviet Union had just launched the world's first satellite, Sputnik, which Mao felt over-shadowed his accomplishments.

He returned to Beijing eager to assert China's position as the world's leading Communist nation. On 1 January 1958, the Communist Party's mouthpiece, *People's Daily*, published an article calling for "going all out" and "aiming higher"—code words for eschewing patient economic development in favor of radical policies aimed at quick growth.

Mao drove home his plans in a series of meetings that changed the Communist Party's political culture. In several extraordinary outbursts, he said that all leaders who opposed "rash advance" were counter-revolutionary—opponents of Mao and the state. As was the pattern throughout his reign, no one was able to stop him.

Having silenced opponents in the party, Mao pushed for the creation of communes—taking control of the land that farmers had been allotted during the violent land reform movement a few years earlier. This included even farm implements like plows and hoes. It now all belonged to the state. People were to eat in canteens and share all agricultural equipment, livestock, and production, with food allocated by the state. The first commune, aptly named Sputnik, was created in Henan province.

Local leaders were ordered to follow fanciful ideas for increasing crop productions, such as planting crops closer together. The idea was to create Sputnik harvests—crop yields that were astronomically higher than anything seen in human history.

This might have resulted in nothing more than falsified statistics, except that the state relied on these numbers to tax farmers. They had to send grain to the state as if they were producing impossibly high yields. Seed grain was confiscated, and storehouses ransacked to meet the targets. Farmers had nothing to eat and nothing to plant the next spring.

Compounding this were equally deluded plans to bolster steel production through the creation of "backyard furnaces"—small wood-fired kilns that somehow were supposed to create steel out of iron ore. Unable to produce real steel, local leaders ordered farmers to melt down their agricultural implements to satisfy Mao's national-level targets.

The result: farmers had no grain, no seeds, and no agricultural implements.

Inevitably, famine set in. In 1959, when Mao was challenged about these events at a key conference at the resort of Lushan, he purged his enemies. Enveloped by an atmosphere of terror, officials returned to China's provinces to double down on Mao's policies. Up to 45 million died in what historians reckon was the worst famine in recorded history. This decimated villages across China but was especially brutal in camps like Jiabiangou, as its inmates told Ai.

"Our food ration was reduced to two hundred grams a day. After the kitchen staff and the cadres took their share, we were left with one hundred and fifty grams. It was cooked into some kind of paste. We ate one helping in the morning and one in the evening. How could one survive on that?"

"They came up with the idea of eating wheat straw. Straw chopped up into pieces, stir-fried in a pan then ground into flour. They cooked gruel with the straw flour. We immediately said this isn't food, but the party officials insisted on making it, saying it was edible. 'Cows and horses eat grass. They can do all kinds of hard work, like pulling carts and ploughs. Eating straw is an invention.'"

"We all suffered from constipation badly. As a result, we used to help each other with twigs to dig it out. That was how we coped with constipation. It caused a lot of blood. Pools of blood. That was how it was."

"Many died of constipation."

"One after the other they kept dying. Endless deaths. It was like everyone was rushing toward hell."

發現了人吃人 那個人叫啥名字
inmates were eating human bodies.

Food parcels often determined who lived and who died. Si Jicai, a prisoner who worked in the camp office—a job that kept him alive—was charged with handing out the mail. He recalls Chinese New Year in February 1959.

"They cried as they ate, and they were all on their knees facing east. I thought, why are they all crying and facing east? Then I realized that many of them had come from Lanzhou," the provincial capital to the east. "They were kneeling toward their homes. All you could do was hear them crying."

"They had something in a bowl. I said what was it. I smelled it. It actually smelled pretty good. I said, 'what are you up to?' They did not tell me, so I took a look. There were black and red pieces. The black was kidney. They said, 'Would you want some?' I asked what it was. They told me to try a bite. And I did. I ate some, too. It did taste good. They told me not to tell anyone now that I had also eaten some. There were bodies left on the flatland. There was nothing to be done. They could not bury them. It was winter. The ground was hard. Almost two hundred corpses were left lying in the ditch. Dogs and wolves came in packs to eat them. The bodies were piling up. So the inmates came. They might try to cut some flesh off the buttocks, but none had any flesh left. So they cut out the offal. That was why I saw things that were red. They were lungs."

"Not a single cadre died at Jiabiangou. Did any of their families die? Their families came to the camp from towns where people were dying because they could eat better. Whose food did they eat? Ours!"

"You look at kids nowadays. They talk back to you if they disagree. Could people in the past do that? Impossible. Whatever you had was granted by the Party. How could you tell between good and bad people? You were told they were bad guys. Then you treated them like bad guys. You can question them now because you occupy the moral high ground. I can ask those questions too: 'Did you have no sense of humanity? Why did you not oppose those things?' People then simply did not think like that. What else do you want? You want to put the blame on individuals?"

The party never made amends for the Anti-Rightist Campaign, the Great Famine, or the events at Jiabiangou. After the survivors were released from the camps, they had to live with the label "Rightist" for another fifteen years until the party ordered that the cases be reexamined in 1978. That meant they spent most of their careers doing menial labor, often while also being persecuted during the Cultural Revolution, which lasted from 1966 to 1976. As for compensation, most of the survivors received roughly five hundred yuan, or less than one hundred dollars.

Part of the reason is that the person in charge of this campaign had been Deng Xiaoping, who became Mao's successor. Most memoirs were censored, and discussion was largely forbidden. That contrasted with the Cultural Revolution, which was discussed and for which the party made some amends—perhaps because Deng and his family suffered under it, or simply that the scale was even larger, making it harder to cover up. Mostly, it was easier for the party to admit that Mao had made one serious error, the Cultural Revolution, than a series of disastrous policies throughout his rule.

This silence began to break in the run-up to the fiftieth anniversary of the Anti-Rightist Campaign. In 2000, the writer Yang

Xianhui, who grew up in the Hexi Corridor, published a series of interviews with inmates of Jiabiangou, retold as short stories in order to avoid censorship. Yang was born in 1946 and was only 12 when the campaign started, but he later worked in the countryside and met survivors. He learned that his high school principal, who had mysteriously been taken away in 1958, had died there. In all, he conducted more than one hundred interviews and published two books of lightly fictionalized accounts. As Yang explained in one of his books:

"As an author, I am retelling the stories uncovered in my investigation in order to reopen a page in history covered by the dust of forty years, in the hope that such a tragedy will not be repeated. Scrutinizing the history of those who preceded us means scrutinizing ourselves."

Yang's book was a sharp departure from previous descriptions of the Mao era. In the aftermath of the Cultural Revolution in the 1980s, party loyalists who had been victimized produced insipid novels that glossed over the hardship of daily life. Many even ended with a hopeful note of political and social rebirth. As early as 1986, the future Nobel Peace Prize laureate, Liu Xiaobo, attacked this "scar literature" as a fake reckoning with the past.

By contrast, Yang had stepped outside the party's channels of rec-
onciliation to "take the unofficial path" of interviewing people. His
work was such a revelation that it spurred an outpouring that continues today. In 2004, the director Wang Bing bought the rights to
Yang's stories and spent a decade interviewing survivors. In 2010, he
released a feature film, "The Ditch," that described a woman from
Shanghai who travels to Jiabiangou to find her husband. She discovers
that he is dead and his corpse partially consumed by fellow inmates.
Wang also made the 2018 documentary "Dead Souls," an eight-hour
series of interviews with survivors. In addition, many survivors began
publishing their own accounts, using computers to write up histories
that could be spread by email, or sent abroad to be published there.

These unofficial works rarely dwell on elite machinations, focusing
instead on the degradation of the individual. They avoid heroizing
the victims—in their desire to survive, they plot and connive against
other inmates. For Yang and others, this is especially relevant as the
victims are the very people who had supported the regime until they
were purged. The implication is that given a chance, they might have
carried out the purges.

Still, many of the former inmates did come to realize the inherent
problems of a one-party state. Even if they had once been its faithful
servants, their firsthand exposure to its cruelty made many of them
recoil and rethink. Some tried to forget the past. But many became
insightful critics, using their personal experiences as a way to undermine the state's efforts at disremembering.

Ai's decision to focus on the present is most obvious in the story of
the survivor Zhang Suiqing. In part five of the film, he has just arrived in Lanzhou, determined to erect a tombstone. He begins to call
up old friends and contacts, asking if they want to join him in a small
protest. But as he dials, he keeps getting the same answer: it's not con-
venient to talk. Sometimes a relative intercepts the call and says the

person is ill. Ai films Zhang. She focuses tightly on the phone pressed against Zhang's ear.

"How many of them were you," Zhang asks.

"Seven."

"How many survived?"

"Two."

Zhang is dressed in a camel-hair overcoat, a dress shirt and cardigan, his hair neatly cut, combed, and parted. He could be a somewhat older entrepreneur negotiating a deal.

"I got it. I got it. Then we won't bother you if we are not welcome. Then I will go. Goodbye."

More calls. Ai pans her camera over the Yellow River, its water high after the spring melting of the snows in the Tibetan plateau. Willows blow, a translucent green awning over the gentle waters. The past seems gone. Then a man named Pu Yiye recounts a recent experience.

"I met a young man before I retired. A strapping young lad. He asked me how to get to Jiabiangou. I asked where you are from, and he said Xuzhou. I said what do you want, and he said he was looking for his father. I asked who his father was. He said his name was Yang Wanhua. I knew him. He used to work at the epidemic prevention station. He was a doctor. He died in Gaotai [a Jiabiangou satellite camp]. I took a look at this young man. He looked like his father—very refined.

"I said 'don't go, you won't find him.'

"He said 'I must. My mother sent me. She cries every single day, from morning to night, missing my father.'"

Pu sent the man back; there was nothing at the site to comfort a grieving widow. The story was common. Early on after the Anti-Rightist Campaign started, many of the wives tried to commit suicide. Others desperately sought their husbands' corpses so they could fulfill a traditional practice of burying the dead in their hometowns. Through the ensuing decades, many spouses traveled to the Hexi Corridor to look for any trace of their partner. For many women, the grief has never ended.

One is Yu Liyin. She dug up several graves, finally identifying her husband by his teeth, his unusually long middle toe, and a sweater that had been preserved in the desert. Yu and a relative wrapped the bones in cloth, put it in a bag, and snuck onto a train. Nervous, she didn't eat or drink for two days until she got back to Tianshui, a city just east of the Hexi Corridor. Knowing that luggage is inspected at major stations, she went one stop farther, to a village station, and walked out the back, up over the mountains, and hitched a ride home on a truck. "That was how he finally came to rest in his hometown," she told Ai.

In the early 1960s, the camp officials tried to make the deaths look natural. They painted the names of the dead on stones with red paint and placed them in the desert as if it were a regular cemetery. Some inmates died, here's their grave, what's unusual about that? Then the wind blew away most of the paint, so the tombstones vanished. And then the wind blew away the sand covering the bodies, revealing the mass graves once again. In 1970 the city of Jiuquan began to build farms in the area, mainly to raise sheep that could eat the scrub. One volunteer said that when he walked out into the desert, he found bones everywhere.

Later, as Ai discovered, the medical school in Lanzhou sent out several big trucks and hired hundreds of local militiamen to dig up the graves and put them in boxes. The bones were bound together with wire. Some of the corpses had been mummified and still had hair and skin. Some villagers came out to pillage and stole a few gold teeth. In other places, shepherd children played with the skeletons.

As Ai films, she walks through the fields filming skulls, femurs, and scapulas that poke out through the sand. Most of the bones seem to have disintegrated but these larger ones survive, bleached so white that they reflect brightly in the Hexi Corridor's light. Ai films slowly, lingering over the bones.

Mr. Zhang's plan called for building a graveyard for family members to honor the dead. In 2013 he almost succeeded; the local government approved his plan to build a small stone wall shaped in a circle around an obelisk. The plan was completed and for a while the black tombstone stood in the desert.

Cenotaph of the Remains of Those Who Died in Disaster

And on the back, he had inscribed

57 Fellow Sufferers from Lanzhou
Respectfully Erected
by
Jiabiangou Survivors
Friends and Family

Then the local government realized that it had made a mistake. Xi Jinping had just issued his statement that the Mao era could not be rejected. Its import was immediately clear—and indeed over the years became seen as one of Xi's first shots against unofficial history. Suddenly, the memorial was sensitive. Zhang and his friends might be sincere but the symbolism—a tombstone to honor thousands of innocent people killed by the party—was too powerful. Within days it was destroyed. Zhang salvaged a corner of the monument with the character *li*, or "erected," visible. Everything he had done had been legal, but his work was destroyed.

Ai's point is clear: the "hit, smash, loot" tactics of the Cultural Revolution that she and her family had experienced were not unique and are not dead; it is how the party regularly deals with people who have different views—especially when they dare touch on Communist Party history.

One elderly gentleman, Li Jinghang, sums up what many of the survivors feel. They didn't seek a quarrel with the party, but the organization could never accept their desire to set the record straight. He was the only survivor of eleven teachers from the middle school and normal college in the town of Tianshui. He figures prominently in Ai's film, usually lying on a bed sidewise like a reclining Buddha, his eyes closed in contemplation. But now he sits up in a chair to make a point.

"Now that the tombstone has been smashed, that means there was no such thing as Jiabiangou. In other words, forget about the past. Human beings don't need to preserve history. If that's the case, then you have to ask what defines humanity? What does it mean to be a human being?"

Throughout most of her filming, Ai was aided by Zhang Suiqing, the man who built the memorial and who kept trying to commemorate the dead. Just as her film was premiering in Hong Kong in 2017, Mr. Zhang was terminally ill with cancer. The chemotherapy that the doctors recommended would have cost 60,000 yuan, or about 10,000 dollars. He and his wife didn't have enough money and had bought a cheaper medicine that couldn't save him. As he lay dying in Lanzhou, Ai watched the film's opening by video from her home in Wuhan. As had been the case for a few years, she was unable to travel to Hong Kong due to government restrictions on her travel, but friends had set up a link and she watched the ceremony, moved that the outside world was seeing her work. By phone and through messages, she relayed the audience reaction to Zhang. Afterward, she wrote him a

piece of calligraphy. It was a poem, "Calming Winds and Waves" by
Su Dongpo, the person who had defied the emperor and written the
poems at Red Cliff.

> *Stop listening to the rain pattering on the leaves*
> *Why not go for a stroll and sing your heart out?*

She doesn't write the final two lines, which every schoolchild
knows, because it would be too crude. Instead, she leaves it as an un-
spoken message, of having found peace:

> *Now that I have arrived, home at last*
> *Nothing stirs me anymore, the glaring sun, the wind, or the rain.*

Memory: Facing Walls

For nearly one thousand years, the city of Dunhuang at the end of the Hexi Corridor was an inflection point of world culture, where Chinese, Western, Indian, and Central Asian cultures merged into one, dazzling innovative style of art. The city reflects this artistic drama: the Mongolian foothills to the north, the Tibetan Plateau to the south, and the "whispering sand dunes" to the west. Seen from a map, the sands look like an extension of the Taklamakan Desert in Xinjiang a thousand miles farther west. It is as if the winds had tried to blow this great desert into the Hexi Corridor, but miraculously stopped at Dunhuang. Rising up like a tidal wave about to crest, they are a marker saying this is the end-point of Chinese civilization and what lies farther west is foreign—even if at times, like today, it is under Chinese control.

The caves are located 10 miles south of Dunhuang, in a small valley less than a mile long. It is housed in the Mogao Caves, carved into the cliffs between the 5th and 14th centuries by pious merchants, nobility, and travelers—a collective effort of peoples and civilizations united by the spiritual aspirations of one of the world's great religions, Buddhism. The site today contains nearly five hundred grottoes filled with a vast array of artwork: fift thousand square yards of wall paintings and twenty-four hundred painted statues. One cave alone had once held one thousand paintings on scrolls and fifty thousand texts written in Chinese, Tibetan, Sanskrit, and a variety of Central Asian languages. About six hundred years ago, political turmoil closed off the Silk Road and the caves were largely abandoned, some sealed off against the elements, others filling in with sand and debris.

Early last century, the caves were rediscovered and many of the works sold off to foreign adventurers and scholars. That caught the attention of an art student in Paris, Chang Shuhong, who read about the discovery in a French newspaper and wondered why Chinese themselves weren't studying the caves. He returned home and in 1944 convinced the Kuomintang government, which was running China at the time, to allow him to set up a research institute. When the Kuomintang lost the civil war to the Communists in 1949, Chang stayed on and made Dunhuang his life's work.

In 1962, an art student arrived in Dunhuang looking for work. His name was Gao Ertai, and he was trying to find refuge from a totalitarian state that, as he wrote in his memoir, "was entirely made up of communes and soldiers." Hoping to get as far away from the Maoist state as possible, he thought of Dunhuang, where he hoped to "find my refuge among the relics of the Wei, Sui, and Tang dynasties, just as Schiller had sought refuge in the Golden Age of Greece and Rome to escape the dark political reality of his contemporary Germany."

Gao was a survivor of the Jiabiangou labor camp. At times during his imprisonment, he had been hauled out to paint portraits of Mao. During those and other commissions he had been able to eat, which gave him the strength to survive the privations of camp life. Released into the city of Jiuquan, he had nowhere to go. He knew of Dunhuang and so wrote to Chu asking for work. Without waiting for a reply, he set off. He hitched rides on coal trucks, slept in open fields, and begged for water until he arrived in Dunhuang.

The town that Gao encountered was far from the glory days of centuries past or the global tourism center of today. It was a dusty settlement of squat, adobe buildings and manure-covered streets. He walked south through stony fields of gravestones toward the foothills of the Tibetan Plateau. As he approached, the land dipped into a valley, which was lined with ancient trees fed by a small stream. The caves rose above the patch of green, dotting the cliff face.

Gao found Chang and his team of forty scholars housed in primitive farmhouses, everyone living cheek to jowl—a dysfunctional clan of infighting archaeologists, art historians, bureaucrats, and Communist Party functionaries. Their mission was to study the very past that the Communist Party was seeking to destroy. But they spent most of their time fighting each other as they tried to survive Mao's erratic directives.

Chang graciously met Gao and immediately agreed to hire him. He told Gao to go look at the caves and make a mental inventory. Gao soon realized that he should stay as far away from the institute as possible. It wasn't as bad as what he had just experienced in the camp, but it was a microcosm of the country's upheavals: bitter infighting, humiliations, and mental torture.

Some of the people Gao met were psychologically disturbed by the struggles of the past decade. One woman wandered through the institute, one arm cradling books, the other dragging a dead tree branch behind her, while she murmured that the tree was dead, dead, dead. A researcher who regularly showed up to work five minutes late made sure people realized that he was only five minutes late. He would mutter that he was just five minutes late, just five minutes, and everything was fine, wasn't it? It was just five minutes, five minutes.

Slowly Gao began to take up responsibilities. According to one record, construction of the caves had begun in 366. That meant that 1966 would be the 1,300th anniversary of their founding. The team's leaders decided to build a new cave that would have Mao seated in the middle, in the same location that the statues of the Buddha would have been located. The walls would be decorated in the same style as the other caves. The west wall, behind Mao would have a history of the Communist Party called "Taking in Our Stride the Perils of Cliffs and Torrents." The south wall would depict the Communist Party's war against Japan and the Civil War, entitled "Long Live the Victories of the People's Wars"; the north wall would depict the regime's achievements, entitled "600 Million in the Divine Land: All Equal to the Ancient Sages," and the roof would show a communist paradise called "The Hibiscus Land Bathed in Morning Sunlight."

Gao worked flat out, spending most of 1965 making sketches of the future frescoes. But then, power shifted. Mao launched the Cultural Revolution in 1966 to combat what he saw as an ossifying political system. That meant that established officials like Chang—especially someone like him, who had once worked for the Kuomintang government—were targeted. Chang and his wife were attacked for lacking revolutionary fervor. Worse, he was charged with promoting scholars based on talent and professionalism, instead of their zeal for communism. Soon, all the senior leaders and experts were under attack by the rest of the institute. As Gao recalls:

Overnight those gentle, reserved people turned into fierce beasts and violently leaped and hollered, suddenly sang at the tops of their voices, suddenly burst into tears, slapped themselves, rose at midnight and yelled "Long Life," or banged gongs and drums to disseminate the thoughts of the "Great Man." In the whole Mogao Caves area, only those icons of Buddha and bodhisattvas maintained their dignity and self-possession.

Many of the staff were physically attacked; Chang was beaten so badly he couldn't walk. Others were sent to do physical labor: cleaning latrines, digging ditches, and fetching water, the monotony broken only by "struggle sessions," when they were attacked for not being revolutionary enough.

Gao himself was vilified as Chang's protégé. From 1966 until he left Dunhuang in 1972, Gao spent most of his time sweeping sand out of the caves. No one checked up on him and so he whiled away the years by staring at frescoes.

For years, he had studied the paintings as a researcher: scouring them for information on life in medieval China. He had seen depictions of "farming, silk-worm cultivation, weaving, building, hunting—everything from marriage and funerals, to begging, butchery, and martial arts."

While the people in the institute down in the valley fought bitterly against each other, Gao wandered the cliffs, looking at the paintings. They taught him the impermanence of life. The Communist Party promised certainty: in its telling, history was proceeding along a set track and the party's victory was assured. But the caves showed Gao that there was no certainty. There was no permanence. He learned to escape the Communist Party's tyranny by realizing that it, too, would pass.

> I walked up and down among this forest of wall paintings. I felt I had entered a dream. I thought how difficult it was, through the chaos of history and with so many contingencies needing to come together over so long a period of time, to allow for the creation of these works of art. I thought how much more difficult it was for them to endure through merciless time, through a thousand years of wind, dust, and the devastations caused by armies. And I thought about the impermanence of the world, how members of my family were dead or scattered and how I was brought back from death and was here face-to-face with this art; how extremely fortunate I was. I felt a grave and overflowing gratitude.

Today, Dunhuang is a popular tourist site. Entrance to the caves is by timed slots. The primitive farmhouses where the scholars lived have been turned into a museum. Chu, Gao's boss who was tortured, is celebrated as a patriot who helped recover Dunhuang studies from the foreigners, who took away most of the scrolls and have dominated study of these texts.

In 1978, two years after Mao died, Gao was exonerated. In 1986, he National Science Council recognized him for his "distinguished contributions" to Chinese history. But he was imprisoned again in 1989 for supporting the Tiananmen protests. After his release in 1990 he fled China and now lives in exile in Nevada, where he wrote his memoirs, *In Search of My Homeland*. They were published in abridged form in China and later in Taiwan.

Starting in the 2000s, Gao's memoirs began to circulate online, some of them with the censored sections restored. His depiction of Dunhuang in the 1960s and '70s run counter to how it is portrayed in the official media, which describes it as a glorious reflection of Chinese culture that the Communist Party now honors and protects. Like hundreds of other memoirs from the past decades of Communist Party rule, his story personalizes the party's persistent misrule, making it possible for people today to grasp parallels to the past.

Compared to other writings on Jiabiangou, Gao focused on his personal thoughts and feelings. He largely ignored the physical humiliations as a way not to forget but to conquer what he experienced, or as he put it:

> *Writing* In Search of My Homeland *was like digging a hole in a wall. This time it was a wall built from chaos, a kind of primeval Nature in the midst of History. Through the hole, I am looking back to the past.*

3

The Sacrifice

Jiang Xue can remember her hometown before it died. When she was growing up in the 1970s, Tianshui was a small city of farms and hills and fields, a sturdy outpost of Chinese civilization just east of the Hexi Corridor. Her family lived on the edge of town in a shophouse that her grandfather had built in the 1930s. It had modern brick walls, but the windows were traditional wooden lattices, and the roof was covered with fire-cast tiles—a mixture of old and new that reflected China's steady transformation in the first half of the 20th century.

Her childhood came decades after the Communists had taken power, but it was still rooted in the past. Jiang Xue's mother was barely literate when she married, but she was diligent, and her husband had taught her patiently. As a child, Jiang Xue remembers that each evening her parents would read together chapters of the classic novel *Dream of the Red Chamber*, her father explaining the rich vocabulary and symbolism.

Jiang Xue had her own lessons. Her father sent her out to walk the fields behind the family home to memorize *The Rhymes of Li Weng*, a book of couplets that teaches children the patterns of written Chinese. On one level they are simply an exercise in rote learning, but they also hardwire young people's brains with words, phrases, and ideas fundamental to Chinese culture. She would walk until dusk, when the smoke rising from nearby farms reminded her that her own family was also readying dinner. Then she would skip home, humming the opening lines, which are built around the verb *dui*, or "to face."

> *Heaven Faces Earth*
> *Wind Faces Rain*
> *Continents Face the Sky*
> *Mountain Flowers Face Aquatic Plants*
> *The Scorching Sun Faces the Blue Dome of Heaven*

The Tianshui of Jiang Xue's youth was poor by today's standards. It had rutted roads, outhouses, and open ditches. Most people owned just a few sets of clothes, rarely ate meat, and were lucky to own a bike or a fountain pen. But it was a picturesque small city of wood and brick, facing the waters of the Wei River.

The sense of rootedness was reflected in place names. Tianshui's central district is Qinzhou, named after the ancient kingdom of Qin, which was founded in a neighboring county 2,300 years ago, and united China under its first empire. The Qin—pronounced "Chin"—also lent its name to the foreign pronunciation of China. Another district was named after the local Maijishan Grottoes, a famous center of sacred art in China, similar in scope and beauty to Dunhuang.

In the 1950s, Japanese prisoners of war had been press-ganged into building a long-delayed railway. The new government also paved roads, built schools, and erected factories. But at heart it was still a small farming city set between the blue dome of heaven and the rushing waters of the river. This juxtaposition gave Tianshui its name: *Tian*, sky, and *shui*, water—the city of sky and water.

Later Jiang Xue would think of this era as the last rays of light arriving from a dead star. When she was in her 30s, she returned home one time to find that her hometown didn't exist anymore. It was served by a high-speed rail that raced above the city like a futuristic vision but had ruined everything below: massive concrete bridge supports sunk into abandoned homes, rubble and garbage strewn underneath the bridge, children playing in dirty puddles, old trees cut down, tap water now so dirty that it had to be boiled. The word that often came to her was humiliation—that everything it had stood for had been laid low and wasted. Even her grandfather's home was hard to find. It still stood but was squashed among ugly concrete-and-tile structures, a strange, awkward, eccentric reminder of a road not taken.

That was when Tianshui's fall was hard to miss. But Jiang Xue knew that its death had begun half a century earlier. It was a time of upheavals and of the awful choices that left China permanently un-moored. For her family, it came down to one impossible decision. In 1960, her grandfather decided that he had to sacrifice one member of his family: he had to pick which one of the six would die so the rest could live.

Tianshui sits east of the Jiabiangou labor camp on the edge of one of China's most distinctive geological features: the Loess Plateau. The plateau is composed of wind-blown, silt-like sand packed tightly into a vast highland the size of Afghanistan. The soil fractures easily, leaving the terrain extremely uneven. Over the centuries, streams have eaten through the soil, forming deep gullies, while some hills have sheared off to create bizarre mini-plateaus the size of a football field. Inhabited for millennia, the land is largely denuded, covered with terraced grain fields and scrub. People responded to the unusual geology by digging caves into the hillsides, building homes several rooms deep, the ceilings supported by cross beams and pillars. Out front, the homes sometimes had a wooden sunroom but overall the caves saved the need for wood.

For devotees of Buddhism, this made the area around Tianshui especially attractive for building grottoes, resulting in the great Maijishan cave complex. Its seven thousand statues and one thousand square meters of paintings are housed in nearly two hundred caves carved into an odd mountain shaped like a wheat stack. Over the centuries, many locals became amateur scholars, writing books about the caves, their origins, and the different styles of art found there. Jiang Xue's father, Zhang Youxuan, was one of them, devoting his private time to researching the philosophy and beliefs that had underpinned Chinese civilization for millennia before it was destroyed in his youth.

Jiang Xue's father had been haunted by his father's choice. It had forced him to leave elementary school. He only resumed it in 1966, just on the eve of the Cultural Revolution, which closed down the schools for years. That meant that he effectively had no formal education after elementary school. In that era, survival was all that mattered.

In the early years of Communist rule, the Zhang family had downplayed their love of Chinese culture. Jiang Xue's great uncle was a locally famous calligrapher, teaching his nephew how to write beautiful script and the ideas behind the great works of literature he was copying out. But after 1949 all of that was hidden away and never discussed. Strangely, in the Cultural Revolution, this knowledge offered Jiang Xue's father a way to survive. In 1969 he was offered a job by the local Cultural Center, a government-run organization that in normal times would offer classes in calligraphy, painting, martial arts, and other pastimes to enrich people's lives.

In the Cultural Revolution it had been turned into a center of Maoist propaganda. Mr. Zhang had been recruited there because of the painting skills that he had learned from his uncle. His job was to paint giant Mao portraits, about three by four yards in size, which appeared around the city at intersections and in front of government buildings. It turned out that Mr. Zhang was good at it and soon he was in high demand. In fact, every "work unit" in Tianshui—every factory, ministry, office, research institute, workshop, kiln, or quarry— needed a Mao portrait, and they all wanted his.

Two years later, officials in Tianshui were drumming up opposition to the Soviet Union after the two former Communist allies had split and recently fought a border war. They came up with the slogan "Overthrow the New Tsar!" to criticize Moscow's new rulers and decided to make use of the great Maijishan Grottoes to make their point. So they sent Mr. Zhang up to the caves to make enormous billboards attacking the Soviets.

At the time, the grottoes weren't open to the public—there was too much risk of the religious imagery polluting people's minds. But every once in a while, a provincial or national Communist Party leader would come and be escorted to the grottoes. The Buddhist artworks stood for everything the Communist Party was trying to overthrow, but they were remained Tianshui's calling card. The officials would come and look politely, commenting on how well the Buddhist art was hidden under the giant billboards that Mr. Zhang had written. The landscape had to be inscribed, not with the famous poetry of Su Dongpo or a meaningful ode to the Buddhist art, but with the barking peasant Chinese that the Communist Party had imposed on the country.

After painting the slogans, Mr. Zhang was asked to stay at the grottoes as a custodian. He used his time to read widely and think about his family's ordeal. Eventually, the Cultural Revolution ended, and Mr. Zhang got a job as a schoolteacher. On several occasions Mr. Zhang had the chance to join the Communist Party, which would have meant promotions and a better life. He explains tentatively why he didn't: "Because of my father's decision. . . . [I]t left a deep impression. I saw it first-hand."

He never became a dissident or activist. But he lived with the trauma of the missing family member. He kept his head down but his beliefs unbowed. He studied, wrote about the grottoes, and tried to raise independent-minded children.

Mr. Zhang met his wife in 1973 and their daughter was born the next year. As is usual in Chinese culture, the daughter took her father's family name, Zhang, and was given the name Wenmin, which was decidedly un-revolutionary for the era. Many children ended up with names like "protect the east" (*weidong*, a reference to Mao), martial words like "struggle" (*jing*), or simply "red" (*hong*). The first character of her name, *wen*, means language, or culture. The second, *min*, means nimble, agile, smart, or quick. Zhang Wenmin: today it is common enough, but back then it was Mr. Zhang's way of rejecting the party's ideology.

But when his daughter became a writer a few decades later, she decided for an even more radical break. She dropped her proper name and became known even to her friends by her pen name, Jiang Xue, which literally means "river snow." It comes from the last two characters of a poem by the 8th-century poet Liu Zongyuan.

> *A thousand mountains and not a bird flying*
> *ten thousand paths and not a single footprint*
> *an old man in his raincoat in a solitary boat*
> *fishes alone in the freezing river snow*

The last three characters in Chinese are *han jiang xue*, the cold (*han*) river (*jiang*) (covered with) snow (*xue*). The word for cold, *han*, is also a homonym for ethnic Chinese people, the Han, making the poem a reflection of government failure—the people are adrift on a snowy river. For Jiang Xue the poem is about a solitary struggle, holding out, alone on a boat, facing immense trials beyond one's control. When she took it, she thought of her grandfather, the forces that he had faced, and his lonely decision one winter day in 1960.

Zhang Rulin was a righteous man, tall and strong, a person so impartial that bitter enemies who would accept him as judge in their case. His decisions were based on compassion and not the narrow application of the law. Before the Communist takeover, Tianshui had a branch of the Whampoa Military Academy, the foremost school of military affairs in the country, run under the iron fist of the Kuomintang Party. One day in the 1940s, a cadet appeared in Zhang Rulin's store, begging for help. He was not suitable for military life, he said, and wanted to go home. He was a deserter and if caught the punishment would be death. Zhang Rulin took him to his home, hid him for a few days, gave him a change of clothes, travel money, and sent him on his way. China had already been through years of war. No one deserved to be killed for not wanting to kill.

Zhang Rulin had been poor for most of his life. Around the time of the Communist takeover he had bought Tianshui's first noodle press, shipping it from the metropolis of Xi'an. He made noodles, flatbreads, and stuffed buns, eventually opening a small restaurant next door. His son recalls hearing the noodle machine working late into the night.

Then, life became complicated. The Communists usually attacked people like him, precisely because they had been pillars of their community. But he was poor and so was largely left alone. In 1958, however, the first communes were established. As a respected person, he was asked to head the one formed on his street. He did as ordered and reported to work. But then he realized that communes meant taking the peasants' land—land that the Communists had just given many of them a few years earlier. The communes also had ideas that were counter to traditional culture, such as eating in canteens and abolishing all private property, even work tools.

"So he didn't do it," Mr. Zhang said of his father. "He went for two days, then returned home."

Like all modernizers, the Communists were obsessed with steel production, because in Mao's fantasy world, steel equaled modernity. Enough steel would mean China had made it into the league of powerful countries. When government technocrats said it would take time to build up a steel industry, Mao insisted it could be done overnight through a form of magical thinking. Peasants would build furnaces and make steel in their backyard. The problem was that the farmers, as ingenious as they were, could only build brick kilns, which weren't hot enough to create steel. Mao went ahead anyway.

Zhang Rulin's son stopped going to school. Students were sent out to dig mud and cart it back to repair the primitive furnaces. These were about ten feet high and often cracked. He spent his days hauling mud to the kilns, where men pasted them on the chimneys. It wasn't just pointless work but economically disastrous. The farmers were no longer farming. And when they couldn't produce steel with their small furnaces, they were made to hand over all the metal in their homes so officials could report that steel had been produced.

"Officials went to everyone's home on the street and confiscated their pots, their knives, shovels, brass door locks, even the locks on dowry chests," Mr. Zhang recalled. The iron and brass were melted down into worthless ingots that counted as "steel" production. More ominously, this meant that farmers had been stripped of the tools they needed to farm.

Famine set in by the second half of 1959. Farmers had been told that they had to achieve yields of grain that were many times higher than any harvest recorded. They failed but were still taxed based on these imaginary numbers. Local officials tried to meet these quotas by confiscating private grain reserves and even seed grain.

In this part of China, people were used to going hungry in the springtime, after the winter stores ran out and when the spring planting still hadn't yielded crops. But this was different. Help was not around the corner. They had no tools. Most important, they had no seeds. Quickly, they dug up edible plants. When these were exhausted, people turned to inedible roots, such as tree bark or a topsoil called "Guanyin soil," perversely named after the Buddhist goddess of mercy. Corpses began to pile up: first the very old, then the sick, then infants, then the strong.

The city went silent. People stopped going out. Many lay in bed to conserve energy. Able-bodied men like Jiang Xue's grandfather, however, still had to work. Zhang Rulin was only 49 years old and like the other men in the commune was press-ganged into building a water diversion project on the outskirts of town.

The only place to get food was in the communal dining hall. Early on, the dining hall had plenty of food and people thought that communal life wasn't that bad—you could eat your fill regardless of how hard you worked. But now the dining hall had next to nothing to serve and no one had any food or grain at home, not to mention cooking utensils.

After laboring on the water project, Jiang Xue's grandfather would walk to the canteen every day and get the family's ration. It was one corn bun, about six inches in diameter. It had to feed six mouths. That was impossible. He pondered how to divvy up the bun. The children needed less than their parents, especially Mr. Zhang, who was still a physical laborer. Could the bun be divvied up according to need? He had always stood for justice, but now what was fair? What was just?

Mr. Zhang had decided many cases in the past, but here was one for which there was no fair compromise. Cannibalism was rampant in Tianshui, but Mr. Zhang recoiled at the idea. For him, his family's fate hung on the one bun that they received each day. His conclusion: at least one of them would starve to death. Rationally, they should decide who so the food could be spread among those who would live. That would maximize their chances of survival. But who would die? How would he tell that person? And how would others in the family accept his decision if he was condemning one of their closest kin to die? It would have to be a solution that appeared fair to everyone so they would go along.

Jiang Xue finishes the story, as her father has told it to her ever since she was a little girl at Chinese New Year.

"Grandfather was a just man. Every day he would take a knife and cut the bun into six equal pieces. One for each person. Each one the same. He weighed each piece on a scale. My youngest aunt, she was one year old, she got the same as her father. But he needed more. He was the only laborer in the family. But everyone got the same. They all survived. He starved to death. He sacrificed his life for us."

Jiang Xue and her father sit in his study on the second floor of her grandfather's house. It is a shrine to her grandfather and the world that died around that time. It is decorated with an enormous, gnarled tree trunk that acts as a massive coffee table. Next to it, a desk is stacked with books, writing brushes, scrolls, and all the other tools of a Chinese scholar's life. Calligraphy and landscapes made by her great-uncle grace the walls. An imperceptible layer of yellow Loess soil weathers the quiet tableau, adding to the sense of time frozen, but also of a rich, deep, shaded life, one rooted in eternal ideas that have survived centuries of turmoil, war, and famine.

They discuss her grandfather's death. He died of constipation in April 1960, his stomach filled with bark and Guanyin soil. He had been weak for four days and couldn't pass a stool. Family members took him to a hospital, but the staff were also starving and had no medicine. He died in acute pain. Because all the trees had been cut down to fuel the furnaces, his wife used the planks from their marital bed to fashion a rough coffin.

His death was why Mr. Zhang didn't return to school when the famine ended. He was the oldest male left in the family and couldn't bear to watch his mother work herself to death trying to feed three children. So he became a field laborer, earning less than a full-grown man but still able to help feed his siblings.

Jiang Xue learned her family history every Chinese New Year. Usually families gather for a reunion and a big feast. But before the Zhang family was allowed to eat, Jiang Xue's father made sure that his father ate his fill first. So he and his wife would bundle up Jiang Xue and her two siblings in their winter clothes and hike up the hill behind their house for half an hour to a small plateau. Back then, graves were discouraged as worthless luxuries, so there was no tombstone to find. But her father knew the location by heart and could find it in the night. He set out a white card with his father's name written out in block letters, a cup of tea, and a platter of food. Then he would burn paper money. The family would kowtow on the icy ground three times: knees, hands, head, hands, knees, then up. And again. And again. Then he would tell the story, starting each time with the words "back when we were starving . . . "

Jiang Xue thinks of the deaths. The mass graves. The lack of coffins. The "soft burials," where the body was wrapped in a sheet and buried in a shallow grave—no one had the energy for anything else. She turns to her father.

"The land is filled with corpses, isn't it? All the land behind the town, it's all corpses."

"You have to be careful when you write articles. Don't write so much about politics."

"How long have you been worried about me?"

"You mother was worried earlier."

"You didn't used to be worried about me."

"I wasn't. It's just in the past few years. I know the Communist Party's methods. If they punish you, if they target you, you can't escape."

"Have you seen my articles?"

"Just try not to involve the party so much."

"You want me to avoid mentioning the party because you're worried about me."

"When you write, just try not to comment too much."

"Dad, do you remember what happened in 1959?"

"They were elementary students. They were so hungry. They were at the end of their rope. One day class let out at noon. One of them was Tang Suiqiu. He was just an elementary school student. He was about 12. He was so hungry. He climbed up a dirt cliff and wrote with his finger in the soil 'Down with Mao Zedong' and 'Down with the Communist Party.' If you looked at the cliff in a certain light, you could see it."

"What happened to Tang?"

"They summoned everyone in the area for handwriting samples. In the middle of the night I was also called and had to write an essay. They couldn't figure out who it was. They had narrowed it to three people."

"Was one of them Tang?"

"No. But just as they were about to arrest one of the three, Tang stepped forward and said he did it."

"What happened to him?"

"He went to jail for eight to ten years."

"He was 12 years old and went to jail for eight to ten years? According to the law, of course."

"Yes, so you see if they want to find a crime to nail on you, they will."

"How did it get like this?"

"He said that we should rewrite history."

"Who?"

"Mao. He said we should rewrite history. But history has happened. If it's a novel, you can rewrite it. But if it's history, how can you rewrite it? Anyone with a conscience will reject rewritten history."

When the 1989 protests began, Jiang was elated. She and her high school classmates wired money to Beijing, addressed simply to "Tiananmen Square students." When the massacre occurred that June 4, they put out white flowers to mourn the victims.

She later attended the Northwest University of Politics and Law in Xi'an, but law bored her. Most graduates became prosecutors, judges, or police officers, but she saw what the system did to the men in her class.

"They had internships and would go to villages to work for the police. Some went to work in jails. They came back and told stories of drinking and smoking and how they'd beat prisoners in jail. I saw them change from nice boys to that. So I knew I wouldn't join the system. I didn't know what to do, but I knew that."

Jiang Xue was always bookish but good looking, with long straight hair, glasses, a poutish smile, and a peaceful demeanor that calmed people immediately. And she was good at writing. In college in the 1990s she had tried her hand at writing articles and discovered she was a fast writer. She felt she had found her calling.

That's when she decided on journalism. For one magical decade starting in the early 2000s, journalism flourished. Before then, Chinese newspapers had been founded on the Soviet model. They were organs of propaganda and made no pretense of informing in any objective or comprehensive ways. Provinces, cities, and local governments had their own papers, while ministries or bureaus also ran media outlets: the national trade union had *Workers' Daily*, the Communist Party's legal affairs office owned *Legal Daily*, and the party had *People's Daily*. In the early 1990s, China further liberalized its economy and began to marketize some of these newspapers. This didn't mean privatizing them—they were still run by state organizations—but most of them had to be profitable. Suddenly, they were motivated to appeal to readers.

Her first job was with *Huashangbao*, or *China Business News*, a formerly small newspaper in Xi'an. Under new management after 1997, it focused aggressively on social and lifestyle stories—accidents, disasters, and crime, but also scandals and investigative pieces.

"You could run around and go from event to event, and you could enter someone else's life and have them tell you what they were doing. At the start, in 1998, as a young person—I hadn't yet turned twenty-four—that was really interesting."

The articles were brash and newsy, but the idea of journalism informed by ethics and standards was only just gaining hold. Many pieces were sloppily researched and sometimes sensational. But, slowly, nationally known figures such as Professor Zhan Jiang of Beijing Foreign Studies University began to lecture and write about the best practices of international journalism. He translated winning submissions of America's highest journalism prize, the Pulitzer Prize, into Chinese, and interviewed top journalists on their craft. Gradually Jiang Xue and her friends began to take their jobs more seriously. But all of this was piecemeal and aimless until 2003, a year that journalists, writers, and thinkers across China often refer to as a turning point in public debate.

That was the year of Sun Zhigang, a student beaten to death in police custody. He had been a migrant and all that mattered to police was that he didn't have his identity card on him, so they beat him, and he sustained fatal injuries. His death galvanized journalists and public intellectuals, who successfully called for prosecution of the police officers and a rethinking in how migrants were viewed. In addition, a new administration under Communist Party Secretary Hu Jintao and Premier Wen Jiabao had just taken power. The outbreak of the respiratory illness SARS also caused people to feel that a new atmosphere was taking hold—the government spent months denying that the virus was a problem until it had to admit that a health crisis was unfolding. Suddenly, it seemed that the media could effect change, even in a partially closed system like China's.

This confluence of events inspired people across China—lawyers, artists, writers, activists, and scholars. Journalists like Jiang Xue took on increasingly ambitious projects. She wrote on corruption, environmental problems, and people evicted from their homes. Her editors sometime banned or toned down her pieces but enough could be published that it made a difference. For many journalists, the job turned into a calling.

Slowly—maybe inevitably—the party began to push back. It regained control over newsrooms, installing more acquiescent editors. By the early 2010s, authorities narrowed the range of topics that could be investigated, essentially ending a decade of crusading journalism. Jiang Xue stayed with the *China Business News* until 2013, when another, more ominous turning point occurred. The once-independent newspaper, *Southern Weekend*, published its annual New Year's address to its readers. For years this had been a clarion call for change—never a direct challenge to the Communist Party's authority, but usually it was an appeal to solve a pressing social problem. That year it called for existing constitutional rights to be respected, which in many ways was in line with the government's promotion of a fair and equal legal system.

Before the article was published, however, senior editors watered it down. That prompted a staff revolt. Reporters and editors took to social media to protest, and crowds gathered outside the newspaper's headquarters in downtown Guangzhou. Jiang Xue joined in from afar. She was now director of *China Business News*'s editorial page, a powerful bully pulpit that she used to publish criticisms of social problems and government malfeasance. She used it to comment directly on the mini-uprising, especially after it was put down and leading journalists were fired. A few weeks later, she, too, was singled out for criticism. Her editors issued an order: focus on reporting on everyday people and how their lives were getting better and better. She was then transferred to work in the newspaper's archives. Feeling that she was being set up to be fired, Jiang Xue quit.

That began her work as a freelance writer, publishing primarily in Hong Kong–based magazines. When they came under fire by authorities there, she took up her current work, which was writing for online news platforms, such as Initium. She also published articles on social media with donation buttons. The support generated by some of these articles—when they weren't censored—allowed her to make ends meet. She wrote about her hometown's changes, or the fate of the families of human rights lawyers. Over time she became more and more interested in the historical roots of China's authoritarian political system.

In 2016, she began to hear more and more about a magazine that had been published in Tianshui called *Spark*. Only a few issues had appeared in 1960 before the staff were arrested and sent to labor camps. An independent filmmaker named Hu Jie had made a movie about it in 2013, and a couple of survivors had published their memoirs. But no one had written in depth about the magazine. Jiang Xue was especially interested in why it still resonated today—why did so many public intellectuals in China seem to know about *Spark*?

She asked her father about it. As a boy growing up in Tianshui, he had heard of *Spark*. It had been a huge case, with rallies held in sports stadiums to condemn its participants. He agreed to help her out. Their first stop: a tractor shed down the street in the village of Mapaoquan.

The main offices of the First Historical Archives of China are located just north of the Forbidden City on a small campus of 1950s-era buildings. This was a brief period when the new People's Republic was trying to develop its own architectural style, and several famous architects came up with a hybrid form: a main structure made of brick, not wood, allowing it to be much bigger and higher, but the roofs tiled, and the eaves curved. At the time, many condemned the style as a pastiche, but these are among the few buildings in the capital that bridge the past with the present.

The archives have a spacious auditorium with red velour-covered walls and bay windows that overlook the sparkling lake of Beihai Park. One sunny February afternoon, the auditorium was booked for a speaker, Liu Guozhong, a Tsinghua University professor who spoke on a topic that over the course of the 2010s shook China's intellectual world: the discovery of long-lost texts from China's Axial Age of about 2,500 years ago.

That era gave rise to some of China's greatest thinkers, such as Confucius, Laozi, Sunzi, and Han Feizi. Many of these thinkers, especially Confucius and Han Feizi, have been used by rulers down the ages to justify hierarchy and obedience. But as Jiang Xue's father knew from his years of studying the texts, they also hold subversive ideas. It was these ideas that inspired him to study the classics, a form of internal exile and resistance to the world outside.

Unlike Maoism, these ideas provided a philosophical framework different from the ruler's—the emperor might have his ideas, but it was Confucianism that provided the moral guidance for officials. And they often made use of it, especially the duty to remonstrate against official abuse. That sometimes came in the form of a protest that saw the official punished, such as Su Dongpo or Sima Qian, while other times it was a quiet withdrawal from public life.

What Professor Liu was discussing was even more evidence that these ancient ideas were inherently destabilizing to authoritarian rule. He spoke for ninety minutes, beginning with simple explanations to make sure his points would be understandable for the lay audience. He said that the Egyptians wrote on papyrus. In Babylon there was no papyrus, so they used clay tablets. In China, an early form of writing was found on tortoise shells, which were heated with pokers until they

cracked. The lines were9 used in divination, much like the lines on people's hands might tell their future. On these shattered shells, questions
and answers were written down, giving them their name: oracle bones.
Those are the earliest known Chinese writing, but they are mainly about
very narrow topics: should the crops be planted on such-and-such a
day, should the king launch a war? Get married? Travel? Through the
oracle bones, a scholar could fathom the daily concerns of a Shang
king's life, but not too much else.

The texts that Liu wanted to discuss had been written later on flat
strips of bamboo. The slips were the size of chopsticks and paper thin.
From the desk where he sat, Liu demonstrated how researchers think
the texts were composed: a strip was placed on the left forearm and
the writer used the right hand to hold a writing brush and compose the
text. This, he said, is presumably why for millennia Chinese wrote their
script top to bottom, right to left.

Even more significant were the topics. These were not minutiae of
court life but the ur-texts of Chinese culture. Over the past twenty years,
three batches of bamboo slips from this era have been unearthed. One
cache was discovered in 1998 in Guodian and has eight hundred slips.
Another, discovered in 2000 and held by the Shanghai Museum, has
one thousand two hundred slips. The one Liu was introducing has a
whopping two thousand five hundred slips. The trove came because
of grave robbers who were likely working in Hubei. The slips ended up
in Hong Kong and were to be auctioned off when a donor stepped in,
bought the lot, and gave it to his alma mater, Tsinghua Univer4sity, in
2008. Liu works at a new center at Tsinghua built to house the bamboo
treasures.

The bamboo slips inspire profound challenges to long-accepted
truths about Chinese political culture. The texts stem from the Warring States period, an era of turmoil in China that ran from the 5th
to the 3rd centuries BCE. This was a time when civilizations around
the world, from the Yellow River in China to the Greek peninsula in
Europe and the Indian subcontinent, were organizing new ways of
political and philosophical order—a period so crucial to world history
that the German historian Karl Jaspers called it the Axial Age. All
major Chinese schools of thought that now exist come from this era.
They include Daoism, which developed into China's only indigenous
religion, and Confucianism, which has been the country's dominant
political ideology, guiding kings and emperors—at least in theory—
until today.

One surprise is that ideas that were only alluded to in the Confucian classics were actually full-blown schools of thought—and these once-lost schools challenge crucial Confucian ideas. One text, for example, argues in favor of meritocracy much more forcefully than do the currently known Confucian texts. Until now, the Confucian texts only allowed for abdication or replacement of a ruler as a rare exception; the norm was hereditary kingships, which justified their right to rule on a combination of divine right and performance.

This is essentially how the Communist Party justifies its right to rule: the Kuomintang had become corrupt and ineffective; thus the Communists were justified in usurping power. The party's continued rule is likewise justified by China's economic development, which proves heaven's support ("history's judgment," in communist parlance). But true to Chinese tradition, the party makes clear that its rule is hereditary. This is true not only broadly in the sense that other parties cannot take power, but narrowly in the creation of a quasi-hereditary class that has coalesced around "red" families that helped found the Communist state, such as Xi Jinping's family. The old texts, however, show that even in ancient China, a significant group of writers disapproved of such practices, arguing for rule based purely on merit rather than membership in a group.

Without viewing the past too much through today's lens, one can also see other intriguing parallels to contemporary society. Back in the Warring States Period, increasing literacy and urbanization gave rise to a class of gentlemen scholars, or *shi*, who advised kings; some thought that they might be better qualified than the person born to the throne— the origins of the meritocracy argument. Today, similar trends are at work, but on a much broader scale. Now, instead of a scholar class that wants a say, it is large swaths of the population.

One might even say that the excavated texts show a more freewheeling society than today's. Here we encounter a past that was home to vigorous debates—a place where Confucians approved of kings abdicating and might even have fancied themselves capable of ruling. Today's China also has such ideas, but like the bamboo slips before their discovery, they are buried and their excavation taboo.

In his talk in the auditorium, Liu was much more circumspect. But the appeal of his talk was obvious. The bamboo slips are being edited carefully, with one volume of a projected fifteen volumes released each year. The project is likely to be finished only around 2030. After each volume is released, there is a media rush to discuss the findings, while

blogs and amateurs—like many of the people here this winter afternoon, or Jiang Xue's father—try their own hands at interpreting these
new finds. The audience followed Liu carefully as he outlined their publishing schedule.

"We'll be publishing until after I'm retired," Liu says, laughing. "But
then you and others will be debating this for the rest of this century. The
research is endless."

Liu concluded and bowed to the audience. He had surpassed tea-
time. The organizers did not allow for questions and began turning off
the lights.

But the audience rushed the stage, peppering Liu with questions. A
man from the Book of Changes Research Society asked him how they
should treat new texts on divination. A graduate student from Peking
University asked about the political implications of abdication. Liu soon
ran out of name cards and people began passing his last card around
to be photographed.

The lights were now off, and the room was lit only by the dim winter
sun. The guards stood at the back of the room, waiting to lock the door.
But the crowd of two dozen would not let Liu leave because he held the
key to how they understand themselves: the past.

4

Spark

On the southeastern edge of Tianshui is a strip of shops and houses with an improbably romantic name, Mapaoquan, or "Horse Running Springs." The name comes from the 7th century, when a famous general was helping establish China's most glorious empire, the Tang. He came through town looking for water and rested for a while. Suddenly, his horse bolted forward and began digging into a mound of yellow Loess soil. A few minutes later, water appeared. The word for an animal pawing the ground, *pao*, is a synonym for "running." But the new name also made sense because it could refer to Tianshui's origins as a cavalry base.

Tianshui's military importance was largely because it was a border town. Sitting at the base of terraced fields of wheat and sorghum, it straddles the last good grain-growing areas before the deserts farther west. These prairies were ideal for herding and training horses for battle, but communication with the court was still relatively easy via the Wei River, which flows east to ancient China's most important capital, Xi'an. That made Mapaoquan a bulwark against enemies of Chinese civilization, its horses just as important to the empire as the nearby fortifications that are collectively known as the Great Wall.

In the mid-20th century, Mapaoquan became the site of an equally momentous struggle: early Communist efforts to impose a totalitarian state. When that battle was launched in the 1950s, the town still harkened back to its earlier history, with fields that ran down the Loess slopes to the river. Shrines dotted the landscape, some dedicated to folk deities, others housing the ancestors of prominent local families—an imaginary, eternal China of fields and farmers, temples and traditions.

In fact, local society was being torn apart. Mao's violent revolution had left the temples empty and desecrated. The size of the plots implied small-scale land holdings, but all land now belonged to the state. And for the sharp-eyed, new buildings hinted at the state's unbridled power. One housed the local Communist Party offices, where Beijing's orders were disseminated to villagers. Another was a new garage, which held a tractor—the first promise of the party's pledge to modernize rural life. The village had just one of the machines, and the farmers shared it. In the past, life centered around communal religious life; now it was to revolve around a new god, science, and its guardian: the Communist Party.

Zhang Chunyuan was the tractor's custodian. Just 26 years old, he was veteran of the Korean War, where he had wounded in action and later trained to repair and drive army vehicles. People of his skills were rare in this backward region, and local leaders felt lucky to have him. They gave him the task of overseeing the valuable tractor. He watched over it, repaired it, and drove it for local farmers because nobody else knew how.

Zhang's skills, though, couldn't mask the fact that he was a social outcast. He was a decorated soldier and a university student, a combination that seemed unimpeachable. But he was in Mapaoquan because he had been caught up in the Anti-Rightist Campaign. In May 1958, he was exiled here along with forty other students and faculty from Lanzhou University. They were among the millions who had responded to the Communist Party's request for criticism by giving mild, constructive critiques of problems that they thought could be addressed--assessments that resulted in their exile. In the spring of 1959, just as the flowers were opening on campus, Zhang and the others were banished to Tianshui to labor in the fields.

The students and teachers were divided into two teams. One group was sent farther west to a neighboring county, Wushan. Zhang and another two dozen were assigned to Mapaoquan. The students and teachers were given agricultural work, such as planting fields or tending sheep. This was when the Great Famine of 1959 was taking hold and the students saw the gruesome effects firsthand. As young, strong men and women they were able to withstand the lack of food, but they saw the elderly, the weak, and the very young slowly die.

The students were also spared the famine's worst because of Chinese people's love of education. Even in a famine, local officials realized that these young people had knowledge that far surpassed anything that existed locally. One official had the idea to use the young exiles to run an open university to teach local farmers how to read. That gave the group respite from the hard labor and the chance to prepare classes in the party's offices next to the tractor shed. They found a rare opportunity to read national newspapers and follow the surreal, disastrous train of events that had led to the famine and which were preventing a change of course.

In August 1959, they read about the record yields in Henan and other miraculous events that they knew were outright falsifications. As one of the students, Tan Chanxue, later wrote in her memoirs: "Grain production was supposedly sky-high, but the people's stomachs were flat, and farmers lived in a desolate, hungry world. Trees were stripped of bark and wild vegetables picked clean from the fields."

Soon, the students began to see examples of cannibalism. Walking down from the mountains in search of wild roots, Tan and her classmates saw a group of people surrounding a man selling meat-filled buns—a miracle! "The next day I heard that someone found a fingernail in the bun. My heart trembled. My God!" Old people vanished, only to be found dismembered and hanging from meat hooks in a cellar. Tan figured that three kinds of people survived: officials, who could use their power to get food; clever people, who could steal and snatch; and those who fled west to the oases of Xinjiang, China's Turkic borderland that still had grain and fruit.

The students often met at Zhang's tractor station. It was conveniently located on the main road, where Zhang was an amiable and thoughtful host. Broad and strong, with thick eyebrows and a square face, he had sensitive eyes and loved to read. His knowledge complemented his war experiences, which gave him knowledge that the bookish students couldn't match. But he didn't lecture or talk down to them, instead engaging them in long conversations about the country's future. One point he returned to time and again was how they, even though just students in exile, were duty-bound to help their country.

"He really opposed those who only thought of themselves," Tan Chanxue recalled. "He never thought that his own liberty counted for much."

Some of the group lost hope and tried to flee China. One was Ding Hengwu, a big, burly fellow who had graduated from the mathematics department. He was perpetually hungry but spent hours at a local reservoir teaching himself to swim, part of his plan to escape. One day, he set off to walk a thousand miles south to the Burmese border. His plan was to swim across the Mekong. No one ever found out what became of him.

The most shocking story was that of their classmate Sun Ziyun. He was a Chinese literature major and a Communist Party member. As the famine claimed more and more lives, he wrote a letter to the party's leading theoretical journal, *Red Flag*, informing its editors of the unfolding disaster. He was proud of his letter, sure that the party was unaware of the true situation at the grassroots level. It would welcome his cautious, loyal advice and send aid. He and the other students waited expectantly.

A few months later, in the autumn of 1959, militiamen showed up and arrested Sun while he was working in the field. In front of everybody else they beat him, trying to get him to confess to counterrevolutionary activity. They hung buckets of feces and urine from his neck until the buckets' metal handles bit into his neck and he fainted. Later, he was handcuffed so tightly that blood circulation was cut off and his hands began to rot. Eventually he escaped and fled to another province. The episode left the students stunned: if even a loyal party member like Sun could be treated like this, the party had no interest in the truth.

Zhang Chunyuan thought through many of these issues. Tan Chanxue related to him the story of the peasant woman in whose home she lived. One night, the old woman had cried out in hunger, asking what the peasants had done wrong. They had supported the Communist revolution but now the Communists were starving them to death. Why?

Tan asked Zhang what they should do. He said they couldn't look away. Reports filtering back to even this remote outpost made it clear that the famine was not isolated to Tianshui or its surroundings. It was a national catastrophe. They had to do something. As another of the students, Xiang Chengjian, put it: "If you do not break out of silence, you will die in silence."

Zhang Chunyuan had all the makings of a loyal Communist. A native of rural Henan, Zhang and his family had only known hard times. The area was always on the verge of famine, and that made many people interested in the Communists' appeal to social justice and economic development. In Zhang's case, the party was also an ersatz family. His mother had died when he was 7 and, in his telling, his stepmother had treated him cruelly.

At 13, he ran away from home, never to return. He worked as an apprentice car mechanic and then joined the People's Liberation Army in 1948 as a 16-year-old. When China entered the Korean War in 1950, he volunteered and was wounded when his convoy was strafed by US fighter planes. His neck was permanently damaged and in 1954 he was discharged. He took advantage of policies favoring veterans and entered Lanzhou University's history department.

That began his disillusionment with how the Communists were running China. He thought a university would have a magnificent library but found that most books were under lock and key. Lanzhou University didn't even possess a complete set of the Confucian classics—the basic texts used over the centuries by all literate people—let alone cutting-edge journals. Teaching was worse, with one lecturer for 100 students.

When the Hundred Flowers Campaign began, Zhang criticized the lack of books and poor teaching. For that, he was accused of trying to overthrow the university and sent with the others to Tianshui.

But he took up his job at the Mapaoquan Tractor Station with gusto, fixing and driving the valuable piece of equipment. At nights he even wrote a film script, "Children of China and North Korea," which talked about the ties binding the two socialist countries. He used a pseudonym to send it to a movie studio that was sponsoring a competition. He won a prize worth 700 yuan, a small fortune back in the 1950s. The script was set to be produced until the studio delved deeper into the mysterious author and realized that it had been written by a convicted Rightist.

Zhang, though, was irrepressible. As a boy he was given the nickname "Screw" for being unbreakable when his mind was set on something. That made him cut out to lead the other students, because he had the toughness to do more than just talk—he could get things done. But his uncompromising attitude also led him to take huge risks.

In Tianshui, he once heard that a classmate was being detained by railway police several hundred miles south for having illegally ridden the rails to escape the famine. Zhang forged an identity card as a Public Security officer and traveled down to straighten out the situation. He bluffed his way past railway guards and local police to get the young man released, returning in triumph, convinced that he could achieve anything.

In more densely populated areas farther east, the students probably would never have been able to meet at a place like Zhang's tractor shed. Tianshui, however, was remote and poor, and the students were working at the open university, which gave them an excuse to meet and travel around the region. These face-to-face meetings, they realized, were crucial. Sun's case showed that working alone resulted in nothing. A pebble can't break a rock, Tan Chanxue said, but perhaps many pebbles tied tightly together could smash it.

Everyone in the group became good friends, but Tan and Zhang were particularly close, later declaring themselves to be husband and wife. A slender 24-year-old with thin, arching eyebrows, Tan came from southern China's Guangdong province near the Hong Kong border. While Zhang was bullheaded and brusque, she was gentle, with calm eyes and a reasonable demeanor. There were many obstacles to a love in a famine-ridden land run by a totalitarian dictatorship, but they would soon risk their lives to prove their feelings.

By May 1959, the group was debating issues such as how to rid China of the Communist Party, or at least the current leadership that had caused the famine. Zhang said there were two options: a top-down coup or a bottom-up revolution. The latter seemed impossible and so they hoped that Mao's peers would act. And in fact, something along these lines is what some people in Beijing were planning. Over the summer, one of China's most-decorated military leaders, Peng Dehuai, challenged Mao, but Mao held a pivotal meeting in the mountain-top retreat of Lushan. Peng was crushed and Mao redoubled his economic policies, causing the famine to deepen.

When Peng's downfall was made public, the students felt certain that they had to act: if even a general at the top could be persecuted for expressing loyal dissent, then the only hope was to foment something at the grass roots. They thought that their best bet was to publish material on the famine in hopes of sharing ideas and opening up officials' eyes to what was going on in the countryside. They began to think of publishing a journal.

The idea remained vague until they came across a remarkable poem. It was written by a student at Peking University, Lin Zhao, who had been in studying in Beijing until she was labeled a "Rightist" for defending friends who were being persecuted. Lin's poems galvanized the students, showing them the power of the written word.

Like Zhang, Lin was more experienced than many of the younger students. She had worked as a propagandist for the Communists shortly after their takeover in 1949. At the time, she went along with their violent policies and participated in the land reform campaigns that saw hundreds of thousands, if not millions, of property owners murdered. But with time she began to see that the Communists were not building a utopia but a tightly controlled authoritarian state. As a young girl in pre-Communist China, she had attended a Methodist girl's school. Now she returned to her faith and experimented with art to express her independence from the party. When her friends were arrested, she wrote a poem declaring:

> *The power of truth*
> *never lies in*
> *the arrogant air*
> *of the guardians of truth.*

Lin later wrote a 240-line poem called "Seagull" and circulated it among friends. One friend was the sister of a member of the group of Tianshui students. The woman mailed a copy of the poem to the exiled students. The group was thrilled by Lin's bold imagery and overtly political message. The poem tells the story of a ship carrying chained prisoners. Their crime: they seek freedom.

> *Freedom, I cry out inside me, freedom!*
> *The thought of you has filled my heart with yearning,*
> *like a choking man gasping for air,*
> *like one dying of thirst lurching toward a spring.*

Zhang decided that he had to meet the author. After being arrested in Beijing, Lin was released after her chronic tuberculosis worsened, and she begun spitting up blood. She moved back to her hometown of Suzhou on China's east coast. She was immediately put under close surveillance. But Zhang once again took another huge risk, using his forged identity papers to travel days by train and then arranging to meet her. Lin urged Zhang not to print her poem, seeing it a risk to the group and to anyone who read it.

But then Zhang read Lin's second poem, a 368-line work called "A Day in Prometheus's Passion." It used Christ-like motifs that reflected Lin's deepening Christian faith. The poem tells of an encounter between Zeus and Prometheus, who is chained to a rock for giving humans fire. Zeus explains that his punishment is necessary because humans must never have such an important tool.

> *But you ought to know, Prometheus,*
> *for the mortals, we do not want to leave even a spark.*
> *Fire is for the gods, for incense and sacrifice,*
> *how can the plebeians have it for heating or lighting in the dark?*

Zhang convinced Lin to let them publish the poem and decided to put it in the first issue of their new journal. Students from Beijing also passed him materials about how Yugoslavian Communists were trying a hybrid form of socialism that allowed for capitalist-style incentives (something the Communist Party would formally embrace twenty years later). Zhang decided to add that material, too, to the inaugural issue, as well as essays by himself and others in the group. The journal needed a name. They quickly settled on *Spark*, based on the idiomatic expression *xinghuo liaoyuan,* or "a single spark can start a prairie fire." Mao had used it in one of his essays, making it widely known.

Two members of the group, physics student Miao Qingjiu and chemistry student Xiang Chengjian, were entrusted with printing the issue. They had been assigned to work at a sulfuric acid plant in the western suburb of Wushan. The plant had an old mimeograph machine, which they could occasionally access. Their jobs also required them to cultivate bacteria used to make fertilizer, a process that required a sealed-off space. This allowed them to bar themselves in the room with the mimeograph machine, claiming that they were making the bacteria.

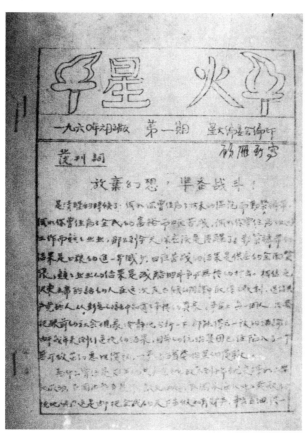

The two spent eight nights in January 1960 carving the plates by hand—there was no typesetting or other equipment available. The process, though, was too slow. Miao and Xiang would eventually have to open their office, which would endanger the enterprise. As always, Zhang came up with the solution. Inside his tractor shed was an old motor. He gave it to Miao and Xiang, who sold it to their factory cheaply. They used the proceeds to buy a used mimeograph machine. The group kept that at the home of Gu Yan, a graduate student in physics, who lived near Zhang. He also carved essays on that machine's drums, and drew the magazine's logo, a torch with a flame leaping upward. They ran off thirty copies. *Spark* was born.

At just eight pages, handwritten, and with no photos or graphics, Spark was primitive. But it was filled with articles that got to the heart of China's conundrum—then and now. The lead article on the first page by Gu Yan set the tone. Called "Give Up Your Fantasies and Prepare to Fight!" it asked questions that have been posed time and again over the decades:

> *Why did the once progressive Communist Party become so corrupt and reactionary less than ten years after coming to power, with complaints and rebellions at home, and falling into an embarrassing situation abroad? This is because the people's world is regarded as its private property, and all matters are managed by party members.*

One key problem was due to "idol worship"—alluding to the personality cult surrounding Mao Zedong. But it also pointed to broader problems, such as the state's unlimited powers: "political oligarchs being arrogant, and perverted. If such a dictatorship insists on calling it socialism, it should be a kind of National Socialism monopolized by a political oligopoly. It is of the same type as Nazi National Socialism and has nothing in common with real socialism."

Writing about the famine, Zhang Chunyuan penned an essay simply titled "Food Matters." He blamed the Chinese Communist Party for exploiting the farmers: "Today's ruler, like any ruler in history, used the peasant revolution to climb Tiananmen Square and ascended to the throne." After that, China's new rulers trampled on the farmers, leaving them no better than serfs. In another essay, he pointed to the lack of land ownership as a key problem facing farmers.

These issues are still surprisingly current. Even today, farmers don't own their land, making it difficult to consolidate agricultural plots. They also cannot mortgage land to finance land improvement or sideline enterprises. Mostly, they are at the whims of officials, who can confiscate their land, force them to move to cities, or to grow certain products that are deemed economically important.

A few months later, the students met again and decided to make *Spark* a regular publication. The goal was to mail it to high-level officials in five major cities—Beijing, Shanghai, Wuhan, Guangzhou, Xi'an—where the students had contacts. They began writing more essays, including Zhang Chunyuan's "On People's Communes," which dissected how farmers lost their property, and Xiang Chengjian's "Letter to the People," a takedown of top leaders.

> *When millions, tens of millions of farmers starve to death on their beds, on trains, by railroads, at the bottom of a ditch, when hundreds of millions (400 million) people are dying of starvation, when the other 200 million are half-starved. When they are full, those animals who "wholeheartedly" serve the people and are "people's servants" can buy any snacks, biscuits, candies. . . . They feasted and walked away (who would dare to ask them for food stamps), and as soon as they arrived, the meal was served.*

Xiang continued in this vein by pointing out the moral relativism of China's top leaders. Decades before Mao's private doctor shocked the world with his tales of Mao's sex with young women, Xiang pointed out the hypocrisy of the older men who led China. While appealing to steadfastness and loyalty, they had taken up with younger women, casting aside their wives who had suffered with them while they were fighting for the revolution. Even worse, information had come to light during the Anti-Rightist Campaign showing that many officials freely took the daughters and wives of persecuted families.

Lin Zhao's "Seagull" was also slotted into this issue. It was engraved onto cylinders in addition to Zhang's "On People's Communes." While they were figuring out the logistics of engraving and then distributing their new issue, they ran off 300 copies of Zhang's article because of its importance in analyzing the root causes of the famine. The idea was to mail out that article first and follow it up with the full issue.

As the second issue neared publication, the group began to debate what to do next. They decided they needed some sort of organization and ways to spread their appeal beyond the narrow group of exiled students. They knew immediately whom to recruit: a far-sighted official named Du Yinghua.

Wushan lies about 100 kilometers west of Tianshui on the edge of the Loess Plateau. The area relies on agriculture, which depends entirely on rainfall. Little wonder that the area is replete in folk religious temples to the Dragon King—the deity who controls the waters.

Du Yinghua's youth was defined by Wushan's poverty and China's wars. Born in 1927, he was 4 when Japan annexed northeastern China and 10 when the two countries went to war. As a teenager he joined Communist Party underground cells that fought the Japanese occupation. The Communists' wartime base at Yan'an was also located in the same sandy, silty Loess Plateau, and word had spread about their promise to help farmers. Du came to believe strongly in the party's promise to use science to better China. After the revolution, he was put in charge of his home county. And when the students arrived in 1959, he welcomed them as talented people who could help spread literacy and modern ideas.

Tan Chanxue was a Chinese literature student but had some familiarity with chemistry. She offered to build a plant that could make sulfuric acid, a key ingredient in fertilizer. Du quickly accepted, treating her and the other students with respect. The students came to trust him. When they received reading material from friends and classmates in Beijing or other big cities, they shared it with Du. The chemistry graduate student Xiang Chengjian took a gamble and lent him the Yugoslav reform program, and later told him about *Spark*. Du was flabbergasted but interested.

In normal times, an official like Du would probably have realized how extremely dangerous it was to even think of an open challenge to the party like *Spark*. But Wushan's situation was desperate. It had a population of 590,000 but in 1959 an estimated 130,000 to 140,000 starved to death. Another 120,000 fled in search of food. That meant that the population had dropped by 50 percent in just a year, a collapse of epic proportions.

One day, Xiang walked across the county to file a report with Du. It was late when he arrived and cold outside, so Du invited him to spend the night in the one-room hut where he lived. Du was a humble, down-to-earth host. He cooked Xiang dinner and boiled hot water so Xiang could wash his feet.

After dinner they went to bed. It was pitch black, cold, and quiet. Xiang thought Du had fallen asleep but then Du began speaking. He said that he had fought to overthrow Chiang Kai-shek and the Kuomintang in order to help farmers. But what had this brought? Just hunger and death. As bad as the Kuomintang had been, it had allowed dissenting voices to exist, people like the author Lu Xun. By contrast, the Communists were more efficient and ruthless, eradicating every dissenting voice. Xiang recalled Du's words:

> *Now all these different voices are gone, and China has become a world of nonsense and lies! Tomorrow, a large number of people will starve to death, but the survivors will be forced to shout every day that the situation is great. What a strange phenomenon! It is unique in ancient and modern times. I don't know why the world has become like this.*

Despite their efforts, the young people felt helpless. Society was collapsing. Cannibalism was rampant. People had nothing to wear. Who could overthrow the Communist Party and restore sanity to China?

The Kuomintang was of no use. It had been defeated and now was holed up in its island redoubt of Taiwan. Someone had to escape from China and find help, or at least get more information about the situation in other socialist countries, such as Yugoslavia. Maybe this would help their country find a way forward.

Tan decided to try to seek help in Hong Kong. She was from Guangzhou, the metropolis not far from the British colony, and she figured she could make her way across the border. The students were some twelve hundred miles away, but China was in such chaos that it wouldn't appear odd if a university student traveled back to her hometown to find food. So she made her way south by train and stayed with an aunt.

The two women decided to flee together to Hong Kong and hired a human smuggler to spirit them across the border. They dressed as peasant women and walked to a village near the border. The smuggler, however, was inexperienced and led the women straight into the hands of the local militia, who detained them in Shenzhen. Back then, Shenzhen was still a village, not the city of nearly 20 million that it is today.

They tried to play the role of peasants, hoping to be let off with a warning for having strayed too close to the border. So when they were allowed out to do manual labor by collecting firewood, the two did so barefoot, although their soft feet were quickly cut by the rough terrain.

Still, no one seemed aware of her true identity until Tan made a fatal mistake. One day, a guard told Tan that if she wanted to post a letter, he would carry it out and post it. She was supposed to be illiterate but decided to use the chance to warn the group around *Spark* that she had been detained. A few weeks later, she realized her mistake. She was taken in for interrogation and asked if she knew a man named Gao Chengqing. This was Zhang Chunyuan's pen name. How did they know about him?

The letter itself wasn't a trap. It had been delivered, and Zhang had quickly heard that his sweetheart had been detained. He decided to rescue her, just as he had helped out his friend a year earlier. He used the same forged identity card, which gave his identity as his pen name,

Gao Chengqing, and traveled south. But the women were being held in a Reform-Through-Labor Facility, which was much stricter than the railway police he had fooled before. They immediately saw through his ruse and put him under arrest. Because they didn't know his real identity, they booked him by his pen name.

Feigning illness, Zhang met a female doctor who was also a prisoner. Feeling he could trust her, he told her that he and Tan were husband and wife and asked her to pass her notes. He wrote several, many of them professing his love and hope for a life after imprisonment. He used an intimate form of address, using only the last character of her given name, *xue*, which means "snow."

> *Snow! It must be a match made in heaven that we can go to jail together. Our feelings will transcend all time and space. May we go out and in, life and death together! The days to come will be long. Take care!*

But the doctor wasn't willing to risk her future for a man she didn't know. She could gain by informing on him and, anyway, he himself might be a ruse to test her. All of Zhang's love letters ended up in the authorities' hands.

The authorities sent a political prisoner to live with Zhang in his cell. The man befriended Zhang, who again fell for the ploy. Zhang confessed everything, not only their hopes to escape but the existence of *Spark*. Soon, Zhang and Tan were on a train back to Lanzhou for trial. *Spark* had lasted only a year and now was extinguished.

By September, the case was cracked. In what became the fourth largest "counter-revolutionary" incident in the country, forty-three people were arrested in connection with *Spark*, including twelve university students, two professors, two graduate students, and twenty-five farmers.

Revenge was swift. The party convened a "Ten-Thousand-Person Sentencing Conference" in Lanzhou to hand down the sentences to those who were still in Tianshui. Zhang Chunyuan got life in prison. The students who carved the drums, Miao Qingjiu and Xiang Chengjian, got twenty and eighteen years. Others got between fifteen and five years, including the official Du Yinghua.

Tan Chanxue spent fourteen years in prison for membership in a "Rightist counterrevolutionary clique." After that, she was forced to take a factory job in Jiuquan, the city near the Jiabiangou labor camp and the satellite launch facility. It was only after her rehabilitation in 1980 that she could leave the factory. She later joined the Dunhuang Research Academy before retiring to Shanghai in 1998. During a trip back to Tianshui in the 1990s, she met people who still knew her case. Once, a woman grasped her hands and said, "You have suffered so!" Tan could only burst into tears.

She was lucky compared to many of the others. The security apparatus quickly picked up those who had fled Gansu. In Shanghai, the physics student Gu Yan, who had come up with the magazine's name and logo, received a seventeen-year sentence. The prison term for Lin Zhao, the poet whose work inspired Zhang to launch the journal, was twenty.

Many fought their fate, especially Zhang. In July 1961, he feigned illness and was admitted to the hospital. During the midday siesta, while everyone was overcome by the summer heat, he changed into street clothes and walked out of the hospital. He hitched a ride to a nearby town, then walked 19 kilometers to a logging camp where a friend worked.

He lived in his friend's logging hut, regained his strength, and then set off to Shanghai to see what had become of his friends. He found that Gu Yan had already been arrested. Then he went to the neighboring city of Suzhou to learn that Lin Zhao had also been arrested. He wrote her a postcard, signing it with her mother's name but figuring that she would recognize his handwriting: "Our life is so rich in materials that we could write a novel that hasn't been seen in ancient or modern times, at home or abroad. I hope you can read this book, this book that cost us so dearly . . ."

Zhang then moved on to the nearby city of Hangzhou, feeling guilty that he was free while his friends were in prison. It's a measure of the turmoil in China brought on by the famine and political instability that he stayed free for so long. But then the inevitable happened. As the famine was brought under control, the government reasserted itself. Zhang was picked up in a street sweep of homeless people. He was identified and sent back to prison in Lanzhou.

A few years later, the party's next convulsion, the Cultural Revolution, proved deadly for some of those in jail. After a brief period of chaos at the start of the Cultural Revolution, the party promulgated new rules to "strengthen public security work." That resulted in harsh crack-downs across the country. Young people were once again sent to re-mote areas to work. Prisons carried out mass executions of convicts.

In 1970, local authorities in Tianshui decided that the new rules meant that Zhang and the sympathetic party secretary, Du Yinghua, should be executed. They had been briefly in contact while in prison, leading authorities to claim that the two were in an "active" counter-revolutionary cell—a capital offense.

For a few months before Zhang and Du's execution, Zhang and Tan were housed in the same prison. Tan wanted Zhang to know, before his death, that she still loved him. She asked someone who de-livered him his meals to tell him that "he will always live in my heart."

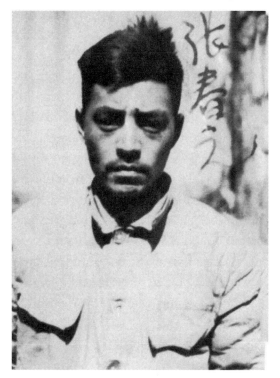

Zhang was sent to the Lanzhou Detention Center to be executed. The prison was nicknamed the "kiln," a castle-like complex with walls 10 meters high and topped with barbed wire. When he entered his final cell, number 12, he was wearing a black cotton prison shirt and trousers, a black cotton cap, and black cotton shoes without laces. Heavy shackles weighing about fifteen kilograms were attached to his ankles, which were wrapped in cotton to prevent bleeding. His hands were cuffed tight behind his back. He could only clutch his sole belongings, a chipped enamel bowl and cup stuffed with a rolled up white cotton towel. He could drop his trousers to urinate or defecate but inmates had to help him pull them back up.

The dozen or so prisoners in the room roused themselves to look at the condemned man. He apologized for bothering them and waited politely for someone to make space for him to sit down. The men were dumbfounded and soon made space.

The prisoner in charge of the room was a man named Wang Zhongyi. He had been rounded up in a sweep of young people and charged with hooliganism. Now he was under orders to make sure that Zhang didn't commit suicide. Over the next three days the men became close and Zhang entrusted Wang with telling Tan how much he loved her.

One of the young men asked Zhang if he was scared. His case was serious, wasn't it? Zhang replied: "Yes, it's serious: active counter-revolutionary activity."

Zhang told the men his life story. Then, on March 22 he was led out to the Qilihe Stadium for a mass sentencing. Before he left, he made Wang promise that somehow, someday, he would find Tan and tell her two sentences: "First, I have a clear conscience toward the party, the country, and the people, and I'm sorry because I can't accompany her to finish the road of life. Second, she must live well; the future is bright and boundless!"

Standing next to Zhang in the stadium was Du Yinghua, the party secretary. They were condemned to death and then led out to Willow Gulley in Donggang Township, where they were shot.

After Zhang's death, a notice was put up in various prisons around the district. One was Tan's women's prison. Tan saw it. Within a month her hair had gone white.

The poet Lin Zhao was equally stubborn. She was released in 1962 on medical parole due to her tuberculosis. Around this time, moderates in the leadership briefly sidelined Mao. Lin was hopeful that change was afoot, so she curbed her criticisms. But once out on the street, she saw that the party hadn't changed. She packed her clothes and informed neighborhood police that she was ready to be taken back to prison.

The party soon obliged. Later that year she was again detained and appeared before a judge, charged with "counter-revolution." She argued that the term was meaningless, and that "the real question" was what crimes China's rulers had committed. She was so blunt that the judge asked, "Are you sick?"

In fact, her mental health was precarious, which is unsurprising given her solitary confinement and mistreatment. The most common form of torture that she and others suffered was handcuffing, with the arms pulled behind the back and the handcuffs tightly fastened, leaving the inmate unable to eat, dress, or use the toilet without help. Inmates like Lin who were in solitary confinement often had to lick their food off the floor and soil their trousers. Some cuffs were so tight that the shoulders would be damaged and the flesh of the wrists would rot, leaving permanent marks. At times, prisoners would beat Lin, or guards would pull out her hair.

For these final six years of her life, Lin didn't leave prison. But when the cuffs were taken off she kept writing, using ink and paper that her relatives sent her. When she was denied writing implements or when the issue was urgent, she wrote in her own blood. She would sharpen the end of a toothbrush by scraping it on the floor and then prick her finger, collecting the blood in a spoon and then writing with a sliver of bamboo or reed. Sometimes she wrote on scraps of paper, other times on her clothing.

Lin's writing was direct, angry, and shorn of nuance. Most famously, she wrote a 137-page letter to the Communist Party's mouthpiece, *People's Daily*. She also used her blood to paint an altar on her prison wall in honor of her father, who had committed suicide after his arrest in 1960. She later used her blood to add images of an incense burner and flowers, and from 9:30 AM to noon each Sunday she held what she called "grand church worship," singing the hymns and saying the prayers that she had learned in the Methodist girls' school.

Like other single-minded dissidents, Lin often gave little thought to the suffering she caused her family. Her mother received a tiny stipend each month, but Lin bombarded her with requests for blankets, food, and supplies. Lin's unwavering opposition also turned her siblings into political pariahs. Her brother chastised her as "the most selfish person in the world."

Lin's obsessive focus came from her conviction that her writings would last. In 1967 she described a recent 30,000-character batch of blood letters that she had sent to her mother in this self-confident way: "In the future, they will make up yet another volume of either my complete published works or a posthumous collection of my papers."

None of her letters reached her mother, let alone *People's Daily*. But prison guards didn't destroy valuable evidence against this enemy of the state. Instead, they methodically filed her writings in her ever-expanding file.

Lin's death in 1968 came during the same phase of the Cultural Revolution that claimed Zhang and Du. In the days before her execution, she was made to wear a "Monkey King cap"—named after the mythical Chinese hero who was so uncontrollable that he had to wear a band around his head that could be contracted to bring him to heel. In her case, it was a rubber hood with a slit cut for the eyes and a hole for her nose. The hood was removed only at mealtime.

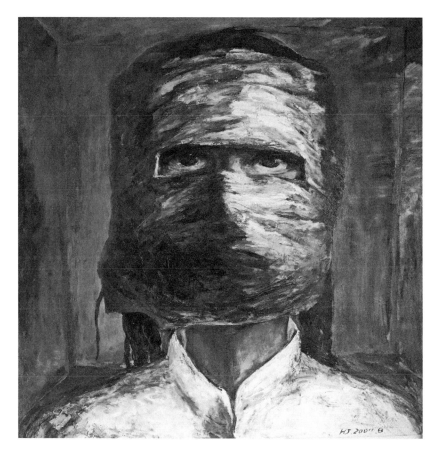

Lin Zhao was executed on April 29—a few days before the big May Day celebrations. Her mother quickly became deranged. She tried to commit suicide by throwing herself in front of a trolley but ended up with a gash on her head and a broken pelvis. Her son became unhinged too and beat his mother. She died in 1975. The students' efforts seemed destined to be buried in the past.

The novel *Every Man Dies Alone*, tells the true story of Otto and Elsie Hampel, a working-class couple in Berlin who took up activities against the Third Reich after Elsie's brother died in action during the invasion of France. Their plans were modest—two hundred postcards of anti-Nazi propaganda, which they placed in letter boxes and stairwells near their home. The effort had no effect; terrified people who found the cards quickly handed them in to the authorities. The couple was easily caught and executed together on the same day, 8 April 1943.

Their case would have vanished if the Nazis' secret police, the Gestapo, hadn't carefully recorded their case and kept the postcards in its files. When Soviet troops captured Berlin in 1945, the couple's case file survived the damage caused by street-to-street fighting and officials' hurried efforts to burn files. Soviet cultural officials turned it over to a well-known German writer, Hans Fallada.

By the time Fallada got the manuscript, he was a broken man. He had spent years in Nazi prisons and now was delusional. When the Soviets contacted him, he was living in an asylum and addicted to opioids. But when he saw the files, he realized that this was a story that needed his full powers. He focused on the book completely for several months, creating a work that only slightly deviated from history. He finished just before he died in 1947, telling a friend, "I have written a great novel."

His friend must have had his doubts. Even in his lifetime Fallada was not seen as one of Germany's great novelists. At this point in his life he must have seemed incapable of writing anything coherent. But Fallada believed in the Hampels' story and willed himself to write a powerful account of why some humans resist. In his telling, the Hampels resisted due to their personal grief and love for each other. But they also possessed an inner quality that some people in every culture possess: a stubborn streak of truth-telling. They just couldn't keep lying. They had to do something.

The survival of their story also owed much to luck. Many people in Nazi Germany tried to resist, but most vanished anonymously into the machinery of terror. But in this one case, fate had determined that the files would fall into the hands of a determined author.

Like the Hampels, the group around *Spark* could have vanished into the void as nothing more than a quixotic effort. *Spark* never circulated nationally. It resulted in no protests or any sort of threat to the government. Over the Chinese Communist Party's three-quarters of a century in power it is one of countless small acts of outrage against the party's unchecked powers. But its story is now familiar to tens of thousands of people. How?

Unlike the Gestapo's files on the Hampels, the Communist Party's files on its past decades have not been released and likely never will be. But over the decades, especially during crises, documents are disgorged from the machinery of government, giving glimpses of China's erased history. One of those periods was in the late 1970s and 1980s, when the Communist Party took tentative steps to redress those wrongly convicted of crimes during the Mao era. Some victims and their families were allowed to see their case files. One of them was Tan Chanxue, the young woman who had been part of the magazine's founding and later spent 14 years in labor camps.

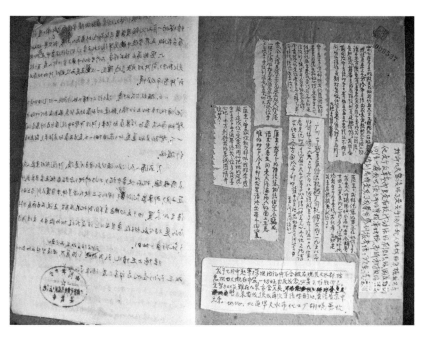

When she inspected her file, she found that police had kept every-thing. That included complete copies of both issues of *Spark*, includ-ing the second issue that had only been partially inscribed on the mimeograph drums. They kept the self-confessions that the members were forced to write under torture. And they even kept the original handwritten love letters from Zhang to Tan while they were being held in the same detention center.

Tan was able to copy these and use them to write her mem-oirs. A few other surviving members of the group did the same. In the 2000s, the underground filmmaker Hu Jie interviewed most of the survivors and in 2013 released online one of his best-known films, *Spark*. Word about the group began to spread to people like Jiang Xue.

The righteousness of the students' cause meant that people kept coming out of unexpected places to keep their memory alive. Wang Zhongyi, the convicted hooligan who had sat with Zhang during his last three days on earth, was later released and tried to keep his promise that he would find Tan and tell her Zhang's last words. He read about *Spark* in a 2012 article that appeared online. He contacted the Dunhuang Research Center to find Tan and they put him in touch with her. He gave her his account of Zhang's final hours, which she later published in Hong Kong.

The most dramatic story was Lin Zhao's. In 1979, Peking University formally lifted the charge against her of being a Rightist. Later, the Xinhua news agency held a memorial service for her be-cause she had once worked as a journalist. The judge who reviewed Lin's file decided to give much of her writing to her family in 1982. He didn't include official court documents, but he released sheets of manuscripts, numbered and bound with green thread, and four notebooks filled with her diaries, as well as ink copies of her blood letters home, which Lin had copied so they would be preserved for posterity.

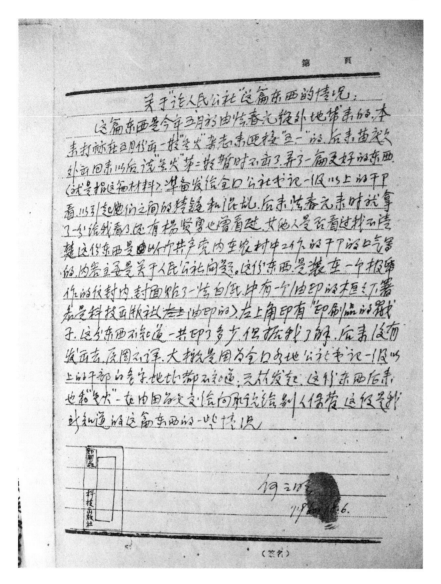

The judge based his decision on aesthetics. He said he was impressed by Lin's poetry and felt that her family deserved to have it. In the early 2000s, Lin's friends edited her writings. They made photos of the blood letters and compiled PDFs that were posted online and went viral. One of the first dissidents to discover them was Ding Zilin, the mother of a Tiananmen massacre victim. A fellow alumna of the onetime Methodist school in Suzhou, Ding found Lin's letters to be revelatory, describing the same system that had also killed her son. She later wrote that they were "a kind of redemption for my soul."

In the 1980s, admirers and family members found Lin's ashes and buried them at Lingyan Hill outside her hometown, the eastern city of Suzhou. Her grave has become one of the most visited pilgrimage sites for China's human rights activists. Every year on the anniversary of her death, April 29, the area is locked down; the rest of the time it is guarded by closed-circuit television.

The documentary filmmaker Hu Jie once again played a key role. His 2004 film *Searching for Lin Zhao's Soul* tells her tale through interviews with those who knew her. Hu's film has disappeared from Chinese websites but has spread through person-to-person contact— people handing each other memory sticks with the film on it. It is also posted on foreign websites, such as YouTube, that many people can access with virtual private network (VPN) software. Through Hu Jie, the Chinese Nobel peace prize laureate Liu Xiaobo came to know of her, praising her, as did the prominent rights lawyer Xu Zhiyong, who called her "a martyred saint, a prophet and a poet with an ecstatic soul, the Prometheus of a free China."

For people like the well-known writer and critic Cui Weiping, these young people from the middle of the last century had managed to identify key problems inherent in one-party rule—and had done so when the Chinese Communist Party was just one decade into power, so apparent were its flaws. Their story showed that the search for a freer, more humane China wasn't new. It was something that Chinese people had been struggling for since the party took power.

For Cui, the effect was electric. Reading their words half a century after they were written, she realized that she wasn't alone in her thoughts. Others before her had also grappled with them. The problems were not unique to one group of people or to one era. They were systemic. That's why when Cui read Lin Zhao's writings, she declared: "Now we have our genealogy."

Memory: Etchings

The prints are from another world: black and white woodblock prints, of men and women dead or dying, of little children pointing out the truth, of sadness, loss, and peace. One print shows people flying over a barren landscape. Below them a child gnaws at a tree trunk. They are souls leaving the earth behind.

The artworks try to capture a reality that few can imagine and, nowadays, that few have witnessed. But the artist has learned about this era from so many hundreds of hours with eyewitnesses that he feels the stories and the scenes are burned into his soul. Drawing them is the only way for them to be released.

These are the artworks of Hu Jie. He is best known as an underground documentary filmmaker, an autodidact who watched classic works such as Claus Lanzmann's *Shoah* over and over again, internalizing the French filmmaker's slow, patient approach to filming the Holocaust, letting the perpetrators speak freely until they had implicated themselves.

He used the same approach in his three most famous films. His first was *Searching for Lin Zhao's Soul*. He had heard about Lin and was captivated by the love story. But making the film was a shocking experience, as he told me one afternoon at his studio in the southeastern city of Nanjing. He was born in 1958 and witnessed nearly 20 years of the Mao era but was still stunned.

"For people of my generation, in elementary school we didn't learn about the Anti-Rightist Movement and in middle school we learned very little. Books about it weren't published. So the Anti-Rightist Movement, or the Great Famine—we didn't understand anything. When I got into contact with this material and talked with Lin Zhao's classmates, they would tell me things, and each time I would be shocked, and I realized that everything I knew about history had been covered up, that the official history was complete nonsense."

He finished the film in 2004 after four years of shooting. But he showed it to only a small circle of friends, such as fellow underground filmmaker and feminist scholar Ai Xiaoming, the samizdat magazine publisher Ding Dong, the film critic Cui Weiping, the Christian essayist Yu Jie, and the future Nobel Peace Prize laureate Liu Xiaobo. Two years later he completed *Though I Am Gone*, about a widower whose wife was murdered by her teenage students at a Beijing high school. And in 2013 he finished *Spark*, a sequel to the Lin Zhao film, that told the story of the magazine.

Hu made many other films, including several with Ai Xiaoming, but those three stand out for their care, their clarity, and their influence. They are gritty and grainy and almost unknown to the outside world—although they have been rereleased internationally thanks to the independent film distributor dGenerate Films.

In the 2010s, Hu continued to film. He made films about a female labor camp in northeastern China. And when I last talked to him shortly before completing this book, he was working on a new film about environmentalists.

But during these dark days of the 2010s and 2020s, he also began to make paintings and woodcuts. Part of the reason was to finance his filmmaking. He knows how the Communist Party attacks people who receive foreign funding. Even though he could almost certainly qualify for prestigious foreign grants and fellowships, he avoids all outside financing, relying on his beat-up cameras and his wife's help. For years she worked in a bank and her income gave them a measure of stability. Now she is his manager and helps arrange sales of his art.

Besides woodblock prints, he paints with oils. Some are pictures of the famine. One of the most shocking (reproduced in the previous chapter) is of Lin Zhao wearing the "Monkey King cap" meant to prevent her from talking. During a series of long interviews in Nanjing, we talked about his work and ways the government makes his work more difficult. One favorite technique is to simply call ahead to interviewees, warning them not to meet him. More than a few times he has driven for hours to find a once-enthusiastic interviewee suddenly "unavailable."

Another reason for his paintings and woodblocks is to fill a void of images from that era. We have images of the Holocaust and many other 20th-century catastrophes. And the Cultural Revolution is well documented visually because it took place in cities and often involved educated people, who were more likely to own cameras. But in the Chinese countryside in the 1950s, few had a camera. His art compensates for this gap in the archive, giving us a visual jolt that texts often cannot.

Hu served in the People's Liberation Army and was sent to the army's arts college between 1989 and 1991. This was the gloomy time after the Tiananmen massacre. He quit the army and moved to the grounds of the Old Summer Palace north of Beijing to live with other artists. New ideas were swirling underground, a time of quiet fermentation not unlike what is happening today. The filmmaker Wu Wenguang, whom we'll meet later in this book, had just released his landmark film *Bumming in Beijing: The Last Dreamers*, a grainy, jerky, hyper-authentic look at people who had dropped out of society. One of Hu's friends had just come back from Japan and had a Super 8 camera. Hu Jie bought it from him and began teaching himself how to film, adopting Wu's rough-cut style of filmmaking to distinguish himself from slick government-made films.

Although Hu made many films and mentored important filmmakers, such as Ai Xiaoming, it was his encounter with Lin Zhao that changed his life. The young woman, fired by the ideals of Christianity, refused to bend while so many had given in.

Hu's films have never been shown in China, but he makes them to document what happened before the eyewitnesses die. He puts all of his films on YouTube and always waives copyrights. Since the Lin Zhao film, he estimates that a dozen important witnesses have died. He also conceives of his films as a message to future generations: that not everyone in China gave in, and that opposition has existed since this state's inception in the mid-20th century. As he put it to me:

The other point is that during this bitter era, this violent era, this most terrifying era, people still tried to reflect on what was hap-pening. They weren't afraid to die. They died in secret, and we of succeeding generations don't know what heroes they were. I think it's a matter of morality. They died for us. If we don't know this, it is a tragedy.

5

History as Weapon

The family of Xi Jinping has its own spiritual genealogy. It is based on "red bloodlines"—people who trace their ancestry back to the founders of the People's Republic. Some members of this nobility became critics because their experiences made them realize the system's inherent flaws. But others, such as the Xi family, drew different conclusions from their proximity to power. Instead of being critical of the Communist Party, they became cautious, respectful, and protective, eager to carry on the party's tradition of using history as a tool to control society.

Like the young people who published *Spark*, Xi's family also hailed from northwestern China. His family members were prosperous landowners in Shaanxi province, but Xi's father, Xi Zhongxun, was radicalized by China's plight in the early 20th century. He joined a student protest group and was thrown into jail for a few months at just 15 years of age. There, he secretly joined the Communist Party and went on to serve as a soldier and officer in a warlord's army.

Four years later, in 1932, he made his way to Shaanxi's north, where extreme poverty and rugged terrain made the region one of the Communist Party's most successful areas for recruitment. It was there that Xi Zhongxun became embroiled in one of the party's first and most significant battles over history. It became a template for how the party controls history, decades later culminating in a power struggle that purged the party's top leadership. That battle cost Xi Zhongxun the chance to rise to the very top of the party and likely influenced how his son saw the writing of history—as a powerful but dangerous tool that could make a career or destroy a person.

When the elder Xi began working in northern Shaanxi in 1932, the region was one of several Communist strongholds in China. But China's central government, run by the Kuomintang, was in the process of destroying most of them. That included one in southwestern China, which was home to the party's central leadership and most of the party's armed forces. The government attacks flushed out Communist officials and troops, who scrambled on a year-long retreat through some of China's most rugged terrain. Known as the Long March, it covered more than five thousand miles over a torturous route that saw the army shrink from roughly one hundred thousand to eight thousand soldiers. The army might have been completely destroyed if it hadn't found refuge in the mountains of northern Shaanxi.

The base was run by a charismatic local leader, Liu Zhidan. He had been trained at China's elite Whampoa Military Academy in southern China. But he returned home to fight for the Communist revolution. In Edgar Snow's hagiographic account of the early Communist movement, *Red Star over China*, he called Liu "a modern Robin Hood, with the mountaineer's hatred of rich men; among the poor he was becoming a name of promise, and among landlords and moneylenders the scourge of the gods."

Liu was a popular and successful leader, but was about to be toppled. As it has been for all of its existence, the party was riven by factions and cliques. One group resented Liu, saying he was too unorthodox because he recruited soldiers from all classes of people, not just the very poor. He also preferred fighting in the mountains rather than in the large population centers. These opponents had the backing of the party leadership in Shanghai. They had Liu, as well as Xi Zhongxun, and another leader, Gao Gang, arrested as part of a huge sweep against their followers. Hundreds of their subordinates had been arrested and many were summarily executed. As the three men sat in prison, they heard the sounds of digging. Guards told them it was preparation for a mass grave—theirs.

Mao's arrival saved the three. Mao had taken control of the party during the debacle of the Long March, which he blamed on the party's central leadership in Shanghai—the same people who opposed Liu, Xi, and Gao. Mao probably saw men as a way to solidify his power base by making local allies in a new and unfamiliar part of China. In addition, Mao sympathized with their ability to adapt to local conditions. His opponents in the party had insisted on the orthodox Communist view that the revolution would be won by mobilizing the industrial proletariat, while Mao—like the three imprisoned men—viewed the countryside as the party's most fertile ground. Using his power as the new head of the party, he sidelined the officials who had purged Liu, Xi, and Gao, issuing an apocryphal order: "Halt the executions! Stop the arrests."

Mao, however, was calculating and cunning in his support. The three were still left with the black mark of having been purged. That meant that their survival depended on Mao's good graces. He had saved the men, but he could still ruin them. This made them even more valuable allies because they would be desperate to please him.

Liu was given a series of inferior military postings with small units charged with dangerous tasks. In 1936, probably seeking redemption on the battlefield, he died in a hopeless attack to push eastward into another province. Now safely dead, Liu was lionized as a martyr. Mao then promoted Gao to head the region, with Xi as a key deputy.

Not everyone was happy with this decision. Some local officials grumbled that Xi and Gao hadn't shown enough accomplishments to be elevated to leadership positions. And so Mao turned to the power of history to secure the men's position. In 1942, he convened a meeting of all senior leaders in the region to write the official history of the northwest Communist base. This history would show that Xi and Gao (and the martyred Liu) had indeed followed the correct policies, while their opponents had been utterly wrong. History would cement their positions.

Xi and Gao were pawns in bigger scores that Mao wanted to settle. Unlike the men who had headed the Communist Party before him, Mao had little formal education in Marxism. He hadn't been to Moscow to study at the birthplace of the worldwide Communist revolution. He also didn't follow the orthodox Communist prediction that a revolution would be led by factory workers in big cities. People like Gao and Xi could be used as symbols of Mao's belief in a more locally rooted communism, while their opponents could be caricatured as following out-of-touch ideas developed in foreign countries.

Mao had already made this point when he took control of the party during the Long March. But many people still doubted Mao. They were not convinced that his ideas about mobilizing the peasantry were original—Liu had already done the same with great success in his mountain campaigns—or that they would work in the long run. Mao was also not recognized as a senior leader by the Comintern, the Moscow-based organization charged with promoting communist revolutions in other countries. In short, he was in charge of the party but lacked the traditional imprimatur of power.

Many of the Comintern's favored candidates were also in Yan'an and wanted to sideline Mao. To squelch this potential opposition, Mao needed a definitive history of the Communist Party from its founding in 1921 until the present. This new history would show that the party's earlier Moscow-led course had been mistaken and that his course was correct. But writing that sort of history would be risky. So he decided to start by rewriting the history of the northwest base. If that worked, then he could turn to his bigger project.

The disputes in the northwest were framed as questions of life and death, with no nuance. Xi and Gao were lauded for following the "correct line," while the Shanghai faction had followed an "erroneous line" that could have led the Communist Party to ruin. The followers of the discarded strategy weren't well-meaning individuals who had made mistakes; instead, they were evil. According to Mao's history of the northwestern base, they were of "debased character," "execrable," "party careerists who aimed to usurp leadership and lord over the party." This defamatory account was endorsed by the party through a resolution. A resolution gave these views the force of law. It became the only accepted version of reality.

Mao's vision was of a black-and-white world—a revolution shorn of camaraderie and fraternity. That histrionic, personal mode of attack became Mao's template for handling the national resolution on party history—and the model for party purges up until today. It was shrill and unpleasant, but for now it was on Xi Zhongxun's side.

Mao now turned to his bigger project, targeting a person who epitomized his real concern: a 38-year-old veteran Communist organizer named Wang Ming. Wang represented everything that Mao hated. He had gone to Moscow in the 1920s to train for four years at the bosom of the revolution. He had mastered Russian, studied Marxist-Leninist theory, taken a Russian name, and worked as an interpreter for Russian representatives of the Comintern visiting China. He had founded a group of Chinese communists in Moscow known as the 28 Bolsheviks. After a brief stint back in China, he had spent another six years in Moscow working for the Comintern. In 1937, the Comintern sent him to Mao's headquarters in Yan'an to help guide the party.

Despite all of these credentials, Wang was no real threat to Mao. His short stay in China six years earlier had been a disaster—he had been arrested and only released because the Kuomintang had never heard of him. He had shown no real ability to organize or lead. But he was admired in Yan'an for his erudition and for having worked abroad. In Mao's eyes this made him his chief rival. Soon after Wang's arrival, Mao wrote several essays against Wang, who countered by praising Mao and trying to avoid the more powerful man's wrath—to no avail.

In 1942, Mao launched his attack, a purge known as the Yan'an Rectification Movement. This was a seminal attack on Mao's rivals, aimed at Wang but encompassing thousands of people.

Officially, the rectification campaign was meant to make sure that party members had a solid grounding in Marxist and Leninist theory.

The reasoning made sense because many of the people in Yan'an were newcomers with little idea about communism or the party's struggles over the preceding two decades. The party set up schools to indoctrinate artists, ethnic minorities, women, scientists, and Communist Party officials. All of these schools taught one key message: the only way to achieve communism was to study Mao's writings.

To this day, the rectification campaign is portrayed in China as a great achievement—indeed, as a turning point on China's path to rejuvenation. It is officially seen as a time when the different people streaming to Yan'an were forged into a unified party that would win World War II, defeat the Kuomintang in the looming civil war, and lead China back to greatness.

Mao began with a purge of writers and artists in 1942 when he held his famous "Talks at the Yan'an Forum on Literature and Arts." This forced artists and writers, some of whom had come to Yan'an seeking an imagined utopia amid the war, to toe the party line. Mao's talks set the ground rules for artistic endeavors that hold true today: ultimately, all art is political and must serve the party and the nation.

Mao then turned to his main concern: the senior leadership. Many party leaders—even Wang—were already extolling Mao in articles and speeches. But he wanted to be sure they had internalized his views, in exact detail, about every twist and turn of party history since its founding. He wanted them not just to kowtow to him but to live and breathe his views.

To achieve this, the party inquisitors working under Mao sought to break down and rebuild people. They created a new vocabulary for this process: "study groups" to isolate and confront people with different views; "struggle sessions" to criticize individuals who resisted; "self-criticisms" that were essentially confessions of every mistake one had ever made, real or imagined; and the final goal: "thought reform."

The intense pressure made it impossible to get through the campaign by simply mouthing a few slogans. Targeted officials had their daily habits monitored. Their diaries were confiscated. They were relentlessly pressured, day and night, to confess and come clean. Self-criticisms were written and rewritten again and again until the person showed enough sincerity, often by admitting to the most intimate of personal failings, and very often after a nervous breakdown.

Brainwashing might be too loaded a word, because many of the people who survived the process later wrote about it critically. But the goal was to create a reborn person who wholeheartedly followed Mao. And if that failed, the reams of self-criticism could be dredged up and used to ruin the person in the future—which was the fate that many victims of the Yan'an Rectification Campaign suffered 25 years later in the Cultural Revolution.

The campaign began in earnest at a meeting in late 1943 when Mao launched a full-scale attack against Wang Ming. Mao's acolytes accused Wang of treason and of collaborating with the Nationalists—absurd, unproven charges but effective as character assassination. Wang's wife, Meng Qingshu, was present at the struggle session and stood up on the podium. With tears streaming down her face, she looked at Mao and asked how he could allow these wild allegations. Mao sat impassively and later banned Wang and Meng from attending further meetings. The point wasn't to reform Wang but to use him to demonstrate Mao's power. If he could do this to the Comintern's prize student, he could crush anyone.

Wang's close ties to Moscow meant he and his wife got off lightly, especially after a senior Soviet official called Mao to ask that he be lenient. Wang was forced to make a confession and a public apology, and then largely dropped from public view. In 1956, he and Meng went to Moscow for medical treatment and never returned.

Many others were not so lucky. The wife of one official under attack died of "mental derangement" after round-the-clock interrogation. Most of China's most powerful leaders were caught up, including the future premier Zhou Enlai. He only arrived in Yan'an in 1943, read the minutes of previous meetings, and quickly understood the danger he was in. He wrote a series of abject apologies and self-criticisms, and doggedly followed Mao's every twist and turn. Zhou's nimble maneuvers allowed him to survive for the rest of his life as Mao's most talented and obedient lieutenant.

Mao capped this purge with the 1945 resolution on party history. This is one of only three resolutions on the past in the party's 100 years of history. One came decades later, after Mao died and Deng Xiaoping wanted to assert his power. And one came in 2021 when Xi Jinping wanted to justify his prolonged hold on power. Each of them drew a cartoonish version of history to justify the new leader's rule.

Because Mao's history resolution was the first, it became the template. That makes it worth closer scrutiny. The document didn't couch Mao's role or importance in obscure language but boldly put him on a par with Marxism's great thinkers. It emphasizes that while Marxism and Leninism are its guiding principles, it is "Mao Zedong Thought" that synthesizes these European thinkers with the reality of China's vast rural population. To emphasize that it didn't need instructions from Moscow, the document states in its first paragraph that "the Party has produced its own leader, Mao Zedong" who "brilliantly developed the ideas of Lenin and Stalin."

The resolution is excruciatingly long—over 50 pages of text in its English translation, including five pages of dense endnotes—and includes minute, blow-by-blow discussions of annual meetings over the period. Mao said he "labored painstakingly" on it, revising it seven times.

When it was finally passed in August 1945, it became Mao's talisman. Over the final three decades of his life, much of it as China's supreme leader, Mao made numerous terrible mistakes that led to war, famine, and turmoil. During this time he was often under attack for his erratic decisions. But he could always use the resolution on party history to prove that Communist Party history was by definition on his side. It was, in the words of one biographer, a "magic incantation."

When the People's Republic was founded four years later, Xi Zhongxun was one of its rising stars. He was promoted to vice premier and moved with his second wife and their young family to

Beijing. He had three children, including Xi Jinping, who was born in 1953. That same year, however, Xi Zhongxun was caught up in one of the new country's first great purges.

Xi's comrade-in-arms from the northwestern base area, Gao Gang, had become one of Mao's closest confidants. Enormously respected in northern Shaanxi, he had mobilized troops and industry to support the Communist armies. When Mao stood atop the Tiananmen Gate in 1949 to proclaim the founding of the People's Republic, Gao was on the rostrum too. Gao later handled logistics during the Korean War and managed communications with the Soviet Union and North Korea. Later, he was put in charge of the Northeastern Bureau of the Chinese Communist Party, making him just one of five regional secretaries in China. (Xi Zhongxun headed one of the others, the Northwestern Bureau.)

By early 1953, these regional secretaries were called to Beijing to take positions in the new central government. Gao was put in charge of the powerful State Planning Commission, while Xi was asked to lead the Chinese Communist Party's Propaganda Department. In Gao, Mao saw an ally in a new court intrigue that he was planning: to damage the widely respected party leader Liu Shaoqi.

Liu was not Mao's direct rival, but like Wang Ming a decade earlier he was widely respected. He had been part of the revolution for decades and had even written a book called *How to Be a Good Communist*. But he and Mao differed on economic matters. While Mao wanted to move quickly toward socialism, Liu favored a slower, more measured approach like that of the Soviet Union—with five-year plans that would build heavy industry and infrastructure.

Mao would eventually depose Liu in 1966 during the Cultural Revolution, allowing him to die in prison. For now, however, Mao simply wanted to take Liu down a peg or two. He encouraged Gao to criticize Liu by attacking one of Liu's lieutenants. Gao miscalculated—thinking that Mao wanted to destroy Liu, he launched a full-blown attack on Liu's deputy. The implication was that if Liu's deputy was this disloyal, so too was Liu.

Gao's attacks, however, caused a backlash. Liu was one of the party's most loyal officials and few believed the charges. Mao realized that the campaign was going wrong so he quickly dropped Gao.

Gao was forced to write a lengthy self-criticism, which his friend and deputy, Xi Zhongxun, supervised—a brilliant tactical move by Mao to make Xi realize that he, too, was vulnerable. Eager to prove his loyalty, Xi was brutal, telling Gao that he had to admit to having fomented a "conspiracy to usurp party power." Gao realized that admitting to this would be signing his own death warrant. He complied but then tried to electrocute himself. He failed but managed to obtain a bottle of sleeping pills. After a conversation with his wife on the night of 16 August 1954, he swallowed the pills and died.

Xi Zhongxun's decision to turn on his friend allowed him to survive a few more years. In 1956 he was promoted to the Central Committee and three years later was made vice-premier. What finally did in Xi was a historical novel.

One day in the late 1950s, Li Jiantong, the daughter-in-law of Xi's old mentor in Shaanxi, the charismatic guerilla fighter Liu Zhidan, told Xi that she wanted to write a novel about her father-in-law. She asked him for help. He refused, saying that the history was too complicated. Li was undeterred and got other people from the region to pressure Xi to help her. Liu was a Communist martyr. He was dead. He had never opposed Mao. And in fact, Mao had elevated him to martyr status in the resolution on party history. How controversial could it be to write a paean to him? Xi reluctantly agreed.

When excerpts from the three-volume novel *Liu Zhidan* appeared in 1962, the work was immediately banned. Even though it was a tribute to a Communist martyr—it didn't attack Mao or call any of the history resolutions into question—the fact that the novel discussed the old Shaanxi Communist base area was seen as a closet effort at glorifying the now-deposed Gao Gang and all the people close to him, including Xi.

Xi came under fierce attack. He was forced to say that the novel was designed to aggrandize himself. He was fired as vice-premier in a purge that affected a staggering twenty-thousand people, many of them in the old revolutionary base areas. In 1965, Xi had to write a self-criticism and was demoted to deputy manager of a tractor factory in central China. When the Cultural Revolution began a year later, Xi was imprisoned. His family was split up. One daughter committed suicide. Xi Jinping was sent to work as a farmer in Shaanxi province. The elder Xi wasn't rehabilitated until 1978, his career derailed by history.

Mao's death in 1976 and the coup that brought Deng Xiaoping to power in 1978 required a new resolution on party history. The first resolution had glorified Mao and made him the culmination of everything the Chinese Communist Party stood for. But three decades later, China was still a poor country. Mao's utopian experiments had cost upward of 50 million lives—up to 45 million alone in the Great Famine, and millions more in the campaign against landlords, Rightists, and the turmoil of the Cultural Revolution. China's small population of educated people was traumatized by the first three decades of Communist rule.

Even for those untouched by the disasters, the failure of the Mao period was obvious. Mao's hand-picked successors were in jail and most of his economic policies had been abandoned, from the communes to the inward-looking self-sufficiency. The party was in the process of giving land back to farmers, welcoming foreign investors, and building an export-oriented economy.

This about-face had to be explained somehow but without making the Mao era a failure. After all, Mao was still the founder of the People's Republic. His mausoleum and a super-sized portrait still dominated Tiananmen Square. The only way to square all of these circles was a new version of history that would plausibly explain what had happened without making the party look too bad. And so Deng undertook the writing of a new resolution, one that would solidify his own hold on power and set the course for the next decades.

Understanding why these resolutions matter requires appreciating a key aspect of Chinese politics. Democracies, in theory at least, regulate society through constitutions and laws, which are passed by bodies of elected representatives. China is different. In the words of a former Chinese government advisor, Wu Guoguang, the Communist Party rules the country by "documentary politics."

This means that a group of leaders—or a paramount leader, such as Mao, Deng, or Xi Jinping—assert their authority by issuing documents that other people have to accept. These can be issued as laws passed by China's party-controlled parliament, and increasingly that is how rules are imposed on society. But very often, and especially for key ideological questions, concepts are promulgated as circulars, resolutions, or white papers. Drafting and revising these documents is time-consuming and involves compromises, but the effort results in a consensus that most factions in the party can support. Once formally issued, these documents become the leader's guideposts for running the country.

This was Deng's goal in 1981. He had to impose his will on the party through a historical resolution that would act like a constitution or statement of principles for what the Communist Party had become and where it was going. It was similar to Mao's efforts in 1945, but for Deng it was more complicated. Mao had been the supreme leader and had already purged his potential enemies. Deng had to contend with people who still supported Mao and many who were adamantly opposed to him, all the while trying to launch a new beginning.

Deng organized a committee to draft the report and gave it three clear instructions: keep Mao as a respected founder of the People's Republic of China, conduct a realistic analysis of the problems and successes of the past thirty years, and lay to rest past controversies so the party could move forward.

The initial draft reportedly infuriated Deng, who said it dwelled too much on Mao's impetuous decisions later in life. This included inciting Red Guards, purging his colleagues, and allowing his wife to make policy. Almost everyone in the government had witnessed

Mao's excesses and many had suffered, making it hard for the drafters of the document to avoid such criticisms. In fact, these views were so widespread in Beijing in the summer of 1980s that rumors began to sweep the capital that a full-blown de-Maoification campaign was about to begin.

Deng sought to save Mao's position. Deng's own son had been pushed—or jumped—from a university dorm room, leaving him paralyzed. Deng had also been purged and humiliated. But he urged the committee to salvage Mao for the sake of the party. The Soviet Union could de-Stalinize without damaging the reputation of its founder, Lenin. Mao, however, was Lenin and Stalin rolled into one. The party needed some core elements of Mao to survive in order for it to maintain credibility. Otherwise, what justification did it have to rule if its founding father had led the country from one disaster to the other?

To quell the rumors, Deng called in the Italian journalist Oriana Fallaci for an interview. She asked him a series of blunt questions, such as why all the blame was being heaped on the Gang of Four— Mao's wife and three associates—who pushed radical policies in the Cultural Revolution. Wasn't Mao also to blame? Deng was sharp and parried her questions by repeating the now-standard formulation that would be found in the resolution: "His contributions were primary, his mistakes secondary."

By September 1980, a new draft met Deng's approval. It was sent to four thousand officials across China for discussion. That was followed by a second scrutiny by fifty-six hundred officials, who filed more than one thousand comments.

The discussions were heated, with many resisting Deng's conciliatory language. Many were outraged about how the resolution dealt with the Great Famine, which was blandly described as having "caused serious losses to our country and people." Some of the party officials were from the provinces and almost certainly had experienced the famine firsthand just 20 years earlier. They said it should be described forthrightly as having caused tens of millions of deaths. Others criticized Mao's writings for being convoluted, unreadable, and illogical.

In the end, Deng had to include more criticisms of Mao and his hand-picked successor, Hua Guofeng, but he held the line at a full-blown critique. He reportedly told two close associates that "discrediting Comrade Mao Zedong . . . would mean discrediting our party and state."

The resolution laid the groundwork for Deng's chief goal: solidifying his hold on power. In June 1981, a party plenum was held that ratified the history resolution. The plenum also reordered a radical shift in the party's highest levels. Mao's successor, Hua Guofeng, was shunted aside as head of the party and replaced with Deng's hand-picked choice, Hu Yaobang. Deng took control of the powerful Central Military Commission.

Xi Jinping's father also benefited from the new history. After being sidelined in 1962, Xi Zhongxun had been rehabilitated in 1978. Deng had sent him to southern China to pioneer the economic reforms that would soon sweep the country. After the history resolution was passed, Deng brought Xi back to the central government—the first time in nearly 20 years that Xi was back in power in the capital.

The elder Xi's long hiatus meant that he was too old to ascend to the very pinnacles of power in China. After serving in several positions in Beijing, Xi Zhongxun retired in 1988, aged 75. But he became a patron saint of early efforts to address the party's checkered past more honestly. He supported, for example, the maverick history journal *China Through the Ages*. Over the years it published pieces calling into question mythic feats of military heroism by the People's Liberation Army, memoirs by close aides to Mao who had been purged, and exposés on blunders in rural policy. Xi endorsed this forthright account of the past, writing a piece of calligraphy that

said, "*China Through the Ages* is doing a good job." For years, the magazine reprinted the calligraphy on its cover as a kind of shield against
censorship.

This was an era that inspired some of China's greatest works of
counter-history, including one that still widely circulates today inside
China: a scathing indictment of Mao's time in Yan'an, written by a
persecuted historian named Gao Hua.

Memory: How the Red Sun Rose

Gao Hua was born in 1954, which in the language of that era meant he was "born in the new society and raised under the Red Flag." It was meant to be a new start for everyone and everything—even the country, which was now called New China. The old society had classes: landlords and peasants, capitalists and workers. Now, everyone was equal under the red flag of communism.

In reality, Gao and tens of millions of others were part of a new class—a caste of untouchables who had political problems. His father had been an underground radio operator behind enemy lines for the Communists. Politically speaking, that should have made Gao like Xi Jinping, who had been born a year earlier—a person with "red bloodlines" or "second-generation red." In fact, the Communists pathologically distrusted idealists who had worked underground. They were almost always persecuted as having collaborated with the Nationalists—otherwise, in the conspiratorial and suspicious mindset of the party, how else could these people have survived? The party preferred people who had been far from the frontlines, for example those in Yan'an, who spent the war making obeisance to Mao. That made Gao Hua's father a target during the 1957 Anti-Rightist Campaign. He was declared a Rightist and sent to prison for several years. As a toddler, Gao Hua and his mother made long bus rides to visit him in prison, a lonely vigil made worse by the Great Famine.

In 1963, Gao Hua tested into Nanjing's Foreign Language School but was rejected because of what the Communists' newspeak called his "class background." Even when he attended an ordinary school, his father's situation came up time and again, causing teachers to isolate him from other students. When the Cultural Revolution began three years later, Gao overheard his father tell his mother that he might well be beaten to death. He fled Nanjing for refuge hundreds of miles north among his kinsmen in Shandong province. Soon after, Gao Hua saw warrants for his father's arrest plastered on the walls around his home.

As Gao grew up, he began to connect his family misfortune with an event twenty years earlier: the Yan'an Rectification Campaign. He had read about it fleetingly in Mao's collected works. Then, when the Cultural Revolution broke out, senior officials in his school and the city government were toppled, with their accusers writing about crimes they allegedly had admitted to during struggle sessions in Yan'an. The teenager didn't understand everything, but it seemed like it had been a brutal event. To his young mind, this moment seemed key to the violence engulfing his life. Instinctively he understood that the violence in Yan'an had been something like the party's original sin, warping it and leaving it unable to function without violence and coercion.

The cruelty he witnessed was mind-numbing. One case in particular stayed with him. Two of his classmates, a brother and sister, lived with their parents in a broken-down shed. Their father had been declared a counter-revolutionary and was banned from working. Their mother was a normal working-class woman. The family was destitute and suffered constant humiliations. One day, the mother cracked and ripped up a portrait of Mao, cursing him. She was arrested and sentenced to death. Everyone from the school, including Gao Hua, the women's two children, and her husband, were made to stand at the roadside and watch the woman, bound hand and foot, be led to the execution ground. "This was called 'being educated,'" Gao later wrote sardonically.

Home was his refuge. Disqualified from serving as a Red Guard, Gao spent his days reading. His mother had fearfully burned most of the family's books, but he managed to pull a few treasured volumes from the fire, including Yang Jiang's translation of the 18th-century French novel *Gil Blas*, Fan Wenlan's *Concise Chinese History*, Alexander Pushkin's *Selected Poems*, and a collection of 300 poems from China's most glorious dynasty, the Tang. Recalling his youth, he later wrote "these books warmed me and served as clusters of light at the end of a long, dark tunnel."

His understanding of China's fate grew exponentially thanks to the quiet courage of an old neighbor. Several thousand confiscated books had been locked up in a warehouse near his home. Its kindly watchman let Gao and one of his friends borrow some. They would carefully choose a few, hide them in their backpacks and walk home. The next week they would go back to borrow more. Gao read hundreds of banned books, including the novels of Ding Ling and the essays of Wang Shiwei, both of whom Mao had purged in Yan'an twenty-five years earlier.

When the Cultural Revolution ended with Mao's death, college entrance exams were reinstated, and class considerations dropped. In 1978, at age 24, Gao tested into one of the country's best, Nanjing University. By then he knew he wanted to study history and would focus on the Yan'an purges. He began collecting memoirs, papers, documents, and other accounts.

He also attended lectures that shaped his views of how to be a historian. He was inspired—"agitated" was the word he used—when he heard a lecture on Sima Qian's "Letter to Ren An," in which the Grand Historian of two thousand years ago explained his motives for completing his work. Castrated or not, he was determined to see his sacred task through to its end. From Fan Wenlan's history of China—the book he saved from his mother's bonfire—he recalled Fan's warning that the true historian must "willingly spend ten years on a cold wooden bench, writing essays without a single empty word."

In the end, he sat more than twice as long. It took him twenty-two years but in 2000 he published his nearly 900-page classic, *How the Red Sun Rose: The Origin and Development of the Yan'an Rectification Movement, 1930–45.* The Red Sun is Mao, and Gao described in rigorous prose how he rose through a series of cruel purges—a template for how the party would operate when it took power.

In a postscript, Gao describes his upbringing, motivation, and research methods. He had to make do without access to official archives; from the start, his project was too sensitive for him to be permitted to see government documents. He was regularly denied research grants, promotions, and the chance for a senior position at another university. Each book and every photocopy were financed on his small salary as an untenured lecturer. Unlike overseas historians, he had no graduate students to do legwork, no fellowships to give him time away from lecturing, no world-class research library at his disposal, and no peer-reviewed journals to help him hone his thinking.

He was familiar with foreign authors and benefited greatly from trips to Hong Kong, where he used the Universities Service Center, the legendary repository of books and documents from China. But he realized that most foreign authors, especially the older generation who bent over backward to be fair to Mao, had missed the point that Mao was central to the party's addiction to violence and coercion. Many also didn't go back far enough to find the origins. Some thought the problems started with the Anti-Rightist Campaign or the Great Leap Forward. Few dared to identify the very early years in Yan'an as the problem, either because they weren't aware or did not want to appear to be too anti-Communist. Gao was an auto-didact, constructing his own counter-archive of papers and memoirs, sometimes incomplete and skewed in various directions. But without having to fit into any tradition—neither the politicized history that was permitted in China nor the conventional wisdom found abroad—he was able to draw original conclusions that are now widely accepted.

He wrote his enormous work at the kitchen table of his family's tiny flat, chain-smoking and drinking tea, his reputation growing through the 1990s as word got out about his epic project. By the end, people made pilgrimages to Nanjing to visit this modern-day Sima Qian, who had accepted poverty and marginalization in order to write an iconoclastic demolition of the Communist Party's political culture. It's no exaggeration to call *How the Red Sun Rose* one of China's most important history books of the Communist era.

Ten years later, Gao was dead of liver cancer, aged 58. His early death robbed him of the chance to write his next book, which his friends said was to have focused on what happened after the Communists, remolded in Yan'an as a tool of Mao's control, had assumed power in 1949.

But in some ways, his life's work was finished. His book punctures what is the Communist Party's founding myth—that it started as a pure, clean brotherhood of idealists fighting to save China. Instead, he shows a group of ambitious, quarreling men whom Mao bullied and dominated into submission. Although banned in China, Gao's book was released by the Chinese University of Hong Kong in 2000 and has since gone through twenty-two printings. It has been translated into English and is available online. Today, anyone writing the Communist Party's history, inside or outside China, reads Gao.

The book is not easy. It is dense, long, and challenging. Gao assumes that readers know many of the endless people who fill his narrative; he gives little background, focusing instead like a laser on Mao. But his achievement is overwhelming, a rewriting of the Yan'an myth that also calls into question the entire Communist project. Here was a Chinese historian, working in China, challenging the party on its most sacred soil.

It is works like this that drive the party's contemporary battle against counter-historians. Unlike Xi Zhongxun and his conviction that the Communist Party's history should be told, warts and all, Xi's son took another lesson from his family's battle with the past. His father had been a victim of history; Xi Jinping would seek to control it.

6

History as Myth

Visiting Yan'an today is a bit like visiting Colonial Williamsburg a few decades ago. The open-air museum in the US state of Virginia was built in the 1930s around a few historic 18th-century structures and many Disney-like reimaginations—its symmetrical facades, pastel colorings, and tree-lined streets meant to symbolize the American Revolution's founding ideals. For decades, it was a must-see for visiting royalty, heads of state, or home-grown tourists eager for a taste of patriotic history. That changed as people began to realize that Williamsburg's past was much messier, with an economy built on the slave trade and an aesthetic that was more chaotic than what was represented. Despite efforts to make the experience more accurate, attendance has now fallen to half its 1984 peak of 1.1 million annual visitors. By the early 2020s, the park was beset by layoffs, leadership turmoil, and an overall feeling of being anachronistic.

Not so Yan'an. The city hasn't so much been rebuilt as overwhelmed by a government-sponsored tourism industry aimed at glorifying the early days of the Communist revolution. Tourists dress in Red Army costumes in front of hammer-and-sickle billboards and visit caves where Mao and senior leaders lived. Children ride stuffed horses and wave replica pistols. In 2021, one of the country's largest property developers, Dalian Wanda, opened a Communist Party theme park featuring mascots dressed as soldiers, shops selling souvenirs, and video installations where children can sit behind replica heavy machine guns to mow down the Red Army's enemies on the screen.

Across the six counties that make up the greater Yan'an area, the government has identified 445 memorial sites and built thirty museums. In 2019, the last year before the pandemic suppressed travel, 40.2 million people visited Yan'an, fueling a local tourism industry with annual revenues of $62 billion.

Almost all countries have idealized places of memory, but in China the lack of critical voices is crippling. Instead of being challenged as nostalgia-induced nationalism, "red tourism" has become a nationwide phenomenon, with 36,000 revolutionary sites that have metastasized across the country. Many are small, sometimes no more than a plaque in a village, but 1,600 are proper memorial halls or museums. Many are extremely active, with a third having more than one large-scale activity or exhibition each week. The party says it uses these for "patriotic education" campaigns—and government figures list more than 840,000 events in 2021, serving 1.4 million study groups.

Red tourism is sometimes depicted as a kitschy curiosity—visit Mao's cave and eat a steamed bun! But it is a serious government priority, reflecting vast government investments. It is driven by the conviction that the Communist Party's version of history should matter to everyone and not just top leaders, which was how Mao and Deng approached the issue back in the mid- and late 20th century. Instead, these kinds of indoctrination campaigns are now to be carried out across China. The goal is to create a population that has internalized the party's view of history, much as officials in 1940s Yan'an had. At times, the state uses coercion—especially for stubbornly independent historians—but it is mostly a campaign that seeps into people's heads through textbooks, social media algorithms, and the patterns of daily life in an authoritarian state obsessed with controlling history.

Even before taking power in 2012, Xi identified history as central to the party's long-term survival. In July 2010, the government convened a national meeting of hundreds of historians who specialize in contemporary China. Signaling the meeting's importance, the government held it in the Great Hall of the People—a Stalinist colossus that dominates the west side of Tiananmen Square. President Hu Jintao paid a visit, but the keynote was held by Xi, who had been designated Hu's successor three years earlier. He laid out a five-point program that called for publicizing the party's history, including its "great victories and brilliant achievements," and the "historical inevitability" of its rise to power. Especially young people, Xi said, had to be made to appreciate the party's grand traditions and the heroism of its leaders, and must "resolutely oppose any wrong tendency to distort and vilify the party's history."

Xi wasn't speaking to a convention of proper scholars, but rather representatives of a vast apparatus of government scribes whose job it is to write history. The size of this bureaucracy is difficult to pin down, but conservative estimates are in the tens of thousands. In the 2010s, for example, one single government agency, the Communist Party Research Office, oversaw 2,836 government institutions with a staff of 17,000.

In addition to that central institution, there is a complex array of provincial, county, and city archives, as well as thousands of record offices that chronicle the work of state enterprises, universities, religious organizations, and large media outlets. All of them are staffed by party-approved employees headed by Communist Party members. Their job is to write histories, organize and cull archives to erase sensitive material, organize exhibitions, and help publishers write textbooks. It was representatives of these organizations who met in Beijing in 2010 and received their instructions from Xi.

Two years later, Xi appeared on the other side of Tiananmen Square to make his first appearance as general secretary of the Communist Party, this time at the National Museum of China. Like the Great Hall, the National Museum is another Stalinist hulk from the 1950s, its severe lines setting the ideological tone for cultural institutions across the country. The museum's anchor exhibition is "The Road to Rejuvenation," a show that explains how the Chinese Communist Party is leading China to national salvation. Xi attended the show flanked by the other six members of the Politburo's Standing Committee, which is the powerful body that runs China. There, he unveiled his most famous phrase: the "China Dream," which he defined as the "great rejuvenation of the Chinese nation." That goal was closer at hand than at any time in its recent history, Xi said, because the nation had learned from its history.

China's rejuvenation could be achieved only through the Chinese Communist Party, and it had to be protected from what Xi saw as its greatest enemy: its own lack of self-confidence. In talks with senior officials that year, Xi pointed to the collapse of the Soviet Union in 1991—an event that has haunted Chinese leaders ever since. To Deng, economics was behind the Soviet Union's collapse, spurring him to launch a new round of reforms in the early 1990s. For Xi, however, the Soviet empire fell because no one believed in its ideology anymore. People began to doubt its achievements. Independent groups like Memorial unearthed evidence of Stalin's atrocities, but the leadership in Moscow didn't crack down. As Xi put it:

> *Their ideals and convictions wavered. . . . Finally all it took was one quiet word from Gorbachev to declare the dissolution of the Soviet Communist Party, and a great party was gone. . . . In the end, nobody was a real man, nobody came out to resist.*

This message became a constant refrain during Xi's first decade in power. The Soviet Union had collapsed because its leaders had allowed alternative versions of history to take root. Later versions of this story, some of them written in books and others told in ominous videos, put the fault much earlier. Instead of Gorbachev being to blame, it was Khrushchev and his de-Stalinization campaign of the 1950s that allowed the rot to set in. In this regard, Xi and Mao were similar. Mao, too, perceived the de-Stalinization of the 1950s as a debacle, a dangerous admission of error that should not have been allowed. For China, the last great communist power standing, this mistake would not be repeated.

Xi's first speeches were more like visions than practical programs, yet they were soon to be implemented. In early 2013, reports began to circulate that Chinese Communist Party members must guard against evils such as constitutionalism, civil society, a free press, universal values, and "nihilistic" views of history. These taboo topics were summarized and made concrete in a government document called "Communique on the Current State of the Ideological Sphere," which is better known as Document Number Nine. The document was circulated in mid-2013 by the party's General Office, which is a clearinghouse for the Central Committee and the Politburo, sending out instructions to tens of thousands of party offices across the country. In a country run by the concept of "documentary politics,") this text essentially had the force of law. That meant a ban on such subjects in the media and even in universities.

Most interesting was the problem of "historical nihilism." The document explained the terms as "denying the historical inevitability in China's choice of the Socialist road," rejecting the party's view of history and denying Mao's importance. "By rejecting CCP history and the history of New China, historical nihilism seeks to fundamentally undermine the CCP's historical purpose, which is tantamount to denying the legitimacy of the CCP's long-term political dominance."

To prevent alternative versions of history from spreading, the government in 2014 banned political books brought in from Hong Kong. Previously, Chinese tourists used to buy books in Hong Kong that could not be published in China, carrying them back in their checked luggage. Airport customs began x-raying luggage, especially from flights arriving from Hong Kong, and confiscating the printed contraband.

The campaign gathered pace in 2016, when the Communist Party's official ideological journal, *Seeking Truth*, explained to its readership of Communist Party members that foreigners were questioning the party's history in order to stop China's rise. China was militarily strong enough to fight off foreign aggression, but it couldn't allow foreigners or Chinese influenced by them to challenge its legitimacy: "Now that weapons can no longer stop China's rise, enemy forces abroad and at home have chosen historical nihilism as a progressive tactic."

One chief target was *China Through the Ages*, the journal of alternative history that Xi's father had endorsed with his calligraphy. It was also supported by Li Rui, who had once served as Mao's personal secretary. Those high-level patrons had protected the journal and allowed it to publish insiders' account of key events. But these ties couldn't save the magazine from Xi's campaign. In 2016, the magazine's editors were fired, and its online archive of back issues deleted.

Later that year, one of the magazine's editors was targeted in a lawsuit for challenging an important Communist Partymyth. Hong Zhenkuai had written a piece questioning the "Five Heroes of Langya Mountain," a communist tale about World War II. According to the government story, Red Army soldiers fought off a much larger group of Japanese soldiers at Langya Mountain, a jagged, sheer peak in the mountains southwest of Beijing. When they ran out of ammunition, they jumped off the cliffs but miraculously survived.

Hong had written in *China Through the Ages* that this story didn't match historical records, or the geography, which he said made it impossible for the men to have survived. Instead of jumping, he wrote, they probably escaped another way. Family members sued Hong and the court found that his research had damaged the soldiers' "heroic image and spiritual value."

Thanks to decades of growing nationalism, the party rarely had to hunt down people like Hong. Instead, it could rely on popular anger, with the Cyberspace Administration of China asking online readers to report cases of historical nihilism to its Illegal and Harmful Information Reporting Center. It set up a dedicated site, as well as a hotline. The bureau said it would accept tips about "distorting party history," attacking the party's leadership, slandering martyrs or heroes, and negating aspects of traditional culture.

Later that year, it gave concrete examples of historical claims-- most of them supported by serious historians--that must be censored, such as :

- the Langya mountain heroes slipped instead of falling.
- Mao's chief speechwriter, Hu Qiaomu, actually penned Mao's most famous poem, "Snow."
- Mao's son, Mao Anying, died in the Korean War because he alerted enemies to his position by cooking egg-fried rice.
- The diaries of the party's most famous hero, Lei Feng, were fake.
- The Long March was shorter than officially claimed.
- The Red Army avoided confronting the Japanese army.
- The party's bloody campaign of land reform had been a mistake, or at least excessively violent.
- America never planned to invade China in the 1950s and thus China did not enter the Korean War in self-defense.

Some of these issues might seem trivial—is it important how Mao's son died, or how long the Long March really was? But in the world that the Chinese Communist Party had created, they were existential questions. Allowing a discussion on these topics would challenge key tenets of why the Chinese Communist Party ruled China. If communist heroes weren't so heroic, if Mao wasn't a gifted poet and thinker, if the Red Army hadn't really fought the Japanese that hard, if even the party's founding act of land reform had been a cruel mistake—then by what right did the party rule?

These moves were part of a broader effort to expand party control so that it did not just crack down on dissent but dominated the ideological field. If in the past the party allowed some form of historical dissent by keeping one eye closed—for example, by tolerating magazines such as *China Through the Ages*—it now kept both eyes firmly open. It wanted complete control of history.

All of this culminated with Xi's own resolution on party history—the first since Deng's in 1981 and Mao's in 1945. In a 2021 speech explaining the document, Xi made clear that he wouldn't revisit the party's errors that took place in the Mao era. The 1945 and the 1981 resolutions, he said, had handled those eras. His new version would look at the past 40 years and set a course for the future.

But even the past decades of the reform era were largely ignored in the new resolution. One of the most profoundly troubling events of that period was the Tiananmen massacre of 1989. That was dealt with in an elliptical way:

> *In the late spring and early summer of 1989, a severe political disturbance took place in China as a result of the international and domestic climates at the time and was egged on by hostile anti-communist and anti-socialist forces abroad. With the people's backing, the Party and the government took a clear stand against the turmoil, defending China's socialist state power and safeguarding the fundamental interests of the people.*

No mention was made of how Deng had to jettison two officials he had hand-picked to run the Communist Party, Hu Yaobang and Zhao Ziyang. And the idea that the protests in downtown Beijing were supported by overseas forces is inaccurate—if anything, foreign governments were caught unaware. Indeed, so eager were countries like the United States to gloss over the events that they quickly restored top-level contacts.

Other crises were likewise ignored. The resolution ignored the crackdown on Falun Gong in 1999 and 2000, which saw regular protests in downtown Beijing for more than a year, including self-immolations and documented cases of deaths in police custody. The resolution also stated that the party "overcame" natural disasters, such as the 2008 Wenchuan earthquake, when in fact corrupt building practices had contributed to tens of thousands of deaths, or the SARS epidemic, which the party tried to cover up for months before finally responding. In previous resolutions, similar crises from earlier eras were at least alluded to, in order to justify the new leader's consolidation of power.

Xi was more circumspect in criticizing his predecessors. He said that by the 2010s, China suffered from "unbalanced and inadequate development" that stymied "people's ever-growing needs for a better life." In other words, the gap between rich and poor had become unsustainable, and the party had to pull back from the go-go policies of Jiang Zemin and Hu Jintao. This makes it easier to understand Xi's hostility toward private enterprise and market forces, and his focus on state-led development.

Most damning was how the resolution blamed previous administrations for corruption:

Moreover, previously lax and weak governance has enabled inaction and corruption to spread within the party and led to serious problems in its political environment, which has harmed relations between the party and the people and between officials and the public, weakened the party's creativity, cohesiveness, and ability, and posed a serious test to its exercise of national governance.

The resolution went on to say that under Xi the party had made huge progress in taking "historical initiative" to solve these problems. This means better self-governance, not allowing outside forces, such as media or an independent judiciary, to monitor government officials.

What interested Xi more than attacking his predecessors was, as he put it in his explanation of the resolution, to "relive the glories of the Party and appreciate how the Party has rallied and led the Chinese people in making magnificent achievements." Hence two-thirds of the resolution focused on Xi's first decade in power, which showed China going from strength to strength.

For a look at how this obsession with history plays on the very local level, consider a temple complex west of Shanghai. Since the 1990s, I have been researching the history of a once-vast complex of Taoist temples in the small city of Jurong. At one point, I wanted to look at government records that might describe their destruction in the early to mid-20th century and their reconstruction decades later. A journalist at the Xinhua news agency put me in touch with a branch of the Jurong county government.

The next day I was invited to the government's office of archives. Jurong is a county-level city near Nanjing with a population of just over 600,000, about 0.5 percent of China's total, and yet ten people worked in the office. Some performed routine tasks, such as issuing birth and death certificates but during my visit almost all were busy compiling a new version of an official local history, known as a gazetteer. The last county gazetteer, the head of the office told me, had been compiled in 1998 and they were about to publish a new version, including a history of the temples. This would become the sole source for all local textbooks and histories, ranging from summaries that tourists read in brochures to accounts taught to schoolchildren.

Individual temples, mosques, and churches might publish their own booklets, but they would take the lead from the official history. What was included—or left out—would define what the public knew of local religious life. And of course this was true not only of religious life but everything that had gone on before: politics, agriculture, industry, culture, and trade. All of it would be smoothed over by the party.

We walked through the office to the desk of a man who was in charge of writing the chapter on the history of all religious organizations in the county. He had interviewed local religious leaders and had collected material from the places of worship. Now he was putting together the final version of his chapter. Before it could be included in the new gazetteer, the official told me, an editorial committee made up of local Communist Party officials and senior government historians would vet it. But because it had been vetted earlier, he was sure that changes would be minimal, so he gave me a copy of his chapter.

When I got home, I immediately looked at the section on the Taoist temples. The temple complex once had hundreds of temples— it was akin to a giant monastery with buildings that sprawled over several mountains and valleys known as Maoshan. Historically, it was one of China's most important centers of Taoism, having given rise to a school of the religion. So the history of this place mattered, much in the way that a history of a great European cathedral matters. I was eager to read how it was presented.

I knew from conducting oral histories in the area that the temple complex had suffered minimal damage by invading Japanese troops. They had set some temples on fire, mainly because communist guerillas had used them as hideouts. But most of the temples were unharmed and were quickly put back into use during the Japanese occupation. The real destruction had taken place in the late 1960s during the Cultural Revolution. That is when Red Guards burned the wooden structures to the ground and dug up the stone foundations, hurling them down the side of the hills. That made the story of the Maoshan temples a key example of how the Communist state had smashed religion and destroyed priceless cultural relics—a process of auto-cultural genocide that had wiped out many physical traces of ancient Chinese civilization.

I'd read the earlier gazetteer from 1998, which had alluded to some of this. It had mentioned that religious services had still taken place in the complex in the 1940s and added that the temple was later damaged by "extremists." The details were vague, but it was possible to figure out what had happened. The new version didn't even have this. Japanese troops had destroyed the temple complex and in the 1990s it had been rebuilt. That was it.

It was no coincidence that the earlier gazetteers were more forthcoming. They had been published closer to the period of destruction and were more accurate. Perhaps this was because so many eyewitnesses still lived and would have called out any sort of absolute whitewashing. The 1980s and 1990s, when many were published, was also a more open era. But I was still shocked at how the new gazetteer had so completely elided the Cultural Revolution.

The local history of Jurong was a precursor of what would happen in 2021 when the party released its *Concise History of the People's Republic of China*. In that book, the few references to earlier disasters were almost all erased. This was opposite to what often happens when one moves further away from an event. Usually that makes it easier to discuss problems more forthrightly, but in China distance led to history being stripped down to a party-approved caricature.

Memory: National Museum of China

The best place to witness the party's endless fiddling with the past is the National Museum of China, a gargantuan stone barracks of a building on Beijing's Tiananmen Square. It was built in 1959, at the height of the Great Famine, as one of the "Ten Great Projects" to commemorate the tenth anniversary of the founding of the People's Republic. A decade ago, it was radically remodeled to tone down some of its Mao-era flavor and create a more pleasing international-style museum. And yet it continues to exist in a permanent state of unease, waiting for the party's next orders .

The museum is located on the east side of Tiananmen Square, across from the Great Hall of the People. That equally oppressive building is the public face of China's political system. It is the meeting place for China's make-believe parliament and various bodies meant to show the open, consensual nature of Communist Party rule. The museum's role is complementary, explaining this myth to the public. Originally, the museum was two institutions: the Museum of the Chinese Revolution and the Museum of Chinese History, but they are now melded into one body, just as Chinese history and the revolution are part of one story.

Of the two, the Museum of Chinese History was relatively easy to curate. Then, as now, the main concept was to stock it with "masterpieces" of the past that would glorify Chinese civilization. The Kuomintang had taken the imperial collection—some of the country's best calligraphy, paintings, pottery, and bronzes—when it retreated to Taiwan after losing the civil war in 1949. But Chinese archaeologists were soon making a series of iconic finds: terracotta soldiers in Xi'an, a jade-covered mummy in Hunan, and a flying horse in Gansu. The museum's status meant it could commandeer these pieces and quickly create an impressive collection of ancient wonders.

The Museum of the Chinese Revolution was far trickier. In his memoirs, Wang Yeqiu, who would become the museum's director, recalls joining Communist troops as they entered Beijing in 1949 and making straight for a prison to secure a scaffold used by a warlord in 1927 to hang Li Dazhao, one of the party's founding members. The scaffold became the first item in the museum's collection. That was an easy decision, but the curators soon stumbled over how to describe Mao and all the other thorny chapters in the revolution's history.

These problems delayed the museum's planned opening on 1 October 1959. Prime Minister Zhou Enlai had visited the proposed exhibition earlier that year and said it did not emphasize strongly enough the "red line"—in other words, the line of thought of Mao. Director Wang was summoned to a meeting two days later and instructed that the exhibition "must show that politics is in command, using Chairman Mao's correct thought and revolutionary line as the guiding principle."

Over the next two years, various senior leaders visited the Museum of the Chinese Revolution, constantly critiquing Wang's efforts to toe the party's fickle line. Deng Xiaoping, for example, was irked that the revamped show had only one photo of Li Dazhao, which he said was "totally unacceptable." That set officials scampering to redo the show again, downplaying Mao and emphasizing earlier parts of the revolution. But when Mao's security henchman, Kang Sheng, visited, he ordered that Mao be re-emphasized.

After several more zigzags, the new building opened on 1 July 1961. Five years later, both museums closed at the onset of the Cultural Revolution. They reopened in 1979, but over the next twenty years were closed more often than open because cultural bureaucrats struggled to find interpretations of the past that their political leaders could accept.

In 2001, the two museums closed for good as officials began to see them as somewhat embarrassing relics of the past. That year, Beijing won its bid to host the 2008 Olympics, but a British research institute rated Beijing a "third-tier" city on a par with Warsaw and Bangkok, largely because it lacked world-class cultural institutions. The report was widely discussed in China, leading to a new emphasis on building opera houses, museums, theaters, and concert halls.

The museums on Tiananmen Square were central to their concerns. These institutions dominated downtown Beijing and set the tone for museums across the country. Their director had the rank of a vice minister and was expected to entertain dignitaries from China and abroad. The location demanded an institution on a par with the Louvre or the British Museum. So officials decided to merge the two museums into the less communist-sounding name "National Museum of China." They hired a prominent German architectural firm to rebuild the structure, explicitly ordering it to add enough exhibition floor space so it would count as the largest museum in the world under one roof.

The $400 million renovation closed the space between the two original buildings with a glass atrium filled with the obligatory cafes and gift stores. With 200,000 square meters of exhibition space, the mu-

seum claims the title of world's largest museum under one roof, sur-
passing the Fifth Avenue home of New York's Metropolitan Museum
of Art by 10,000 square meters. Most of the space was created by
adding huge new galleries that fill out the back of the structure as well
as a gargantuan underground exhibition on ancient China. This show,
which sprawls over 50,000 square meters, duplicates the old Museum
of Chinese History. Besides displaying famous archaeological finds, it
aims to prove that all 56 of China's ethnic groups have always worked
together harmoniously. Even the Mongolian empire, which conquered
China in the 12th century, is made part of the story; it is referred to as a
precursor of today's multicultural China.

The galleries at the back of the museum are stocked with a be-
wildering array of shows. Some are timely and interesting: folk art to
celebrate the Chinese New Year, or ancient astronomical instruments
to show how past eras calculated time. But many are more politically
motivated. One large chunk of space is given over to a warehouse-style
display of art that Chinese leaders were given on overseas trips, all
piled next to each other with no apparent message other than to show
that foreign countries respect China. Other halls house vanity-project
displays of works by politically well-connected artists, calligraphers, or
architects, most of them open for just a couple of weeks—probably as
a way to honor the artists but with no real expectation that the public
will visit or learn anything (other than the rewards of going along with the
system). For a few years in the 2010s, these galleries also housed loan-
shows from leading museums in Italy, France, and Germany designed
to build good ties with China. Even these are highly politicized; the first
foreign show after the museum's reopening was on the Enlightenment
in Germany, but it explicitly avoided mentioning some of the key ideas
from that period, such as universal rights.

But the new museum's heart is located in front, directly to the left
of the main entrance. It is a newer version of the old Museum of the
Chinese Revolution, now called "The Road to Rejuvenation."

The general story line, well-known to a generation of Chinese
through textbooks, movies, and television, is that China was humiliated
by Western powers. Then, some well-meaning but misguided patriots
took up the fight but failed to make progress until they were properly led
by the Communists, whose inevitable victory in 1949 started China's
recovery. The Cultural Revolution, not surprisingly, gets exactly one
photograph and three lines of text, while the Great Famine is not mentioned at all. Instead, we see the 1927 scaffold, photos of the Long

March, paintings of Mao declaring the founding of the People's Republic, and newer artifacts such as a cowboy hat that Deng Xiaoping wore on a visit to Texas, and a safety vest worn by Hu Jintao when visiting the 2008 Beichuan earthquake.

For many Chinese (and certainly for the museum's directors), the exhibition is now best known as the backdrop for Xi Jinping's coming-out party in 2012. It was here that he proclaimed the China Dream, declaring that he would lead China back to glory. Indeed, the museum's own website now makes his speech central to the museum's story. In his greeting to visitors, Director Wang Chunfa hailed the show as "the place where a new era of socialism with Chinese characteristics began."

In 2018, the museum opened a sequel to "The Road to Rejuvenation," on the "new era" that was announced in 2017, when Xi abolished term limits and signaled that he would rule for the foreseeable future. This new show features displays that highlight the accomplishments of Xi's time in office, such as models of new military hardware, satellites, and train lines. Videos show Xi giving speeches or out on inspection. Vitrines hold copies of the dozens of books he penned. Evidence is displayed that he is a man of the people, including restaurant expense receipts showing his frugality. The display cases revolve around one that displays the constitution that Xi held when he was sworn in as general secretary.

Xi's supremacy can be seen on the museum's homepage. The English version has information on new shows and exhibitions. But the Chinese site features a photo gallery of Xi: visiting the museum in 2012, visiting it in 2018 for the new show about his accomplishments, and returning to show foreign dignitaries through the exhibits. Xi had become the show, a blockbuster whose end date has been extended indefinitely. The party's control of history seemed complete.

PART II

The Present

Defeating the bandits in the mountains is easy; defeating the bandits of the mind difficult.

Wang Yangming, 1518.

7

The Limits of Amnesia

In early 1990, China's most famous dissident sat holed up with his wife and son in the US embassy in Beijing, watching their home country convulse in violence and retribution. In June of the previous year, authorities had crushed student-led protests centered in Tiananmen Square, killing hundreds and sending many more into exile. Fang Lizhi had escaped to the embassy and was waiting for a deal that would allow him to leave. He would eventually move to Arizona, but only after he and his family had spent thirteen months in the embassy, living in a windowless room that had once served as a clinic.

In the depths of his despair, Fang wrote "The Chinese Amnesia," an essay that explained why tragedies kept befalling his country. The Communist Party, Fang wrote, controlled history so thoroughly that the vast majority of people remained unaware of its endless cycles of violence. The result was that people only knew what they personally experienced. If they had lived through the Cultural Revolution, they would be aware of that event but not the Great Famine a decade earlier. He recalled that the young people who had just participated in Tiananmen didn't know about the Democracy Wall movement just of the 1970s, let alone the Cultural Revolution or the Great Famine. Each new generation was ignorant of the past, Fang wrote, making people susceptible to the party's indoctrination campaigns.

In this manner, about once each decade, the true face of history is thoroughly erased from the memory of Chinese society. This is the objective of the Chinese

*Communist policy of "Forgetting History." In an effort to coerce all of society
into a continuing forgetfulness, the policy requires that any detail of history that
is not in the interests of the Chinese Communists cannot be expressed in any
speech, book, document, or other medium.*

Fang was writing in an era when the party's control of information
was so absolute that only the very best-connected people, probably
just a few thousand in a vast country of more than 1 billion, knew
all the traumas of the People's Republic. The party had released some
information about the Cultural Revolution, but it was selective and
not widely distributed. Other events, such as the Great Famine or
the millions killed during land reform in the early 1950s, were taboo.
Most people knew what they had experienced but little else—which
was exactly the party's plan.

Fang's essay seems more current today than ever. The party's control of history is now backed by a powerful, technocratic state led by
a leader fully committed to whitewashing the past, creating stories
that many people have internalized as real. China's amnesia seems
complete.

And yet this is wrong. Fang accurately described China of the early
1990s. But in the years that followed, a new trend began to emerge
that has usurped the government's monopoly on history. The party's
increasingly draconian efforts to control history proves the potency
of this insurgency, which is enabled by new technologies that have
created a collective memory for many of China's most influential
thinkers.

In his study of ancient civilizations, the German Egyptologist Jan
Assmann identified two forms of memory. One is "cultural memory,"
or the sacred texts and beliefs that held a society together. These didn't
have to be real, and very often there was no expectation that they are
completely accurate. But people shared these myths and stories to
relate to one another. In times past, Egyptians believed that pharaohs
were god-like beings. Greeks believed that Athena was the guardian

of the city named after her. Jews, Christians, and Muslims believed in the Great Flood and how Noah saved mankind. Chinese believed that Yu the Great tamed the waters. These cultural memories helped answer basic questions about human origins and they bound people together. They were written down by specialists—scribes, holy people, or court-appointed historians—and passed down from generation to generation.

The other kind of memory is "communicative," or memories that people or their families experienced directly. These events usually happened within three generations, meaning they were directly witnessed by a person, or their parents or grandparents, and could be directly communicated, usually orally. The two kinds of memory usually did not conflict: cultural memory held the ur-stories that created a civilization while communicative memories were individual accounts of the present.

The Communist Party, however, mixes the two, using myths to explain the recent past. This clashes with people's communicative memories—in other words, the reality that they know to be true, either through their own direct experiences or those of people still alive who have talked to them. Until recently, this wasn't a significant problem for the party because it only created pockets of disconnect. Although millions of people knew that the party used extreme force in clearing Tiananmen Square, the party's control over textbooks and the media kept these groups isolated and unconnected. The result was that most people believed the government's version of events. As witnesses of a catastrophe aged and died out, their memories evaporated and only the government's version remained. That led to the state of amnesia that Fang described.

Two things have changed since then. One is that long after a person has died, that individual's memories can now be preserved and transmitted to new generations, even by people who do not have access to the mass media. The other is that isolated groups now have the ability to link up. This has allowed large groups of people to understand that they are not alone in observing a disconnect between the official version of reality and their lived experiences. This was what the Chinese critic Cui Weiping meant at the end of chapter 4, when she realized that the existence of the magazine *Spark* meant that she and others were not alone.

This inflection point is caused by digital technologies. This does not mean "the internet," in the way people thought of it a generation ago. Back then, the Web was seen as an uncontrollable, almost magical force that would evade censors and spread truth across the globe. As soon became evident, authoritarian states were quickly able to control online content through censors and software.

But digital technology can still allow people to share their experiences in ways that were once impossible. *Spark* is again a good example. Soon after it was launched, it was closed down and all copies confiscated. When the Cultural Revolution ended and a handful of survivors could look in their personnel files, they saw police copies of the magazine and photographed the material. But it remained in their personal possession or circulated among only a few dozen fellow survivors.

These groups, which in memory studies are called "carrier groups," could have had an immediate influence in China if they had had access to the media. For the most part they have not, but their knowledge has spread nonetheless thanks to the rise of digital technologies. In the case of *Spark*, it allowed members to scan the magazine into PDF format and email it to other people. Slowly but surely this has snowballed until the magazine has become widely known. Memories that had once been personal became collective memories—not for all Chinese but for a significant number of people in the country, many of them highly educated and influential.

This is what another memory theorist, Aleida Assmann, calls the difference between "stored" and "functional" memory. Digital technologies allow items to be stored against time's natural decay or the censor's paper shredder. But they become functional only when they can be used. Assmann likens it to a museum that transfers items from its storage vaults to its display cases. The government archives and, later, the work of victim groups allowed the memory of *Spark* to survive, but it remained stored memory that the public could not access. Digital technologies have made it functional, allowing thousands or even millions of people to learn about it through films, books, and articles.

These technological transformations make it easy for certain Chinese people to see through the government's self-serving accounts of history. Government propagandists can flood the media with their version of reality or slow down unwanted information. This sophisticated form of censoring means that most people will still agree with the government version of events. And yet enough people now have access to alternative interpretations of the past that questioning has become widespread and persistent, despite harsher and harsher crackdowns.

The rise of China's counter-historians is significant because it is taking place in a tightly controlled political environment and challenges Communist Party legitimacy. But it is also part of a global trend. In fact, if we look at our own countries—in Africa, the Americas, Asia, or Europe—we can see that we are all in the midst of a memory boom— an ever-expanding number of books, movies, exhibitions, and works of art that try to make sense of the present through a past. And more often than not, this past is increasingly recounted by eyewitnesses.

In Western countries, that trend began in the aftermath of World War I. Mass literacy, cheap publishing, and the new movie industry helped millions of people understand this traumatic war through the concept of shell shock. Even people who hadn't participated in front-line combat felt that their generation had suffered a kind of combat trauma. This melding of identity and trauma become the norm around the world. Over the past few decades, shared trauma has grown to help define not just generations, but groups of people and even nations: the Holocaust for Israel, the Nanjing Massacre for China, and the genocide for Armenia.

Some of this remembering takes place in the tangible realm of battlefields, museums, novels, poetry, and letters. Nowadays, however, this remembering also takes place in what the scholar Jay Winter calls "theaters of memory"—a virtual world of film, television, or video-recorded war crime trials. More often than not, they prioritize oral histories, which many people see as a more authentic account of past events than scholarly reconstructions.

Memory, though, is a fraught term. As we know from our own lives, memory shifts as we age. This malleability is especially true of the concept of "collective memory." It is sometimes used to mean something like an unchanging recollection of suffering that lies embedded in a nation's collective psyche. As originally conceived in the 1920s by the French philosopher Maurice Halbwachs, however, the term has a more precise and useful meaning: when people remember in groups, they form a collective of individuals sometimes numbering in the millions, but each with their own focus and interpretation of the past. As these people die out, collectives can dissolve and memories fade. These groups do not have to include all or most of a society; smaller groups can have collective memories too.

In this sense, the term applies to China's underground historians. Through digital technologies, they have formed a collective memory, and as a loose, shifting group of people they are trying to rewrite the history of the People's Republic of China. Going back to Aleida Assmann's analogy, these memories are now out of the storage vault and in museum display cases, even if most Chinese cannot enter the show. This process has taken place slowly, over decades. One way to understand China's move from silence to speech is to examine one of China's greatest writers of the past half century, the novelist Wang Xiaobo.

Throughout the late 1970s and 1980s, Chinese writers grappled with the traumas of the Mao period. As in the imperial era, most

writers had been servants of the state, loyalists who might loy-
ally critique but never seek to overthrow the system. And yet
they had been persecuted by Mao, forced to labor in the fields or
shovel manure for offering even the most timid opinions. Many
wrote what came to be known as scar literature, recounting the
suffering of educated people like themselves. Almost all of it was
self-pitying and insipid: the output of people who were aggrieved
but not reflective about having served a system that had killed
millions.

Then, in 1992, an unknown writer named Wang Xiaobo published
a strange novella that parodied these earlier works. It told the hilarious
and absurd story of two young lovers exiled to a remote part of China
near the Burmese border during the Cultural Revolution. There they
have an extramarital love affair, are caught by officials, forced to write
endless confessions, tour the countryside in a minstrel show reenact-
ing their sinful behavior, escape to the mountains, return for more
punishment, and so on until one day they are released, unrepentant
and slightly confused.

The novel was immediately popular for its sex, which was omni-
present, funny, and farcical. After the sex, what was most shocking was
how intellectuals were portrayed. In Wang's novel, they are almost
as bad as the party hacks who control them. The novel's hero cons
his lover into bed, picks fights with locals, dawdles at work, and is as
tricky as his tormentors. The title added to the sense of the absurd. It
was called the *Golden Age*, leaving many to wonder how this could
have been anyone's or any country's best years.

The author was equally perplexing. He lived and worked in Beijing
but was not part of the state writers' association. His novel hadn't even
been released in China. But after its publication in Taiwan, the *Golden
Age* was published in China and became an immediate hit. Wang followed it with a pent-up torrent of novellas and essays. He was especially popular with college students, who admired his cynicism, irony,
humor—and of course the sex.

Wang was strongly influenced by his wife, Li Yinhe, who is best known as China's leading expert on sexuality. She has researched and written about China's gay and lesbian movement, and in recent years has stood up for transgender and bisexual citizens.

The two met in 1979 and married the next year, drawing on their experiences of the Cultural Revolution in their works. Li was part of a new generation of sociologists trained after the discipline had been banned in the Mao years, and the couple went to the University of Pittsburgh, where Li earned a doctorate. They returned to China and co-authored a groundbreaking study, *Their World: A Study of the Male Homosexual Community in China*. Li eventually took a position at the Chinese Academy of Social Sciences and Wang taught history and sociology at Renmin and Peking universities.

The 1989 student movement came and went. Wang was friends with Ai Xiaoming, the feminist scholar and documentary filmmaker whom we met filming the Jiabiangou labor camp, and the two shared a silence about the protests. Both had been scarred by the Cultural Revolution and were unsure about the amorphous student movement . Who was leading it? What were its goals? Like many of their generation, they were wary of large, sometimes chaotic movements.

Staying silent became the theme of his most famous essay, "The Silent Majority." Wang describes how the Mao era silenced people by the ubiquity of the great leader: his thoughts, his ideas, and his words rained down day and night. That left a scar, which for Wang meant: "I could not trust those who belonged to the societies of speech." The struggle to find a voice became a personal quest and an allegory for China as a whole.

This is what drew Wang to gay people in China. Disadvantaged groups were silent. They had been deprived of a voice. Society sometimes even denied their existence. Then Wang had an epiphany: much of Chinese society was voiceless—not only people with a different sexual orientation but students, farmers, migrants, miners, people living in old parts of Chinese cities about to be torn down, and so on. These weren't just a few special interest groups but represented a huge swath of Chinese society.

> Later, I had another sudden realization: that I belonged to the greatest disadvantaged group in history, the silent majority. These people keep silent for any number of reasons, some because they lack the ability or the opportunity to speak, others because they are hiding something, and still others because they feel, for whatever reason, a certain distaste for the world of speech. I am one of these last groups and, as one of them, I have a duty to speak of what I have seen and heard.

The most prominent scholar of Wang's ideas, the Paris-based historian Sebastian Veg, believes that Wang was shocked by the 1989 Tiananmen massacre and questioned his own failure to support the protesters. He came to realize that the protesters, as noble as they were, had represented an older way of doing things that he could no longer support. They saw themselves as classic intellectuals who wanted to influence the state and were angry that they had been ignored. Wang saw society differently. Its core problem was that it was fractured into groups that were too weak to oppose state power. This was why China was silent. Finally, he realized what he had to write.

In 1991, Wang finished the *Golden Age*, which he had been working on since returning from Yunnan in 1972. Unsure how to publish it, he sent a copy to Professor Cho-yun Hsu, a well-known historian who had been his advisor in Pittsburgh. Professor Hsu sent it to *United Daily News*, a prominent Chinese-language newspaper in Taiwan that sponsored an annual literary prize. Wang won and entered what he called a "yammering madhouse"—the world of speech.

The success of the *Golden Age* turned Wang into a prominent public intellectual. His fame lasted only five years because he died of a heart attack in 1997, at age 44. But during that time he became an early adopter of the internet and wrote prolifically for Chinese media. Directly or not, he influenced a generation of people, such as his friend Ai Xiaoming. Others, such as the writers Yan Lianke and Liao Yiwu, also began describing the most vulnerable members of society, such as prison inmates or victims of the Mao era. One of China's greatest filmmakers, Jia Zhangke, often mentions Wang as the writer who inspired him to tell individual stories rather than the collective narratives favored by the state.

Wang himself was influenced by many thinkers. As a youngster growing up in Mao's China, he secretly read the works of Bertrand Russell and internalized his idea of personal liberty. In Pittsburgh he also read Michel Foucault and his description of power relations between individuals and the state. Besides his influence on Wang's thinking, Foucault is also useful in explaining Wang's own role in Chinese society. Foucault describes how intellectuals moved from pontificating on universal themes—freedom, morality, existence—to specific areas in which they possess specialized knowledge. Using this expertise, they can intervene effectively in public debates, often on behalf of vulnerable groups, such as the poor, immigrants, or sufferers from HIV/AIDS.

In the West, this began in the mid-20th century, but in China it was only possible with the digital revolution. This allowed Chinese thinkers to shoot films or publish independently of government-controlled studios or publishing houses. Since the late 1990s, these counter-historians have produced groundbreaking historical journals, documentary films, and articles. Almost exactly following Foucault's description, they intervene in areas where they have gained specific expertise. And by working to uncover neglected or lost history they also create new information for others to use.

Not coincidentally, it is among these "grassroots intellectuals" that we more easily find female voices, such as the poet Lin Zhao the filmmaker Ai Xiaoming or the writer Jiang Xue, and minority voices, such as the imprisoned Uighur intellectual Ilham Tohti. Their voices were often excluded from the male-dominated Confucian tradition of intellectuals or the macho world of big-name Chinese fiction writers.

In his essay describing his personal journey, Wang described another important reason behind his decision to speak out. It wasn't to join the Confucian tradition, with its often-patronizing concern for the nation or the people, but for selfish reasons. "The one I wish to elevate the most is myself," he writes. "This is contemptible; it is also selfish; it is also true."

He shares this motivation with other grassroots intellectuals. The journalist-turned-historian Yang Jisheng watched his foster father die of starvation during the Great Famine and decided that his life's work would be documenting it. The video blogger Tiger Temple worked as a slave laborer on a railway and later decided to document that. Ai saw women being oppressed. Jiang learned about her grandfather's death. Others had their homes expropriated or suffered because of the government's mishandling of the Covid-19 pandemic. All of them decided for these personal reasons to stand up. This can be seen as narrow or parochial, but as Wang recognized, it is also how societies change: by people trying to understand and describe their own lives.

Memory: A Landlord's Mansion

Yangjiagou is a Loess Plateau village like no other: its streets are paved, its cave dwellings clean, and its residents wealthy. The reason for this prosperity is Mao, who moved there in 1947 for several months to lay the groundwork for the Communist Party's victory in the civil war. Encouraged by articles in the government press, red tourists regularly come to experience the place that Mao called a turning point in the war, an idyllic period of four months when his troops began to push toward total victory.

But why did Mao come to this village? One reason was strategic. Yangjiagou lies near the Yellow River, giving Mao an escape route if the campaign went badly. But it was also attractive because it was home to one of the most spectacular cave complexes in China: the Ma Family Mansion.

The Ma clan had moved to the village in the 18th century and carefully built up its landholdings. By the early 20th century, the family was wealthy, and its children had been sent to some of China's best universities and even abroad to study. One of them was Ma Xingmin, who studied architecture at Shanghai's Jiaotong University and later went to Japan for further training. He returned to his home village in 1928, his mind filled with progressive ideas about modernizing China.

Shortly after his return, a great drought struck the land. Starvation set in. In the traditional world order, Ma was meant to play the role of benevolent patrician and help his tenants. He melded that responsibility with his love of architecture by building a new family home, paying workers in rice from his grain reserves. Using elements from Western architecture, he built a long rectangular entrance hall that united under arched roofs the entrances to 11 cave dwellings. Over the next decade, the new home took shape in fits and starts, with Ma slowing the project during good times and ramping it up when the local economy was weak.

Meanwhile, one of Ma's brothers had developed close ties with the Communists, who were now based in nearby Yan'an. The family astutely financed the party, which flattered him by naming him an "enlightened gentleman" (*kaiming renshi*). It was one of the many titles that the party bestowed on people it otherwise would not tolerate. It didn't mean permanent acceptance but a tactical approval that could be recalled when the party didn't need that person any longer.

According to the story that tourists hear, when Mao left Yan'an and was heading east in search of a place to stay, Ma offered him his grand new cave complex. To prove Ma's communist-loving bona fides, the party shows tourists a song that Ma wrote praising the Communists, with one of the lines going: *The party is like a sun, and I am a flower, the flower grows tall by following the sun.* According to a government website, he left the village in 1948, settling in the western metropolis of Lanzhou. He was "happy in his old age," and died of natural causes, aged 71, in 1961.

Perhaps not surprisingly, the reality is different. In early 1947, the party was still two and a half years away from taking control of China, but in the areas of western China under its control it launched a program of land reform. In Yangjiagou, party officials issued bonds and bought land from the landowners, then distributed the land to the farmers.

This pragmatic and peaceful program irked one of Mao's most notorious lieutenants, Kang Sheng. He oversaw the party's internal security and surveillance in the 1940s and would do so again, twenty years later, in the Cultural Revolution. To Kang, the point of land reform wasn't simply to redistribute land but to do so violently. The farmers needed to have enemies and had to learn to hate the landowners. So the party labeled them *dizhu*, or landlords, and caricatured them as blood-sucking leeches who had impoverished their neighbors. Some of this was accurate, but the point wasn't to punish abusive landowners. Instead it was to create a nationwide class of enemies that had to be eliminated. That, according to radicals like Kang, would foster gratitude toward the Communist Party.

But that wasn't what the farmers in Yangjiagou wanted. In fact, they wanted to first struggle against the Communist Party officials, then against the landowners because party officials were seen as corrupt and unfair in how they distributed land. But the party insisted that landowners be targeted. People like Ma were "struggled against" in show trials and expelled from their land—in Ma's case, from his newly built cave complex.

In addition to taking the property owners' land, the party also sought to destroy their prestige. Their ancestral temples, which were the equivalent of a village church or town hall, were demolished, as were one of Yangjiagou's most distinctive features, ornamental archways, or *pailou*. They were ceremonial gates built over the streets, about two stories tall, and richly decorated with carved wood and calligraphy especially to mark success in the imperial examinations. Yangjiagou once had more than a dozen *pailou*—a remarkable number for a single village, and a sign that its wealthy residents had helped others by building schools. The *pailou* were all destroyed.

Tourists of course do not learn this history when they visit Yangjia-gou, but China's counter-historians have unearthed most of it through oral histories. The most important of these writers is Guo Yuhua, an anthropologist at Tsinghua University in Beijing. Her 2013 book *Narrative of the Sufferers* was set in Yangjiagou and based on years of fieldwork in the region.

One of Guo's key findings was that the hunger and famines of the Mao era weren't temporary phenomena, such as they were when Ma built his caves. Instead, farmers suffered through three decades of famines, from the late 1940s until the party finally allowed a return to private cultivation of land in the late 1970s.

Guo saw parallels between this violent history and events of today. Clans and religious organizations had provided structure in Chinese society. The party's goal was to smash these old pillars so that its new methods of social control could function unchallenged by any institution or person from the pre-Communist era.

It also substituted the old rituals, such as religious festivals and holidays, with the party's own rituals. Instead of the pailou's gentle instructions in Confucian virtues, loudspeakers blared out announcements. Instead of ritualized attacks on demons during a religious festival, real people in the form of landowners were beaten to death. Instead of the hereditary power of sprawling families and their complex obligations, the party apparatus force-fed society a uniform set of rules and regulations drawn up in remote centers of power.

The process involved more than substituting one set of structures for another. Pre-revolutionary China had been a place of eclectic thoughts and competing groups. The emperor and his emissaries were far away, and local society was based not on the ruler's own ideology but on Confucianism, which was higher than any one ruler's thoughts. That allowed for independent moral action that could challenge authority, even if this was often fraught with difficulty. In post-1948 China, even this slender possibility was obliterated. The party merged with the state, creating an authoritarian bent that the People's Republic has never been able to leave behind.

In Guo's oral histories, local people called themselves "sufferers," or *shoukuren*, because anyone who farmed suffered from droughts and famines. In the title of her book, Guo uses it to refer to these poor farmers, but she also uses it metaphorically. Similar to the novelist Wang Xiaobo and his idea of a "silent majority" of victims, she saw the sufferers of Yangjiakou as emblematic of how Chinese society had been brutalized by the Communist revolution.

Her research turned Guo into one of China's most outspoken advocates of victims of state power. She kept her position at Tsinghua but like many counter-historians has not been permitted to ascend to the highest ranks of her profession. She was never given tenure or faculty housing, which is an essential benefit in a city like Beijing with high real estate prices. Instead she and her husband bought a place in the city's remote suburbs, and she commutes into the campus. She also was never given graduate students to supervise and only allowed to teach basic courses. In 2022 she was forced to take early retirement.

But throughout the 2010s and '20s, she has remained one of China's most influential public intellectuals. Back when she first published her book in 2006, it was easy to see the campaigns that roiled Yangjiagou as something from the past—the Mao era that was already a generation or two removed from the present. Guo always insisted, however, that the state's totalitarian side had never vanished. Its legitimacy has never been based on democratic or popular support but by enforcing its policies through public campaigns, be it to rally support for the Olympics, or diplomatic slights and grievances. She published widely and traveled around China, speaking at small gatherings of like-minded public intellectuals, especially one in the former imperial capital of Xi'an.

8

The Lost City

The ancient capital of Xi'an was built in a web of waterways
protected by some of China's most rugged mountains. It lies
south of the great Loess Plateau, which sheltered Xi'an from the nomadic tribes who once roamed down from modern-day Mongolia.
Holding it like a cupped hand are the Zhongnan Mountains, the
legendary home of mystics and hermits that divides northern and
southern China. It is far from the coasts, but its waterways weave their
way around the city, nourishing and connecting it to the rest of the
country.

In ancient times, the most notorious of these rivers was the Ba in
Xi'an's eastern suburbs. Even today, it is synonymous with sadness: the
final crossing after which a friend or loved one would truly have left
the capital for one of the empire's far-flung outposts, often never to
return. The 8th-century poet Li Bai wrote:

> *The Ba River flows vast and grand*
> *Up above, ancient trees without flowers*
> *Down below, the sadness of spring grass.*

Today the area represents another sorrow: the drab uniformity of
Chinese cities. The Ba still flows vast and grand, but the space above
it is filled with 15-story housing blocks encircled by razor wire, while
the ground below is a grid of broken sidewalks and parked cars. One
elevated subway line serves the area, its station roof made of corru-
gated iron that was being hammered by rain one September morning
when Jiang Xue arrived to visit a friend.

She took a tiny trishaw for half a mile to an apartment complex that was only twenty years old but aging unnaturally fast, its concrete already cracked and its paint discolored. The building's appearance suggested that in only a few years it would be torn down, just like the farming villages and towns that it had supplanted.

One of the towers was home to a gentle 65-year-old man who was, as Jiang Xue put it, her *qianbei*, or elder: Zhang Shihe, a pioneering citizen journalist. He was most prominent when he lived in Beijing in the 1990s and 2000s making short video films about the hinterland. He had been driven out of the capital during the 2011 crackdown resulting from the Arab world's revolt against authoritarian leaders. Nervous that something like that could spread to China, officials began to break up the vibrant scene of independent writers, documentary filmmakers, and artists who had congregated in Beijing during the first 30 years of the reform era. Zhang returned to his hometown of Xi'an, which is also where Jiang Xue went to university and now lives.

Zhang's apartment was a cozy mess. The tables were covered with overflowing ashtrays, smeary tumblers, and random bits of camera gear scattered on tables and chairs. A strange glassed-in balcony curved around the outside of the unit like a breezeway, allowing visitors to pass from the living room to the bedroom unannounced. The corridor was stocked with crates of water, beer, and a battered bicycle that he had used to ride through China, filming and interviewing people along the way. His prize possession hung over the living-room sofa: a red paper lantern emblazoned with four characters: *gong min she hui*, or "civic society."

Another proud purchase was an ultrasonic eyeglass cleaner that sat in the middle of a table strewn with beer glasses and peanut shells. At Zhang's urging we surrendered our spectacles for a few minutes while the machine worked its magic. Afterward, his apartment suddenly seemed bright, sharp, and sparkling.

Jiang Xue looks up to Zhang with the affection one might have for an eccentric uncle whose honor caused him to exchange a life of privilege for penury. Born in 1953, Zhang does in fact come from a kind of nobility: the "red aristocracy" that founded the People's Republic in 1949 and whose children now largely run the country with Xi Jinping as their head man. Zhang's father had been a senior official in the Ministry of Public Security and the family enjoyed all the perks of China's early Communist era: a spacious apartment, cooks, drivers, and flunkies—in other words, servants, just like in the pre-Communist era.

But power became a liability in 1966. That year, Mao launched the Cultural Revolution, in part to prevent this new oligarchy from keeping power permanently. Zhang's parents were imprisoned and his formal schooling ended. Eventually, he was forced to work, as he puts it, as one of "Mao's child laborers" building a dangerous railway line through the mountains. Scores of children died, some believing they were sacrificing themselves for the revolution, others simply press-ganged into service.

When the Cultural Revolution ended a decade later, people like Xi made up for lost time by climbing furiously upward to regain what they saw as their rightful place at the top. Zhang and many others, however, tried to understand and change a system that had give rise to Mao. He ran one of China's first independent bookstores in the 1980s, but the 1989 massacre convinced him that he needed to do something more concrete. In 1993, he left for Beijing to join a growing community of activists hoping to effect change.

By the mid-2000s, Zhang made a name for himself as a citizen journalist—a breed of campaigner who used newly emerging digital technologies to record interviews and post them online, thus bypassing traditional forms of censorship. He adopted the online name of Tiger Temple, or *laohu miao*, which is still how most Chinese know him.

Beijing became Zhang's base for long bike rides into China's hinterland. One year, he spent five months following the Yellow River and producing more than 40 videos on people's daily lives, pollution, and corruption. About 30 can still be seen in China. The others are censored but available on YouTube.

"Everyone wanted to travel but few had the time," he said. "Everyone was busy making money. I thought: I have time but no money. So I thought I'd travel poor."

Those films made him nationally popular, but the crackdown on the internet through the 2010s made such work impossible. That hasn't deterred Zhang. Here, back in Xi'an, he is spending his later years out of the limelight, filming documentaries and oral histories of the events he has seen—messages in a bottle to be read in a future China.

Xi'an feels like the last place to find contrarians like Jiang and Zhang. Over the past two millennia it has been the capital of ten dynasties, including some eras in which it was one of the most cosmopolitan cities in the world. But in recent decades, tradition has seemed more like a burden: for many people its medieval walls, heavy industry, and surrounding countryside of dusty, yellow earth made it the epitome of China's grimy, backward interior.

Its reputation was cemented by one of the most famous novels of the post-Mao era. Published in 1993 by the writer Jia Pingwa, the book was set in a thinly fictionalized version of Xi'an called Xijing, or Western Capital, which he described as a once-great capital turned into a filthy backwater. Jia titled his novel *Ruined City*.

The story was notorious for its sex scenes, which was assumed to be the reason it was quickly banned. But the sex was just part of an overall cynicism that propel the main characters, who use each other mercilessly to satisfy their lusts. The hero, Zhou Min, is a ne'er-do-well from the provinces who comes to the big city seeking fame. He wins over a minor writer who helps him out by forging a letter by a more famous writer recommending Zhou for a job at a prominent literary magazine. Zhou gets the job, though he never reads books. Then he decides to write his first article about the famous writer. He writes a puff piece but also mentions the writer's sexual conquests; at one point, he describes a girlfriend dismissively. That prompts the woman in question to file a lawsuit.

This legal battle forms the main plot line, but mostly we watch the characters as they indulge in sex, gambling, and alcohol. The only rule is looking out for oneself, which the novel implies was due to a breakdown in social relations. Superficially this can be seen as due to the go-go years of the early economic reforms, but as the characters reveal themselves, it is obvious that they abandoned morality during the violence of the Mao era. At that time, the only way to survive was to sell one's friends down the river, or so their stories imply. It was this amoral era that set up the anything-goes mentality of today's China.

Another key theme is censorship, which superficially is about the novel's sex scenes. Jia tells readers that parts of the book have been censored, using blank spaces—in Chinese they look like boxes 口 口 口— to represent characters he voluntarily (or not, he does not say) cut out of the text. The use of the boxes is not random; throughout Chinese writing in the 20th century, writers have used them to indicate censored words. After each cut, Jia added a phrase telling readers how many characters were cut: "the author has deleted n characters."

But the cuts seem to have little to do with sex because they usually follow very explicit scenes. Instead, the implication is that something else is being cut. What, is left purposefully vague.

The book is set in the supercharged political atmosphere of the 1980s, when one campaign after the next buffeted people in the cultural world, culminating in the 1989 massacre. This context, however, is completely missing from the book—in fact, politics of any sort is rigorously absent even though almost everything else is discussed. That makes it hard to escape the conclusion that the □ □ □ boxes are about politics, and not sex.

The novel was then subject to another, more insidious form of censorship. In 2009, it was reissued by the Writers Publishing House, a prestigious organization founded in 1953 that is home to some of China's best-known official authors. It seemed a vindication of Jia's social critique—finally the book was back in print. But it came at a cost. Instead of the boxes, which explicitly indicate censorship, the new version uses ellipses, which in Chinese do not imply censorship. They are followed by the words "and here the author has made deletions" without mentioning how many words had been cut.

As the scholar Thomas Chen has argued, the blank boxes were a way for the public to evaluate the act of censorship. The boxes explicitly meant censorship, and Jia told them how many words were cut. The new version left it vague: something was cut but what and why aren't clear anymore—the omissions could simply be artistic ambiguity. The censor's handiwork is now close to invisible.

With so much of China in the grips of Xi Jinping's forever crackdown, Xi'an still felt more vibrant than the national capital. Unlike Beijing, whose intimate neighborhoods of alleyways have been replaced with fascist gargantua, Xi'an's walls and temples still form a coherent urban space. It has one of the highest concentration of universities and institutes in China, but its distance from the capital and its traditions seemed to give it a small bit of leeway.

As I wandered through Zhang's apartment, looking at posters of his films, his old bikes, and his gear, I asked Zhang if this explanation made sense. He took my glasses and once again stuck them in his ultrasonic contraption, hoping I would finally see things clearly.

"No!" he said with a deep laugh. "The reason why we can do anything here is it's a stupid city. The officials don't get what the [central] government is trying to do. And the police are stupid. If the police here were to train in Beijing, they'd come back way fiercer!"

Jiang and Zhang argued for hours, trading stories about the Mao era, he as an eyewitness and she as one of its children. I asked Zhang if his work made him a dissident. The word doesn't have an easy translation in Chinese. One cumbersome approximation is *chi butong zhengjian zhe*, or "someone who holds a different political viewpoint." A more compact translation is *yiji*, with the character *yi* meaning "different, strange, or unusual" and *ji* meaning "oneself." The meaning can be "dissident" but also "alien" or "outsider"—someone who doesn't belong. That makes sense when people like Zhang are compared to the mainstream, but it's a word he doesn't like.

Instead, he sees himself as someone inspired by another character also pronounced *yi*, which means "righteousness." This concept has moved people in Chinese for millennia, including heroes, bandits, and generals, all of whom in various circumstances can fight for a good cause, even if they are also imperfect people. These people were often forced to the backwaters of China's geography, which made the term *jianghu*—literally "rivers and lakes"—a synonym for a place where righteous outlaws held sway. Throughout our talk, Zhang returned again and again to the character *yi*, or righteousness, which as in many cultures has been one of China's most powerful ideas through the ages.

"Politics? Don't bring that up. But righteousness . . . ," he said, trailing off as he sought to define what it meant, and then did so with an example: "Because I'm one of those people who gets really angry when he sees something wrong. I have to speak up."

One of Zhang's main projects is helping a local academic, Chen Hongguo, make videos. Chen had been a prominent legal scholar and public intellectual before deciding to quit teaching and strike out on his own as a freelance intellectual. He set up a library and salon where he used to hold public discussions with prominent writers, scholars, and artists.

For six remarkable years until 2021, Chen, Zhang, and Jiang Xue showed the sort of public work that intellectuals in China can do if they are given just a tiny bit of space. From the start, they knew their work was on borrowed time. And so Zhang documented their every meeting with videos that are now posted online, an archive of what Chinese civil society can look like—a message to the future about a more hopeful time in the recent past. In 2018, I visited the space, and spent a week in this circle of socially engaged people.

At nighttime, a spotlight in front of Xi'an's Great Temple of Promoting Goodness illuminates four huge characters: *mi zang zong feng*, or "The Esoteric Repository of the Faith's Traditions." At its height twelve centuries ago during the Tang dynasty, the temple was a center for spreading foreign ideas. Buddhist missionaries from India lived there, translating texts from Sanskrit into Chinese and advising emperors on their faith's new ideas about life and society.

Nowadays, the temple keeps the hours of a tourist site. Daytime visitors snap selfies and pray briskly for good fortune; in the evening, it is dark except for the spot-lit characters. For several years in the late 2010s, the building across the street burned brightly. It was nondescript but featured an unusual sign: "I Know I Know Nothing."

In Chinese, this Socratic paradox is rendered as *zhi wu zhi*, which is the official name of what in the 2010s was China's liveliest public forum. An arts and culture space, Zhiwuzhi offered daily lectures, a dozen reading circles, live broadcasts of its events (which are still housed online thanks to Zhang on foreign websites such as YouTube). Its rooms plain and simple, it drew in people through the power of ideas .

One rainy Saturday evening in 2018, I stopped by and watched thirty people listening intently to a former university professor talk about Shakespeare's "King Lear."

"King Lear had three daughters," Chen Hongguo said. "Two told him what he wanted to hear. They weren't being honest. He didn't listen to the other one."

The rain pattered against the windows and cars whooshed through the flooding streets. More people began arriving in the small space, strewn with easy chairs, sofas, and stools.

Soon, the seats were taken, and people focused on Chen, a fidgety 45-year-old with a permanently mischievous smile, and a passionate, slightly hoarse voice that hammered home his points. He slouched in his chair on the podium, conducting the crowd with his right hand while his left held a remote that advanced a slide show of movie stills, Shakespearian quotes, and bullet points.

"The problem with King Lear? He didn't listen to his honest daughter. He didn't have to. Absolute power: this is a political problem that Lear faced, but he didn't recognize it."

Chen spoke for nearly two hours, but no one fidgeted or left. This was in the midst of China's most repressive political era in decades, but many still yearned for something more, and on this evening they kept coming: a journalist who had lost his idealism but recognized it in Zhiwuzhi; an off-duty policeman curious about morality; a high school teacher upset by her students' apathy; a successful entrepreneur who felt that society needed different voices to thrive. None were familiar with King Lear, but they knew that whatever the topic, at Zhiwuzhi it would become vital.

"So I want to ask you one question," Chen said, as he prepared to open the floor to questions. "Are the politics of our era 'when madmen lead the blind?'"

When Chen arrived in Xi'an in 2006, it felt like exile. A native of southwestern China's Sichuan province, he had tested into China's elite Peking University. There, he studied with famous professors and landed a job at Xi'an's Northwest University of Politics and Law. It wasn't bad for an ambitious young academic, but back in the 2000s Beijing was open and vibrant while Xi'an was a backwater. So Chen began inviting guest speakers, including prominent public intellectuals such as his Peking University professor He Weifang, the economic and social reformer Mao Yushi, the independent historian Wu Si, and the civil rights lawyer Pu Zhiqiang.

But still he was dissatisfied. Over the past decade, most universities in China have been moved to remote campuses, where they enjoy more space, but students are cut off from faculty and society. Teachers commute from the city on school vans, arriving just in time for class and departing soon after.

To forge a closer tie with students, Chen set up a book club, and they began reading Milton's *Paradise Lost*, de Tocqueville's *The Ancién Regime and the French Revolution*, as well as *Democracy in America*. Because the administration wouldn't grant him a classroom, students met in his office. When that got too crowded, they gathered in the stairway. Soon, sympathetic articles in the Chinese press began appearing about Chen's "stairway lectures."

Public security, though, opposed his activities. In 2010, they briefly detained him when he tried to travel to Hong Kong for a conference. In 2013, he quit his job, much to the consternation of everyone he knew.

"No one supported me," he told me between lectures one day at Zhiwuzhi. "My wife? Forget it. We sat down and cried about it. Everyone worried that in China's system I'd find no work. Professor He Weifang called me and said, 'Don't resign.' But I did."

Later that year the Communist Party issued Document Number Nine, banning universities from teaching certain foreign ideas, including constitutionalism—exactly the topic Chen taught. "They'd have fired me, so it was fortunate that I did quit." The restrictions on university life were part of a broader move to reverse tentative steps toward a more open society. Chen wondered what to do.

After a year in Beijing taking stock of his future, and six months doing more of the same in Hong Kong, Chen launched Zhiwuzhi in the summer of 2015. People like Zhang Shihe and Jiang Xue were already in Xi'an and were willing to lend a hand. Besides recording his talks, Zhang helped with publicity and other online work, while Jiang Xue hosted events.

Even though the space eventually closed, Chen has kept lecturing, with Zhang posting the lectures online, where they can generate revenue. Chen is still sure that quitting and striking out on his own was the right move.

"At the university, I could only give a few lectures a month and the authorities still had to approve everything. If I tried to lecture, the students' advisors would try to convince them not to attend and would record who attended. Now, we give on average ten lectures a week."

I asked what his goal was. Foreigners always want to know how long these sorts of efforts will take to "change" China, and usually think in terms of election cycles or foundation grant programs. So

I asked him how long it would take to change Chinese society into something more open, however he wanted to define that.

"China has a saying that it takes ten years to grow a tree, but a hundred to cultivate a people. Real social transformation takes time. A scholar wrote four characters to describe our work: *jing shen chong jian*, which means 'spiritual reconstruction.'"

Chen's own spiritual life includes religion. In 2009, he converted to Christianity, part of a wave of "cultural Christians" who were interested in the faith. Many were attracted by the concept of immutable God-given, instead of capricious government-granted, rights.

Chen isn't a regular churchgoer but he says the faith's ideas underlie his life. One is that small acts have larger consequences. When I asked him what he meant, he recited a verse from the Gospel of Luke. It was the parable of a man sowing seeds: some fell on rocks or were eaten by birds, but a few landed on rich ground and sprouted.

"One seed can make a difference," he said. "Who knows what grows from it?"

For a center of intellectual activity, Zhiwuzhi was small. Exiting the elevator, one large conference room lay to the left, while to the right was a small coffee bar selling campy merchandise—tote bags with a red-bearded Socrates and mugs emblazoned with its logo. The main room was dominated by a low-rise stage facing shelves of books and an open area of chairs, stools, and sofas. One wall featured bold calligraphy of the center's name, *zhi wu zhi*, written by Chen's mentor, Professor He of Peking University. Other walls were filled with dozens of photos of speakers, most of them critics of the system such as such as Guo Yuhua who wrote about the Communist Party's use of ritual to rule, the filmmaker Hu Jie, and Ai Xiaoming. Interspersed were Hu Jie's woodblock prints.

The space had several patrons, including Li Tao, a former journalist and later editor of a newspaper. When the newspaper was censored into irrelevancy, he began to invest in real estate and coal mining.

"I left idealism far behind, but Chen Hongguo still pursues it," Li told me, looking lost in thought. "I must support him."

At every event I attended, I met a thickset man in his 40s who went by the name Zijia.

"I'm in public security," he said to me as we made small talk one evening.

"You mean, private security, like guards in front of buildings?"

"No, I mean Public Security," and he laughed, pointing to an imaginary badge on his shoulder and saying in English: "Police!"

"Is this work?"

"No. I learn a lot. It makes me think."

"How?"

"Today I saw a man on the bus with a big knife in his satchel. I could have just arrested him. Job done, commendation, boss happy. You know what I mean? He was wearing a [Muslim] skullcap." He eyed me significantly. China was in the midst of a campaign against Islam, with Muslims often tossed in reeducation camps for the slightest infraction. "But then I decided, no, let's talk to this man.

"So I talked to him. He was on his way to work. He runs a halal butchery. So I said to him, 'Brother, you really shouldn't carry such a knife on the bus but go on to work and carve up lambs. Leave the knife there and don't carry it on the bus.' We parted with smiles.

"I don't know. It's like sometimes you try to talk to people and understand their viewpoint a bit more."

"And so you come regularly?"

"I think it's amazing that there's this thing here. Some people say, 'Oh it's sensitive,' but it's just lectures."

The same year that Chen quit his job as professor, Jiang Xue also quit journalism. Both realized that the instructions from on high made it impossible to carry on their work to the same high standards of the past. And both were lucky to have family and friends who supported them.

Since then, she has been spending her savings to write long profiles of people who resist the system. One is the wife of Pu Zhiqiang, the famous lawyer. She also wrote a portrait of the wife of Guo Yushan, the mild-mannered founder of Transition Institute, a private think tank. Another focused on wives of human rights lawyers. But the pieces are almost immediately blocked. And of course she carried out her research into *Spark*, collaborating with Zhang to record and post online some of her interviews.

"I feel I have to write them," she said. "In the past you were always being told you can't write this or that. Now I can write."

To keep engaged with other people, she volunteered at Zhiwuzhi. She suggested speakers and filled in occasionally for Chen as an on-stage host. With Zhiwuzhi closed, she spends most of her time writing and filming, even though the outlets are shrinking.

Zhang is also more inwardly focused. The government's bans on the sort of short, political observations he used to record on social media—for example, while bicycling along the Yellow River—can be understood as a success for Xi's campaign against free thought. And yet the ban has driven Zhang inward to make deeper, longer films—ones that might mean more to Chinese people in the future.

His most ambitious is a series of video interviews with others who also slaved as children on Mao's mountain railway. Several thousand died from the harsh working conditions but none of their families and survivors received compensation or an apology. Every few weeks a group of them comes to Xi'an to petition the provincial government for redress. They often stop by Zhang's apartment for a meal and a bottle of grain alcohol.

Zhang knows that his videos of these people will never be shown in today's China. But he hopes that he is creating a record for future generations, an ark that can survive the current flood.

"You keep asking me why, but I'm not so good with those theoretical questions," he said. "I just know I'm going to keep going; it's my responsibility to history."

Memory: Snow's Visit

The camera jerks hurriedly behind Jiang Xue as she gets out of a taxi at Xi'an's main train station. It is cold and dark. Her voice overlies the video. She explains that she is returning to her home province of Gansu to research the story behind the magazine *Spark*.

The forty-minute film was released in 2016 and rereleased on YouTube in 2022. It shows some of the ways that Jiang Xue works: her quiet questions, the patience that underlies her longer-form work. She shot most of the video herself and at times it is extremely jerky, with a bit too much zooming in and out. But the film was edited by Tiger Temple, who adeptly focused it on one person, Xiang Chengjian, who was one of the young Lanzhou University students who printed the first and second issues of *Spark*.

The film was part of Jiang Xue's new persona as an "independent recorder" (独立访问者) of events who writes outside the mainstream media. She links her work, both video and written, under the name *xue fang*. "Xue," her given name, means "snow," while "fang" means "interview" or "visit." The intimacy of much of her work makes it seem a bit like a social call, and in this case, Jiang Xue is indeed the quiet listener, only occasionally prodding the old man as he thinks back to the events of his youth.

After some scattered interviews with other people involved in *Spark*, the film hits its stride for the last thirty minutes when we are alone with Xiang. He sits on his sofa, his back supported by large red cushions. His hands are clasped behind his neck. He looks forward, his eyes closed.

Who does he most miss from that time?

至于张春元那是不用说的

He thinks of old friends like Feng Zhejun, Hu Shoujun, and of course Zhang Chunyuan, the charismatic leader of the group who had been older than the rest.

"I miss them all very much. Sometimes I just think about them in my head."

"Is it often like that?"

"Very often."

"You think of their voice and their smile . . ."

"Yes."

"The way they were when they were young."

"Yes. I will never forget them. Until the day that I disappear from this earth I won't forget them."

"Because these people . . ."

"They were all extremely kind-hearted. They were sublime."

"So we should remember them."

"I wish that this country can draw on its historical tragedies and not repeat them. We should draw on these lessons. I hope that young people can develop a sense of justice and carry forward the virtue of having a sense of justice."

"People should dare to act?"

"But not make unnecessary sacrifices. People should cherish their lives but be brave when they need to. Otherwise you're not truly a person."

Xiang puts his hands on his head and covers his eyes. He lets out a sigh and then repeats a poem by Lu You from the 12th century, a poem that admits impending defeat while hoping for ultimate victory. The poem begins with the narrator acknowledging the Buddhist idea that life is empty and that earthly matters are of little consequence. But he still regrets that the nine provinces of traditional China are divided by Mongolian conquerors. He is confident that a famous general will unite the country's heartland but knows it won't happen in his lifetime. That is why the poet addresses his son and asks that after he has died, the boy will tell him of the final victory in his prayers.

I know that everything is empty,
But I'm sad at not seeing the Nine Provinces reunited.
One day the army of Wang Shibei will control the Central Plains;
Don't forget to tell your father when you carry out the family sacrifices.

It is a poem that most educated Chinese know, and Xiang only has to start reciting it for Jiang Xue to let out a sigh. Hearing it, she wonders: China might not be whole again in this old gentleman's lifetime, but will it be in mine?

9

The Gateway

In 1938, the battle for China was in full fury. Japan had devastated government forces under Chiang Kai-shek in Shanghai and then again in Nanjing, leading to the infamous massacre and an exodus of millions toward the interior. Most outsiders expected China to capitulate in a matter of months.

Then, a small miracle happened. Chiang's forces stiffened around the central plains city of Xuzhou, holding out for a full month. After exacting tremendous casualties on the Japanese, the defenders executed a clever withdrawal of more than three hundred thousand troops to the Dabie Mountains, one of the many ranges that radiate out, north to south, like natural defenses of the interior. The Chinese soldiers fought rearguard actions, linking up with other troops. Their goal: to make a last stand at the gateway to China's vast interior, the industrial metropolis of Wuhan.

Wuhan's strategic importance goes back millennia. It sits at the confluence of China's greatest river, the Yangtze, and the country's most important north-south river, the Han, which starts nearly a thousand miles north near Xi'an. In the past, Wuhan was made up of three cities: Wuchang, the ancient political and economic capital of central China on the south bank of the Yangtze, and across the river the cities of Hankou and Hanyang that sit on either side of the Han. In imperial times, the governor of this region was one of the most powerful officials in China, controlling a complex web of waterways and wetlands. For centuries it has been called *jiusheng tongqu*, or the pass to nine provinces.

By 1938, the three cities had been merged into Wuhan, by far the most important city still under Chinese control. For most of that year, it was also an example of how vibrant China can be when its people are unfettered. Desperate to unite the country, Chiang's Kuomintang party permitted a free press and free artistic expression. His censors and his secret police backed off, allowing the city to come alive. Newspapers sprang up and began reporting on problems in the government and the flood of refugees. Writers such as the novelist Lao She came down from Beijing to escape Japanese occupation and chronicle China's resistance. They were joined by famous photographers, filmmakers, and writers from around the world, who arrived to witness the looming battle. These visitors included the Hungarian-born photographer Robert Capa, the Danish film director Joris Ivens, and two British writers, the poet W. H. Auden and the novelist Christopher Isherwood. Spain had just been lost to fascism and now Wuhan was up next—in Auden and Isherwood's memorable description, a bellwether for the era and an oracle for the future.

> This is the real capital of wartime China. All kinds of people live in this town . . . generals, ambassadors, journalists, foreign naval officers, soldiers of fortune, airmen, missionaries, spies. Hidden here are all the clues which would enable an expert, if he could only find them, to predict the events of the next fifty years.

Wuhan once had two hundred lakes, the remnants of a giant, prehistoric sea that has yet to completely fill in. Although all but 30 have been paved over, its nickname is "sponge city," with sinkholes that pop up during construction, roads that flood, and parks that are often waterlogged. When it rains, the drops of water falling from the heavens meld with the factory smoke streaming upward from the earth, enveloping the city in a smoggy cloud.

It was on one of those late-summer days that I went to visit Ai Xiaoming. She has lived in the cold world of Beijing and the subtropical swelter of Guangzhou but always seems to gravitate back to her hometown in China's center—a family history born of war, displacement, and government power. Her life has been made up of juggling these different homes, where she lives out her different personas: dutiful daughter, attentive mother, prolific academic, social activist, underground historian.

Each role is centered in a different location. From 1995 to 2012 she lived most of the year in Guangzhou because of her teaching job. Her students and many of the activists she knew were based there. Her first films were also set there: *The Vagina Monologues*, which she shot with Hu Jie, and her 2005 film *Taishi Village*, which documents how authorities systematically deny rural citizens their rights. Her home was a semi-public space, where activists and visitors could come to screen films or crash when they lacked a place to stay. She was something like a mother hen, taking guests out to the market to shop for food in the morning, coming back for discussions or work in the afternoon, and then cooking up a big meal in the evening, which often was the focal point of the day.

She retired from the university, age 55, in 2008. This was not early retirement but typical for that era in China, where talented people were shunted aside, often at the peak of their abilities, in order to free up positions for young people—a sleight of hand that kept young people employed and older people marginalized. She kept her Guangzhou flat for another dozen years, selling it only in 2020. By then, she had long since moved her life back to Wuhan, especially after her final graduate students left the university in 2012.

In Wuhan, Ai has three separate apartments for three very different roles: activist, daughter, and wife/mother. These spaces were made possible by her younger brother, Ai Luming, one of Wuhan's best-known private entrepreneurs and philanthropists. Holding a PhD in economics, in 1988 he founded Wuhan Contemporary Technology

Group, which started in biotech but is now a conglomerate that includes a real estate arm. In 2019, the Chinese wealth tracking firm Hurun estimated his personal wealth at nearly $1 billion.

In Wuhan's lake-dotted south, near the Third Ring Road and subway line 2, Ai Luming developed a subdivision where the family lives. Built in the 2000s, by today's standards it is hardly luxurious, but it is still an attractive set of twenty three-story buildings, each one with about four units, depending on the layout. The buildings are on a tree-lined, narrow street jammed with cars parked in assigned slots. And of course it has bulletin boards and banners exhorting people to follow the latest party campaign—"red education," for example, was being pushed when I went to visit the first time. The complex, like most in China, has guarded entrances, which are meant to keep out peddlers and through-traffic and keep track of who is visiting whom.

One large unit became the family home. The siblings' mother had already passed away in 1997 and so they gave their father one wing of the house. Ai spends most days in this home, looking after her bedridden father and working out of a study that is reserved for her use. A caregiver helps with the heavy work, but Ai is in charge—something she does gladly, despite the stresses. Born in 1957, her brother is four years younger, and she loves him dearly. Especially because he has not retired, she willingly takes on the responsibility of caring for their father.

In addition, she has a smaller house for her own family, whose privacy she guards carefully. She and her husband have a son, who has studied abroad and now works for his successful uncle. For many years, Ai also had another smaller apartment in the same complex where she met activists and dissidents. The idea was to keep these three worlds separate and not implicate her nuclear family, or her extended family. Like all entrepreneurs, her brother is a Communist Party member, and she understands that he cannot get involved in her work. She takes no money from him but is very proud of his charitable work and the fact that he built his company from scratch.

Her study in her brother's home is lined with computer monitors and screens so she can edit her work and keep abreast of events in what is her fourth space: the virtual world of social media, email, and communication apps.

These worlds swirl around her, all competing for her time. We sat in her study and chatted for hours, interrupted only when she needed to go downstairs and visit her father. Even though her public persona is of a severe defender of rights and the downtrodden, in person she tells jokes, and laughs—especially at herself. Looking at the different phases of her life, she can see the absurdity of so many twists and turns: the fanaticism of her youth, the apolitical academic pursuits of her 30s, and the slow turn toward feminism and activism as she got older, a time when most people head in the other direction.

In other ways, too, her life has come full circle. The first twenty-five years were spent in the Mao era, when nothing was permitted. Then came a period of reforms and increased possibilities for Chinese people to shape their lives. And now she is constrained again, with politics back in command. Through it all, one thing has remained constant, her bloodlines, a family history that set her on a path toward conformity and caution, which she was able to leave only with great difficulty.

Despite the world's attention, Wuhan fell in late 1938. The battle, however, changed the course of World War II. Japan had expected a quick victory that would allow it to turn its attention to the rest of Asia. Instead, Chiang stopped Japan's march westward, allowing him to establish a permanent wartime capital farther upstream in Chongqing. His soldiers tied up hundreds of thousands of Japanese troops through the end of the war.

At the time, however, the loss of Wuhan seemed like another in an endless series of Chinese defeats. Certainly, the human cost was unimaginable. The number of dead and displaced people quickly ran into the tens of millions, while a disastrous decision to slow Japan's advance by blowing river dikes destroyed hundreds of villages and vast farmlands. But what gave the catastrophe a human face were the hundreds of thousands of orphans. Aid agencies launched campaigns at home and abroad to find them new families.

Chinese government officials tried to set an example, among them Tang Shengzhi. He was a general who at one point was Chiang's rival. The year before, Chiang had given him the hopeless task of defending Nanjing. Just as Chiang probably hoped, Tang took the blame for the debacle, retiring to rural Hunan province in southern China to study Buddhism and focus on his family. But he had only one child, a daughter named Tang Renqun, who was already married to an air force instructor. The general responded to the call, and adopted eleven children, who lived and studied near the family compound at an academy that he had established in southern China's Hunan province.

Soon after, Tang's son-in-law died in a plane crash. The general's widowed daughter and one-month-old granddaughter moved back to the family home and got to know her adopted siblings. One of these was Ai Renkuan, a 13-year-old who was six years her junior. By the late 1940s, Ai was a military cadet and the two secretly fell in love.

Their affair was complicated by the government's pending loss to the Communists. The family had a chance to flee to Taiwan, but the general had had dealings with Mao in the 1930s and had not participated in government campaigns against the Communists. He felt safe and decided to stay. The Communists rewarded him handsomely, declaring him a "democratic personage" and giving him the largely honorary job as deputy governor of Hunan province.

In the true fashion of a patriarch, the general's decision applied to all family members, including his daughter. Ai Renkuan had a chance to flee to Taiwan but stayed because of his love for Tang Renqun. The two married in 1950. Ai was allowed to join the People's Liberation Army, and later the Chinese Communist Party, his sins of being a young government officer seemingly forgiven. He was transferred to Wuhan and a few years later demobilized. He landed a job in the city's commerce department and then became an elementary school-teacher. Thanks to his education in General Tang's private school, his English was above average and so he tested into a better job as an English teacher in a middle school.

In 1953, the couple's first child was born, a rambunctious daughter that they named Ai Xiaoming. It was a cliché name from that era, one meant to show fealty to the new regime. "Xiao" means dawn or day-break and "ming" means bright. Under the Communists, China was starting a bright new day.

Ai Xiaoming, her 14-year older stepsister from her mother's first marriage, and a few years later her brother, grew up as "the general's grandchildren." It was a quiet life of small privileges: they suffered less from rationing than many others, and people were respectful of their family background. But the family knew that their position was pre-carious. Millions of people associated with the former government had been purged or killed in the Communists' early campaigns. Their existence depended on the party's goodwill.

Growing up in Wuhan in the 1950s and '60s, Ai recalls being surrounded by silence. Her mother, Tang Renqun, was psychologically
fragile and prone to fits of schizophrenia. Her gender became the
focal point of the general's complicated family life. He had married
previously, but when his wife had been able to give birth only to
Tang Renqun, the general divorced her—the general needed a son
to carry on the family lineage. After the divorce, Tang Renqun lived
with the general and his new wife. As his second wife also did not
bear him children, the couple dressed Tang Renqun like a boy, pre-
tending she was the son they coveted. When she was 10, Tang Renqun
broke down, screaming for her mother. She was then sent off to live
with her mother and later was married off to her first husband, the air
force pilot. After his death, her return home, and her marriage to Ai
Renkuan, she was finally with a man she loved. She was psychologically stable. And yet social pressures were again pressing in. Once again,
bloodlines were at the center of the family's troubles.

Her parents knew that their personal biographies made them closely
associated with the old regime. So they tried to distance themselves
from their children, hoping to protect them from guilt by association.
They told Ai and her siblings that they couldn't advise them how
to be good citizens. Their main advice was to draw no attention to
themselves and to fit in with the surrounding society.

"My father was very strict with us, but that strictness was not so that
we would get ahead in life or make a career," Ai recalled. "Instead, he
didn't want us to stir up trouble, or think independently. He wanted
the family and the children to be safe."

In 1966, her father's fears proved accurate—and his years of cautious
conformity inadequate—with the launch of the Cultural Revolution.
General Tang was arrested and sent to prison, where he died in 1970,
aged 81. Ai Renkuan was attacked for being the adopted son (and
son-in-law) of a Kuomintang general. He wasn't just a "historic
counter-revolutionary" —communist jargon for someone who had
made some sort of error before 1949. He was also called a "current

counter-revolutionary," meaning he had actively opposed the government since then.

As proof, the party found examples from his English class. On the blackboard, he was accused of having written, in English, "Mao Zedong was born in China," and also "Lei Kai is a sharpshooter." In his confession, Ai Renkuan wrote that the two had nothing to do with each other. The first sentence came from a textbook. The second was about a former student who was now a sharpshooter and had come to the school to report on how his study of Mao led him to become an excellent shot. There was no hidden meaning or implied threat to Mao.

No matter, Ai Renkuan was fired from his job, beaten, and his head shaved; he spent the next years cleaning toilets. Later, because he was so good with his hands, he was allowed to repair tractors, watches, and other equipment. He also worked in the kitchen as a cook.

His wife Tang Renqun, the general's daughter, was also beaten, detained, and forced to write self-criticisms. Besides denouncing her father, she also examined in depth a mistake she had made at the high school where she worked as a librarian. Eager to make a chili sauce, she used her ration coupons to buy chilis from the school cafeteria. This was a serious mistake, she said. She had only been able to afford the chilis because she had extra food coupons as her father was a famous general. Her willingness to use her food coupons to acquire this luxury showed her poor understanding of her privileged position.

She had to write and rewrite the self-criticism while her father and husband sat in jail and Ai Xiaoming and her younger brother were left at home without their parents. (Their older stepsister, whose father was the dead air force instructor, had married and left the family.) Eventually she was released but reassigned to a new job sweeping up at a tourist site. Her schizophrenia flared up again, and she would sometimes run out to the neighbors and bang on their doors, asking why her family had been destroyed.

The same day that her father was denounced, 12-year-old Ai Xiaoming became a target. She was on her way to the school cafeteria. Two students blocked her way, telling her that she had to distance herself from her father. She had been unaware of the events and felt struck by lightning. In a daze, she rushed home.

That night, she took a newspaper and wrote in thick calligraphy strokes a denunciation of her father, primarily accusing him of being a tyrant at home. It wasn't a serious accusation, and her poster wasn't huge, but it was the only way she knew to cut ties with her family. The next day she went back to the cafeteria, climbed up on a chair, and pasted the poster up on the wall.

Inside, she was in turmoil. She still went to class but was like a robot. Her father had disappeared, and her mother spent the days confessing her crimes about chili peppers, or commuting to the tourist site and sweeping all day. Ai and her younger brother were left to fend for themselves.

One day her teacher called her over.

"What did you write in the composition book?"

"Just writing."

"Did you write about Ai Renkuan?"

"I did not!"

"We know all about your father. You haven't been able to cut off. Why not? What did you remember? Think!"

The teacher took out Ai's composition textbook and turned it over. On the back was written "Ai Renkuan is good." It was handwritten in pencil. The writing was crooked, but it was clear. That afternoon the students had been listening to a propaganda show broadcast through the school's loudspeakers, which were located in each classroom. She recalled holding her head in her hands and almost dozing off, despite the din. Had she written it?

The teacher wrote up a report and put it in the girl's official record: Ai Xiaoming had written counter-revolutionary slogans.

But Ai still fought to become a good new citizen of new China. She attempted to join the Red Guards, was rejected because she wasn't from a good family, but eventually joined another group when entry rules were relaxed. She learned a revolutionary dance. She changed her given name. Instead of Xiaoming, she chose "Weidong," which means "defend the east," with the east being Mao. When her group of Red Guards were about to see Chairman Mao at Tiananmen Square in Beijing, she wrote in her notebook: "My parents gave me life; Chairman Mao educated me."

In 1969 she had finished elementary and middle school. But then came a reality check: she was denied entry to high school because of her bloodlines. Her family's political problems meant her education was over. The next year she changed her name back to Ai and was sent off with millions of other urban young people to labor in the fields and learn from the farmers.

When she thinks back on it, she laughs at the absurdity. She spent her teens planting crops and reading Mao's works. One day, when we were talking about it, she couldn't help blurting out: "It was a waste of time!"

Then, her bloodlines saved her. In 1974, the Cultural Revolution was still two years away from ending, but the party had already begun to restart higher education. The university entrance exam would not be reinstituted until 1978, but a form of Maoist university opened for the children of top officials, even those who had been killed by Maoist violence. This is how Xi Jinping obtained his university education and it was how Ai got into university without a high school diploma. Her grandfather had been General Tang Shengzhi. That was enough.

But unlike people such as Xi, who used the head start as a stepping-stone to powerful careers, Ai was slowly transformed by her learning. She was admitted into Central China Normal University, a Wuhan-based school that like many institutions of higher learning had been forced to relocate to the countryside. So she was still stuck far away from her home, and the classes mostly involved reciting Mao's poems. But she and other students found novels by foreign authors, such as

Tolstoy and Stendhal, and circulated them. They also read classical Chinese works, with their profound ideas on morality and thought.

The messages sank in only slowly. When Mao died in 1976, Ai begged to join the party, writing her application in blood. She was rejected because of the black mark in her file—for having written the "counter-revolutionary" slogan about her father being good. But she persisted and eventually joined in 1984. She later described her thinking: membership was a "safe box"—a way to protect herself in the future.

In 1985, she moved to Beijing to work on a PhD in Chinese literature at Beijing Normal University. She needed just two years to finish her dissertation, on leftist literature—the first woman to obtain a PhD in literature after the Cultural Revolution. She began working at the China Youth University of Political Studies. This school was under the Communist Youth League, which is one of the party's most important organizations—a conduit for new, young talent into the system. It was a job that probably would not have been possible without party membership.

That could have set her up for a smooth career as an educational apparatchik. Ai, however, was slowly changing from within. She befriended outsiders, such as the novelist Wang Xiaobo, listening to his idea of a "silent majority" of people silenced by the Chinese Communist Party. Ai wrote sympathetically about Wang and helped edit a volume that came out after his early death, in 1997, of a heart attack. When his corpse was placed in a coffin at the crematorium, it was Ai who put in his hands a collection of his essays that had just been published.

In 1988 she spent a year in Hong Kong working on the ideas of Milan Kundera, translating his work *The Art of the Novel*. She returned in 1989, just as the student protests were about to begin. But her work was still largely academic, and her life revolved around her newborn son. Like Wang Xiaobo, she wasn't sure what to make of the chaotic scenes on Tiananmen Square and the unclear demands of the students.

"Those of us who went through the Cultural Revolution wanted to keep a distance from political movements. So '89, the student movement, in my heart I rejected it," she said, laughing at how funny that sounds today—she, the political activist of today turning her back on the biggest political protest in contemporary Chinese history. "My views are now different, but back then that's how I thought. I supported democracy, but we'd been through a lot of movements. So I didn't like any movement."

But Ai defended the students' right to free speech. Many people deserted the square after the Communist Party declared martial law, a decision that made clear its intentions to use force to clear the square, but it was precisely then that Ai showed her true colors.

"Maybe I was influenced by Kundera. You can't use those methods against students. I had to stand up."

She went to the square to see the protests and brought blankets to the hunger-strikers. The massacre, though, caught her off guard. "We never thought they would do that. It was inconceivable."

After the massacre, her school launched a purge against anyone who had participated in the protests. She escaped much criticism but realized that she had no future at her university, which was so tightly tied to the Chinese Communist Party's political structure. Fed up with politics, she accepted a job in 1994 at Zhongshan University in Guangzhou, a major Chinese city not far from Hong Kong. She took a job in the Chinese literature department, later switching to comparative literature. Her focus turned toward women's issues. She told me that she always felt there was something odd in her department.

"For example at academic conferences there were few women scholars, especially high-level scholars. In our department there were very few female professors. And even excellent [female] scholars couldn't become heads of departments, or administrators. It made me realize that everything we were talking about in terms of women's issues was evident in the school."

A turning point came in 1999 when she spent an academic year at the University of the South in Tennessee.

"American universities weren't just about research. They were about serving society and changing society. It had a big impact on me. This was the first time I'd thought about this. I really liked the democratic, equal form of education.

"I attended a lot of events on campus. The school emphasized pluralism. There were a lot of events, like African American musical groups and commemorations of Martin Luther King, Jr. It made me think that a university should be like that."

She also used the year to teach herself about film. She borrowed two to three videotapes almost every day, sometimes arriving at 7:30 AM to get a film and only returning the last one at night.

While in America she watched "The Vagina Monologues," a play about sexual experiences, reproduction, mutilation, menstruation, and other topics related to women that often are downplayed as inappropriate or marginal. When she returned to China in 2000, she translated the play into Chinese and had her students perform it.

This was a new period of intense intellectual ferment in China. Reports of social problems became common, including the 2003 case of Huang Jing, a woman who died after her boyfriend forced her to have sex. Ai spoke out about Huang's case, coming to national attention. She was also inspired by the 2003 death in police custody of a young man, Sun Zhigang. The case caused a change in how police handled migrant laborers. Suddenly, a more unfiltered kind of politics became possible.

Ai's decision to make so many films on so many sensitive topics brought her to the government's attention long before Xi took over. In 2008, she was one of the first people to sign Charter '08, the call for moderate political rights drawn up and circulated by future Nobel Peace Prize laureate, Liu Xiaobo. The next year, she wrote a letter to the Communist Party saying she wanted to withdraw her party membership. Since then she feels that she is no longer a party member, although the party does not allow people to leave it, and it is impossible for her to know whether they consider her a party member.

Since about then she has also been unable to leave China. In 2010, she and the feminist lawyer Guo Jianmei were awarded the Simon de Beauvoir Prize for Women's Freedom. She was invited to Paris to receive the award, but police rejected her application to renew her passport, a tactic they would use for many people in later years—including most of the Chinese population during the Covid-19 pandemic.

In one of her earliest films, Ai introduced viewers to Tan Zuoren, an activist from Chengdu who was the first to make a clear link between shoddy building practices and the death of thousands of children whose schools collapsed on them during the 2008 Beichuan earthquake. About twenty thousand people died in Beichuan and another forty-nine thousand across the region. Tan wrote a famous essay called "Longmen Mountain" that described how the earthquake was actually the second man-made disaster to have befallen Beichuan.

The first had come in 1935 when the Red Army was on its Long March, heading north toward their eventual base in Yan'an. After staying in Beichuan for one hundred days and recruiting fifteen hundred locals into its ranks, the army withdrew, leaving the town vulnerable to government troops who moved in to seek revenge. Worse, the Red Army implemented a scorched-earth policy that destroyed a dozen villages, a priceless temple from the Tang dynasty, and most of the roads and bridges that locals had so laboriously carved out of the mountainous landscape. In the end, more than half the population of 46,000 was killed.

Tan investigated the building projects and posted his findings online. He called this work "New Citizen Movement"—the idea being that people in China should strive to be citizens and not subjects. Ai made people like Tan the focus of many of her films, especially in the 2000s. These were people who were defending their rights, such as the "rights-defender lawyers," who took government laws at their word and tried to stand up for rights enshrined in China's constitution and laws.

Ai said the problem with this strategy is that it is based on a tolerant government, one that will respond to peaceful protests. That was an ideal after the Cultural Revolution when people talked of "bringing order out of chaos." That might have been permitted for a time but it gradually became taboo. By the 2010s, as Ai put it, many of those who tried this kind of moderate reform had been "smeared and punished, one after the other, and the government had changed—back to the way things were in the Mao era."

"The severe political pressure unleashed through governmental response has made it clear that it is unshakable, it does not need to listen, it has idolized itself. What happened in the past, the demonization of those critical of the government, is taking place once again."

The scholar Zeng Jinyan has written extensively on Ai, including a PhD dissertation in 2016. She notes that Ai has gone through four phases of stigmatization. First, she was the daughter of a politically persecuted person, meaning her childhood was marked by her own suffering at the hands of state-orchestrated violence and ostracization. Then after a brief period of fitting in during the late 1970s and 1980s, she became a scholar viewed by many as too radical because of her focus on feminism, which in China is a controversial topic. Although respected in the feminist community, her work attracted no support at her university, which did not offer her the chance of teaching past the mandatory retirement age of 55—something it sometimes does to scholars who are popular or acceptable.

The third phase came when she started making documentary films, which were often seen as too radical. Before they were shut down in the early 2010s, underground documentary film festivals often did not invite Ai to participate. Many preferred more aestheticized films and were worried that the advocacy nature of the films would get them in more trouble. Zeng, for example, writes in her doctoral thesis that she was invited to a feminist film festival to speak, but the organizer cautioned her not to speak about Ai.

To avoid political risk, we did not invite teacher Ai (Xiaoming). If your speech is about her, it might not be appropriate. . . . It is better to talk about research on (other) Chinese female directors. Teacher Ai (Xiaoming) is too sensitive, (talking about her) might cause the closure (of the event).

Of course, the irony is that this caution did nothing to save this or other independent film festivals. Early on, Ai recognized the pointlessness of trying to compromise, resulting in one of her most famous actions. In 2013, she wanted to protest the sexual abuse of children at a school in China. After the government arrested an activist who uncovered the abuse, Ai asked Zeng to take a picture of her topless, holding a pair of scissors, and with her body covered in calligraphy protesting the government inaction. She posted it to her Chinese microblog, which immediately banned it, and to Twitter.

That image has since become one of the best-known protests of the past decades, but also a sign of the desperation that people like Ai feel in trying to effect social change. With their books and movies about current events banned, how to change the system?

By 2014, Ai was increasingly interested in the past. Her films had always been about the most immediate of concerns: a woman's rape, villagers protesting for democracy, or citizens uncovering corruption. Her next project was the epic documentary on the Jiabiangou labor camp. That look back in time consumed most of the next few years, paralleling a growing interest in Chinese social media about that earlier era, and especially one of its most insightful essayists, Yu Luoke.

Like Ai Xiaoming's youth, Yu Luoke's life was defined by bloodlines. He was born in Beijing in 1942 to parents who had studied engineering in Japan and been denounced as Rightists in 1957. Two years later, Yu graduated from high school with high marks but was denied entry to university because he came from a tainted class background. He moved to a suburb of Beijing to farm and noticed that the discrimination in the countryside was even worse: there, children of one of the five black categories were denied even primary education.

With the help of a friend he got a reading pass to Beijing's main library and threw himself into a self-guided course on the philosophy of freedom. At the time, foreign authors were not banned, and he read European Enlightenment thinkers, especially Rousseau. In 1964 he moved back to Beijing but could not obtain a regular job. Instead, he worked as a provisional teacher at an elementary school and lived at home.

This was a seminal moment in 20th-century Chinese intellectual history. One of the most important historians in modern China, Wu Han, wrote a daring play that became the initial shot in the Cultural Revolution. Much like Ai Xiaoming's grandfather, Wu had backed the Communists when they took power and was given the largely honorary position of vice mayor of Beijing. The play was called *Hai Rui Dismissed from Office* and described a minister in the 16th century who was forced out of office for criticizing the emperor. Wu Han's intentions are not clear, but he began working on the project in 1959 at the height of the Great Famine. Many immediately saw in it an allegory for Mao's dismissal of the upright general Peng Dehuai, who had dared to warn Mao about his disastrous policies.

By 1965, Mao was eager to purge another moderate in the party, his deputy Liu Shaoqi. One of Mao's followers wrote an essay attacking Wu Han's play, saying it was meant as an attack on Mao. The idea was that attacking Wu Han would weaken the Beijing mayor, Peng Zhen, who himself was a loyalist of Liu. The strategy worked, and by 1966 the Cultural Revolution was in full swing. All three men were purged, with Wu Han and Liu Shaoqi dying in prison in 1969.

This high politics made Yu Luoke's involvement all the more remarkable. Immediately after Mao's acolytes attacked Wu Han in 1965, Yu wrote a rebuttal, saying that the arguments were superficial. Because the Cultural Revolution hadn't yet been launched, he managed to get it published in a Shanghai newspaper. But it cost him his job and he ended up working in a factory.

As the Cultural Revolution unfolded, Yu lost outlets to publish and turned toward his diary. He noted that the workers, peasants, and soldiers who supposedly were behind the party were simply creations of the propaganda apparatus. He also noted that the Red Guards were children of top-level officials. At the time, people began writing their thoughts in "big-characters posters"—handbills, mostly, which they pasted up on notice boards or the walls of buildings—just like Ai Xiaoming's denunciation of her father. Yu did the same, taking advantage of the growing chaos to spread his ideas.

As he investigated the issue of state violence, Yu heard of a massacre that had taken place in Daxing County, the same place where he had worked as a farmer after being denied entrance to university. Using his contacts, he found out that hundreds of people had been murdered, all of them members of the *heiwulei*, or "five black categories": landlords, rich farmers, counter-revolutionaries, rightists, and a catch-all group known as bad elements.

Incensed at the massacre, Yu wrote one of the most famous essays of the Mao era: a ten-thousand character (about thirteen thousand words) essay called *chushenglun*, or "On Family Background" (sometimes translated as "On Class Origins"). In it, he warned that the "five black categories" were becoming a permanent underclass, while China's rulers were from the *hongwulei*, or "five red categories:" poor and lower-middle peasants, workers, revolutionary soldiers, revolutionary officials, and revolutionary martyrs, including their family members, children, and grandchildren. He warned of a new ruling class based on bloodlines. His essay was colorful, with many vivid examples of how the Communist Party was misruling China. But where to publish it?

The solution came far away from Beijing. His brother, Yu Luowen, had joined millions of young Chinese who used the anarchy of the time to ride the rails to the far ends of the country. He ended up in southern China near Hong Kong. Next to the school where his group of friends was staying was a printing press. One day, he observed how workers used a simple method to etch characters on wax paper and print handbills—the same method used by the students a decade earlier when publishing *Spark*. He had brought his big brother's essay with him, shortened it to three thousand characters, and ran off hundreds of copies. He and his friends posted it at busy intersections, prompting heated street corner debates. He mailed a copy of the article to his big brother back in Beijing, including a summary of how he had printed it.

Yu Luoke then ran off copies and distributed it around Beijing. Others began to take note. Two students borrowed 500 yuan, a small fortune at that time, and helped the Yu brothers print the essay at a proper printing shop. The printers said the essay would take up three A4 pages, with the last one blank. The two students decided on the spot to turn the blank page into a cover. They named it *Journal of Secondary School Cultural Revolution*. In January 1967, about thirty thousand copies were printed, and the young men began distributing them around the capital, selling them for two cents a copy. They were sold out in a few hours. In February, they printed another eighty thousand copies.

Soon, hundreds of letters each day arrived at Yu Luoke's local post office—so many that he had to go collect them in person. The missives detailed how the Communists' policies had caused them to suffer. People traveled from across China to visit them at their home, excited that someone finally had uncovered how the Chinese Communist Party ruled. The editorial board was expanded to twenty people, and the group sponsored debates and seminars.

These remarkable events were a another in a chain reaction of similar underground publications, from *Spark* a decade earlier to the Democracy Wall movement a decade later, the Tiananmen uprising a decade after that, the rise of Internet-based blogging of the 2000s and early 2010s, and the citizen journalism during the 2020s Covid-19 era.

As with these other eruptions, the Yu brothers were aided by sympathetic officials. In this case, some in the government thought the Communist Party shouldn't rely solely on the five red elements and the creation of a nobility. So for a few months, at least, the brothers were allowed to publish, lecture, and debate. Also, as in later eras, they took advantage of new technologies or temporary chaos before the government got a handle on the situation. But like those eras, the Yus' several months of free thinking came to a sudden halt. The *Journal* was closed down in April 1967. Yu Luoke remained free and began to write on economic inequality—which then, as now, was a significant problem that the party downplayed. In January 1968, he was arrested.

In jail, he continued his inquiry into Communist China's congenital problems. He borrowed different editions of Mao's works, analyzing how different editions were radically different from each other, implying that Mao had engaged in ad hoc reasoning that he later went back and corrected. His conclusion: Mao and the Communist Party "are very confused about their policies. They are anti-Marxist."

Two years later, on 5 March 1970, Yu was executed by firing squad at Beijing Workers Stadium in the now-fashionable Sanlitun part of town.

Yu Luowen wrote several accounts of the family's story. In 2016, he opened his WeChat app to find what he called a "hurricane" of people commemorating his brother's detention—something that would be repeated four years later during the Covid crackdown on the anniversary of his execution. In an essay, he tried to explain why people still cared about his brother.

Many people in China are trapped by their family history, he wrote. Farmers are allowed to work in cities but never to send their children to school there. Income disparity is larger than ever, and the college-entrance exam is structured so that children of poor people have huge disadvantages in applying for a university slot. Bloodlines still matter.

"To this day, Yu Luoke's name is still banned in official Chinese publications," he wrote. "Keeping people from knowing about Yu Luoke shows that the theory of bloodlines is still useful to those in power."

10

Remembrance

On the last stretch of flatlands north of Beijing, just before the city runs into the Mongolian foothills, lies the satellite city of Tiantongyuan. Built during the euphoric run-up to the 2008 Olympics, it was designed as a modern, Hong Kong–style housing district of three hundred and fifty thousand people, with plentiful shopping and a subway line connecting it to the city. But the project had been a rushed job, and planners had neglected to put in parks, open spaces, or anything for the public other than the one subway line and a cat's cradle of roads. Construction had been pell-mell, and the area aged supernaturally fast. Its towers leaned into the northern winds, crumbling and cracking, resembling a hastily recruited army rushed to a remote front.

This rootless suburb is home to *Remembrance*, an underground journal that consists of a seventy- to ninety-page PDF mailed out every other week. *Remembrance* has no proper address, let alone bustling editorial offices. But if it has a home, it is here, in one of Tiantongyuan's concrete apartments, a dark, ground-floor unit lined with bookcases and stacked with boxes of books—a fittingly anonymous home for a publication that officially doesn't exist.

Over the past decades, Chinese counter-historians have produced a half dozen other samizdat publications that explore the past through the lens of personal experience, many of them published over many years. They include *Scars of the Past* (*Wangshi Weihen*), *Annals of the Red Crag* (*Hongyan Chunqiu*), and *Yesterday* (*Zuotian*). But while most of them have closed for various reasons, *Remembrance* continues to be published like clockwork, thanks in part to Chinese scholars residing overseas, who help with formatting and distribution.

One Saturday, several of *Remembrance*'s regular writers stopped by the Tiantongyuan apartment for a pot of Pu'er tea and a chat with the journal's co-founder, the retired film historian Wu Di. As they arrived piecemeal over the course of the morning, Wu leaned back in his chair and gave a running commentary on each. Among them were a computer data specialist at a technical university ("the greatest specialist on Lin Biao!"), an editor of the Communist Party's flagship *People's Daily* ("obviously he has to keep a low profile"), and a befuddled professor who had to call Wu three times to get directions ("what an egghead—he knows everything about violence in the Cultural Revolution but doesn't know how to hail a cab on his phone").

Born in 1951, Wu is trim and energetic, favoring denim shirts, leather jackets and black baseball caps—a look somewhere between a retired cop and an aging hipster. His undyed hair is still black, with only a few flecks of gray to set off his dark eyes, which glimmer and sparkle. But he is also a cautious man, who positions himself as a just-the-facts recorder of history.

"I simply write true things," he told me, as the visitors pulled up chairs to a big wooden table, pouring themselves tea and cracking sunflower seeds. "No one says you can't sit in your own home and do a little research in history."

The group began discussing its controversial effort to encourage people to apologize for violence they committed during the Cultural Revolution. Some thought that *Remembrance* had done a good job by publishing articles and even organizing a conference, but others said they understood its critics, who claimed that the publication had taken sides in one particular case of a mob of girls who had beaten to death a high school vice principal in 1966. That topic would return again and again during the course of the day—a sensitive issue that has divided intellectuals inside China and abroad. But first the group discussed potential contributors, and the mood lightened while names were suggested.

"He's good—if he drinks, he talks a lot."

"He's retired."

"Dead."

"That means he can't get into trouble—a good pen name!"

"One guy in our work unit, we see him in the yard walking alone each night. He published a book on (the) June 4 (1989 Tiananmen Massacre) in Hong Kong called *The True Story of June 4*. After that no one dared to talk to him."

Everyone laughed uneasily. Wu smoothed over the awkward moment by announcing that he'd arranged lunch at an odd little restaurant that aims to promote traditional Chinese values. Before we left, Wu pulled me aside: "You might be interested in politics, but I'm not. I am just a historian."

Compared to counter-historians such as Ai Xiaoming, *Remembrance* is more academically oriented. Its articles are footnoted and strive for objectivity. And it seeks to interact with international scholars who work on similar topics. But like Ai and other people based in China, its writers are motivated by personal experience.

For Wu Di, it came when he was a 17-year-old, in 1968. Like most other young people from that era, he was exiled to the countryside, a move that allowed Mao to restore control after the anarchic early phase of the Cultural Revolution. Wu was sent to Inner Mongolia and lived among the herders and horsemen of the great steppes north of Beijing. One day, a man in his tent was robbed and another falsely accused of it. Wu spoke out in favor of the accused and was immediately arrested.

He was thrown into a jail cell about the length of a living room filled with twenty men. They were accused of having organized a plot for Mongolian independence centered around the ethnic Mongolian communist leader, Ulanhu. After a month, Wu was reassigned to a cell with just two men. The men were also accused of being part of the plot but were considered suicidal. Wu was ordered to make sure the men didn't take their lives.

"At first, I was just excited to be away from the overcrowded cell and didn't care about the men," he said. "But then I began talking to them and started to learn about the Cultural Revolution in Inner Mongolia."

When he eventually returned to Beijing, he got a university education, became a teacher, and explored the outside world through foreign films, which became his specialty. He published widely on the topic, including an amusing book on foreign and Chinese cinema, which could be translated as *East-West: Apples and Oranges*.

Yet the memories of his youth stayed with him. He knew he had witnessed history and he spent the 1980s carefully writing down what he had heard, corroborating information with eyewitnesses. A key finding was the degree of ethnic hatred that underlay the violence. Official figures show that during the Cultural Revolution in Inner Mongolia 22,900 died and 790,000 were imprisoned, but there was no atonement and no discussion of the fact that most of the perpetrators were ethnic Chinese or that the victims overwhelmingly were Mongolians. Wu's conclusion was that this unresolved era continues to underlie ethnic tensions in the region.

But the manuscript was unpublishable and there was no *Remembrance* to get even the gist of it published in China. It lay in Wu's desk drawer, a fading memory of the windswept Mongolian steppes.

The only way to get around Tiantongyuan is by car, so we drove to the restaurant through the bleak northern streets, ending up at one of the suburb's luxury compounds. The houses inside were called villas, but they were little more than cookie-cutter concrete blocks, with blue-tinted windows protected by rusty bars. Out front were BMWs and Land Rovers—expensive anywhere but exorbitantly so in China due to high tariffs. Rich people lived here, but they seemed trapped in their small homes, as if they had bought into a lifestyle they didn't understand, or maybe even want.

After half a mile of winding through the subdivision, we arrived at a small parking lot. I had expected a grand restaurant, but it was a simple, pre-fab building with big windows. Inside, two volunteers stood behind a card table, ladling food out of two stainless steel buckets. The choice was vegetable or tofu stew, and the staple was millet porridge or steamed buns that had gone cold. It was 12:15 but already late by Chinese standards and we were alone.

On one wall was a large portrait of Confucius above an altar table with fruit and flowers. Across from it were elegant Chinese bookcases, the shelves of different length and height. They were stacked with books and DVDs, free for the taking, extolling traditional Chinese religions. One was called *Lectures on Confucianism, Buddhism and Daoism* given at the Palace of Golden Horses Hotel in Kuala Lumpur. Another was *The Hidden Truth: See Truth, Treasure Life*. The restaurant's simplicity and its free literature were signs it was a center for proselytizing traditional values. I asked Wu who ran it.

"It's a businessman," he said. "He's doing this as a charity. It's an act of benevolence."

Nothing is truly free, and we paid by having to listen to a DVD of a man lecturing from an enormous flat-screen television at full volume. He wore a gray collarless jacket and stood before a backdrop of a sky and field of cartoonishly bright colors. The topic was a Buddhist classic, but he was free-associating about death, morality, and national affairs.

"How can you tell a country's condition?" he said. "By the virtue of its leaders."

Virtue, he said, means being not corrupt. If leaders are not corrupt, they are virtuous. If they are virtuous, they should be respected.

The *People's Daily* editor laughed and shrugged, as if he were listening to one of his newspaper's circular editorials.

"The usual line from Chinese tradition—everyone should be respected and virtuous," he said. "But what to do if the leaders aren't virtuous?"

We ate quickly and drove back to the apartment. The men reassembled around the big wooden table to talk, but I wandered to a back room to chat with Dai Weiwei, one of *Remembrance*'s editors and contributors. Like Wu, she is a volunteer but works at it more or less full time.

Born in 1964, Dai is a tall northerner, with short curly hair and a soft voice. Her parents had been senior editors at the Xinhua news agency, which meant she grew up in a housing compound with other children of the elite, leaving her with an almost encyclopedic knowledge of who is married to or related to whom. She joined *Remembrance* in 2011, three years after it was founded.

"This is a chance for us to look into our own history," Dai said to me. "*Remembrance* is ordinary people looking at history, not the government."

Wu's idea had been to find a publication to allow people like himself to publish. His own manuscript on Inner Mongolia had stayed in his desk drawer until the 1990s, when he met one of the West's foremost scholars of the Cultural Revolution, Michael Schoenhals of Lund University in Sweden. He published it in an English-language monograph series of excerpts under the pseudonym "W. Woody." In 2000, Wu published the book in Hong Kong.

In 2008, he launched *Remembrance* with the Chongqing historian He Shu. In the inaugural edition, the men wrote that most research on the Cultural Revolution had been done abroad, by scholars such as Schoenhals, or Harvard University's Roderick MacFarquhar. Now it was time for Chinese to look at their own history and publish their findings in China. In 2011, the two men split amicably, with He focusing on his own unofficial publication that specializes in southwestern China. Wu needed help editing, and Dai volunteered.

In 2012, the magazine changed its sixteen-character mission statement from studying the Cultural Revolution to including most of the

20th century. Wu and Dai's rule of thumb, however, is that history stops in 1978, the year Deng Xiaoping ascended to power and established the current political system of state-led capitalism and strict political control. That means *Remembrance* avoids sensitive contemporary issues such as the 1989 Tiananmen massacre—a topic that would guarantee the editors' detention and *Remembrance*'s closure.

Still, *Remembrance* publishes articles on some of the most controversial topics in the Communist era. These include pieces looking at the still-murky plot by Mao's favorite general, Lin Biao, to depose the dictator; accounts of political campaigns; and histories of strikes in the 1950s—the supposed golden era of Communist rule when the party claims it enjoyed mass support.

I asked Dai if *Remembrance* had a *kanhao*, the government-issued registration that all periodicals must obtain to be illegal.

"No, but we aren't a publication," she said. "We are just a PDF newsletter that goes out to just 200 people."

According to arcane rules whose origin no one knows but which everyone accepts, China's public security classifies emails to fewer than 200 people as a private distribution list; anything more is a publication, which means censorship and oversight. So officially, *Remembrance*'s writers are just hobby historians sending out an email every once in a while to interested friends. It's not their fault if *Remembrance* somehow reaches many of China's educated elite and is avidly read and collected by researchers abroad. Forwarding is beyond Wu's control.

Outside, we could hear the men arguing. Their voices rose, until the discussion sounded almost angry; one man seemed to be shouting. The topic was the apologies to victims of the Cultural Revolution, a topic that had riven China's social media in the 2010s. No one could agree whether it was a good thing or not. I prepared to go over and listen in. Dai looked up.

"They get heated, but it's a chance for a release. They teach at universities but can't teach this to their students. Think about that."

In downtown Beijing, just a little over a mile west of the Forbidden City, is one of the country's most illustrious high schools. Its graduates regularly attend China's best universities or go abroad to study, while foreign leaders and CEOs make pilgrimages to catch a glimpse of the country's future elite. Founded in 1917, it has been lavishly rebuilt over the past few years, with a sleek new gym, dining hall, and classrooms—a monument to a rising, future-oriented country. But to many Chinese people of a certain age, the Experimental High School Attached to Beijing Normal University conjures up another image— that of a group of fanatical girls torturing their vice principal to death.

For years, the event has had an almost mythic pull on foreign scholars of the Cultural Revolution, a *Lord of the Flies* story that has attracted academics investigating female violence, documentary filmmakers tackling the mindset of the Red Guards, and researchers trying to piece together how many people were killed, by whom, and how. In China, the story is more veiled. In official accounts it is only mentioned as an example of the chaos that the country should avoid, and heavily censored to excise key elements—such as that many of the perpetrators were children of the Communist elite, and today are prominent members of society.

Led by *Remembrance*, accounts of violence—including the principal's killing—are being set down, published, and passionately debated. More remarkable, for a period of time in the 2010s, people apologized publicly for their actions, setting off long-overdue discussions about how China should deal with its violent past. How should one address the past, especially when many of the victims are dead? Is it best to forget, which the country has largely done, or is there merit in digging up the past? And is it possible to have a cathartic coming-to-terms-with-the-past in a country with no real public sphere? Although these public discussions were eventually throttled by the party, they show the urgency of history and the influence of China's underground historians.

During this time, primarily in 2013, the apologies came in rapid succession. One man in Jiangsu wrote in a magazine about how he had informed on his mother, leading to her execution. In Beijing, an editor wrote an account about how he'd beaten a peasant who he had thought hadn't shown enough enthusiasm for Mao's ideas. And in Shandong, a man took out a small advertisement in a magazine, saying he had beaten and spat on teachers but now, approaching old age, "I cannot forget what I have done wrong."

The most widely reported was an apology by Chen Xiaolu, the son of a famous general. Chen had said he had led a Red Guard–style police unit but failed to protect teachers at his school from being humiliated and beaten savagely by students. Chen had been widely praised for his apology, but after about a month, censors had closed down discussion because the issue was too sensitive. In an interview, Chen said one motivation in speaking out is he is afraid that many behavioral patterns haven't changed much in China.

"In 2011, people were beaten during the anti-Japanese protests," he told me. "People still have that violence, that anger."

None of the apologies has touched a deeper nerve than one made in 2013 by a reluctant 67-year-old woman—one of the girls who had stood by as her vice principal was sadistically tortured to death. Song Binbin had been one of the school's student leaders as the Cultural Revolution unfolded starting in May 1966. The daughter of a famous general, Song Renqiong, she took the lead in writing vitriolic "big character posters" denouncing the teachers and administrators of what was then an all-girls school. Taking their lead from China's god-like leader, Mao Zedong, she and other classmates focused their attacks on authority figures, who Mao said had betrayed the party.

In the girls' school, that meant the top suspect was the school's vice principal and party secretary, Bian Zhongyun. A 50-year-old mother of four, Bian was a staunch communist who had joined in 1941 and worked in a guerilla base before the Communist takeover in 1949.

At the start of the summer, Bian had been beaten but the violence had eased. Mao had left Beijing and moderates had tried to get a grip on the situation by sending "work groups" to factories and schools to restore calm. But when Mao returned in July, he recalled the work groups and urged students to resume their attacks on authority. Bian was beaten badly on 4 August. That evening she told her husband that the girls would kill her. He urged her to somehow escape but she was proud, and certain she was a good communist. The next day when she left for the school, she formally shook her husband's hand, as if to say farewell.

Bian was tortured all day. In a moving and detailed documentary on the killing by the underground filmmaker Hu Jie, witnesses say the girls wrote slogans over her clothes, shaved her head, jabbed her scalp with scissors, poured ink on her head, and beat her until her eyes rolled into her head. When she started foaming at the mouth, they laughed and ordered her to perform manual labor by scrubbing the toilets. She collapsed and died there, her clothes soaked in blood and feces. Hours later, some students carted her away in a wheelbarrow. When students mentioned Bian's death to party officials, they brushed it off as not inconsistent with Mao's orders.

Song's direct role in Bian's killing is unclear. She has never been credibly linked to the beating, but as she was one of the student leaders, many assumed she must have at least known about it. Still all accounts show it had been an anarchic and confusing day, and she might not have done any worse than the scores of other girls who were in the school that day but did nothing to stop the violence.

Song's case is special because of what happened in the next few weeks and how she dealt with it in the following decades. At a mass rally of Red Guards on August 18, she met Mao on the rostrum of Tiananmen Square, pinning a Red Guard armband on the 72-year-old's sleeve. Mao chatted her up, asking what her given name meant. Song replied that Binbin meant "refined," "gentle," or "elegant," and Mao suggested she change it to "Yaowu," which means "be militant." Photos and films show Song beaming as she talks to Mao, ecstatic that she has been allowed so close to the great leader.

The next day, an article under the byline Song Yaowu condoned extremism, saying "violence is truth." Schools across China were renamed "Yaowu," and Song became one of the most famous Red Guard leaders, just as one of the most violent phases of the chaotic decade began. In Beijing alone, 1,772 people were killed that August, with Principal Bian's murder usually reckoned to be the first. For years, many believed that Song killed Bian as well as others.

Like other Red Guards, Song was eventually sent to labor in the countryside when Mao decided that their chaos had gone too far. Her family connections, however, ensured that she didn't suffer as badly as others. Most urban youths were able to return home only after the Cultural Revolution ended in 1976. But like other children of top Communist officials, such as Chinese leader Xi Jinping, Song returned to Beijing in the early 1970s to attend university.

In the 1980s, she emigrated to the United States, changed her given name to Yan (which means "stone"), earned a PhD from the Massachusetts Institute of Technology, worked as a civil servant in the Boston area, and married a wealthy businessman. A 2012 Bloomberg News investigation showed that her extended family had become fabulously wealthy over the past decades, typical for the aristocratic-like clans that stem from the founding generation of Communist leaders. In 2003, she returned to China.

Song remained famous; she steadfastly refused to give interviews but did give some hints as to her views on the past. In the 2003 film *Morning Sun* by the US filmmaker Carma Hinton, she consented to be interviewed, portraying herself as an unwitting girl who had been almost tricked into meeting Mao on the rostrum. She also said she didn't write the article condoning extremism and abhors violence. Hinton, who grew up in China and participated as a Red Guard at another Beijing school, was a gentle interviewer: in the film, she doesn't ask Song about Bian's killing, and allowed Song to be filmed in a dark room so her face was obscured. Instead, Bian's death was discussed by one of Song's classmates who had not been present at the school that day. She started her account by saying that Bian had been in poor health, implying that this was an important reason for her death.

That same year, Song threatened to sue the University of California Press for a book, *Chinese Femininities, Chinese Masculinities: A Reader*, which made several assertions about Bian's murder, including that Song "led" the students in torturing Bian to death. The two sides reached an agreement, with Song not pursuing legal action in exchange for the press issuing an errata to the book and promising to make corrections to later editions. The editors and authors also issued an apology for presenting Song "as responsible for violent acts that occurred near the start of Cultural Revolution. Including these statements in the book was a serious error in judgment."

A few years later, Song again surfaced in the media. To celebrate its 90th anniversary, the school published a picture book of famous alumni, including Song, and prominently featured the picture of her meeting Mao on the rostrum. Almost perversely, the facing page has a picture of Bian, with no mention of the link between the two women. Pictures taken at the event that circulated online show Song looking at the book with no apparent shock or remorse. Other pictures show a banner her classmates made for her that flew outside the school. It is adorned with photos of her youth, including the Mao picture. The photos were widely circulated in China, eliciting scorn and anger among many victims of Mao-era violence.

But friends close to Song say she was troubled by being associated with violence, especially Bian's death. That led to the involvement of *Remembrance* and Wu Di.

One day, Wu and several writers who contribute to *Remembrance* met at the magazine's offices in Tiantongyuan to debate the apologies. They gathered around a big wooden table, drinking tea and cracking sunflower seeds, trying to figure out how these apologies had become so emotive. They had triggered an outpouring of anger and empathy that was so overwhelming that the government eventually banned the topic from government media.

Wu told me that Song had long wanted to speak out about the violence but was discouraged by her husband. When he died in 2011, she participated in a roundtable discussion that was reprinted in *Remembrance*. Later that year, the magazine also published a piece by her called "The Words I've Wanted to Speak for Forty Years." In it, she recounted the circumstances surrounding Bian's death, explaining how she urged her classmates not to be violent and only found out about Bian's death later, after which she tried to get her medical help. The article went on at length about how Song hated the given name "Yaowu" (be militant) and had suffered for being associated with violence. Reading it is an unsettling experience. One senses that Song's feeling is honest but muddled, a misguided attempt to equate her sufferings with the atmosphere of terror and violence that she helped create.

Song's article was criticized as an attempt by Song to whitewash her role in Bian's death. Wu and *Remembrance*, too, came in for criticism for giving Song a platform. Wu told the group of us at the table, however, that this had been his goal. By giving Song a place to air her views, he hoped to spur the discussion on responsibility.

"What I had hoped for was a Willy Brandt moment," Wu said to the group, and the writers nodded at the reference to the former West German chancellor who in 1970 fell to his knees before a monument to the Nazi-era Warsaw Ghetto Uprising, a signal moment of penance in Germany's post-war rehabilitation. "But it became more complex than I thought."

As Wu had hoped, the discussion did heat up after 2012. Wu urged Song to take the next step and apologize formally herself. Several classmates said they would join her and several teachers from that era, now in their 90s, agreed to participate.

Early the next year, Song returned to her old high school, where a bronze bust of Bian stands on a pedestal in a conference room. Bowing before it with several other classmates, Song pulled out a written apology, saying she felt "eternal regret and sorrow" for her actions. At first, Song largely reiterated her 2012 article, saying she'd tried but failed to disperse the girls.

But then she went further, trying to explain her actions that day. She said that she had been scared. People who had sided with the moderates were being accused of not following the correct political line. Worried about the consequence for herself, she "followed those making errors. . . . [F]or this, I have responsibility for the sad death of Principal Bian."

The next day, Wu organized a conference to discuss the violence at the girls' school. Song sat hunched over a MacBook Air, and gave her account again, as did numerous other participants. A few weeks later, Wu dedicated an issue of *Remembrance* to Bian's killing, including essays by Song and some of her classmates describing their experiences that summer, the violence and how it happened.

In some ways the apology was remarkable. Unlike the statement by the general's son, Song's apology is more detailed. She describes her actions and how, in effect, she had been too cowardly to defend her teacher—a plausible explanation given her age and the totalitarian atmosphere.

But Song wasn't quite entirely convincing. Crucially, she doesn't explain why she would assume that the girls wouldn't beat Bian when they had disobeyed her once, or how she could not have known that Bian was being beaten after she left the girls—the campus is not that big and other eyewitnesses say the atmosphere was so tense that people hid during Bian's torture. In essence she does explain these points by alluding to the fear that possessed her, and one can read between the lines and understand that she probably knew what was going on but didn't act. Yet her circumspection left many observers dissatisfied, especially given her previous history of avoiding discussion of Bian's death and even celebrating that era.

Bian's widowed husband, for example, rejected the apology. Chinese media reprinted a statement attributed to him calling the apology "hollow." Many liberal intellectuals in China and abroad chimed in, primarily questioning Song's claims that she pleaded for calm. Some online cartoonists created parodies. One—not explicitly mentioning Song but circulating online after her apology—showed a cartoon of a tear-shedding crocodile in a Red Guard's uniform. Another had a police officer asking a group of people why they're admitting to having aided in torture and murder—are they here to turn themselves in? "Oh no," they say. "We came here to apologize."

From the government's perspective it was more unwanted publicity about who did what during the Cultural Revolution—a not obscure topic given that Chinese leader Xi Jinping and other leaders came of age in that era and that some may have participated in the violence. Xi himself was not implicated in violence; because of his father's persecution, he was banished to a village in western China. One of Deng Xiaoping's daughters, however, was one of Song's classmates, as was a daughter of another former leader, Liu Shaoqi. After a brief flurry of reports, the government issued a circular to editors banning news on Song's apology and ordering websites to take down posts about it. What had started as a way to put Song's conscience to rest had had the opposite effect, turning into a public debate that the government has had to squelch.

Wu is happy about the resulting public discussion but not how Song was attacked. "I thought liberal intellectuals would applaud us for trying to get this discussion going," he said to our group. "But after all this criticism of Song Binbin, who's going to apologize again in the future?"

The writers gathered around the table began talking at once. Some supported Wu, saying he had done his best. Others said they could understand the unwillingness by some to accept Song's apology, noting that Song and her friends still wouldn't even say which of them actually had beaten the vice principal. The group argued back and forth.

"The point is if they were Red Guards they were under Song's control."

"They know who did it—why don't they say?"

"What purpose would that serve? It would end in suicide."

"Chinese society can only accept an apology and not an explanation."

"She excused herself, but she did apologize."

"Higher levels don't want this because they think it'll cause conflicts. That's why no one reports on the apologies anymore."

"Don't forget that Bian was the highest Communist Party official at the school. If you put it this way—they beat to death the highest Communist Party official at the school—haha, so if you think of it like this, the West can accept it. The people who beat her to death were anti-Communist heroes!"

Everyone stopped and looked at the person who had made that dark joke. He looked down a bit embarrassed. "Just a jest, sorry."

After hours of discussion, the meeting was almost over. The tea leaves were spent, and no one bothered adding more water. Soon the men would disperse, heading back from this faceless subdivision to the city proper, down where the Cultural Revolution had started nearly half a century ago.

But first, Yin Hongbiao spoke. He is a Peking University international relations specialist who also writes on student violence. Like almost everyone who contributes to *Remembrance*, Yin holds no official position in this field because universities, even famous ones like Peking University, discourage or ban research and teaching of recent Chinese history. But he has written extensively on the subject, and the others listened attentively. Yin reminded them that people like Song had been teenagers at the time.

"Children can commit crimes, but you have to ask who raised them?" He spoke slowly and looked up at the others who had gathered around the wooden table. "Who encouraged them?" he continued. "We want them to apologize, but shouldn't others, too?"

The room went silent, everyone lost in thought. Then they started speaking, incoherent but passionate and urgent, as China's past collided with its future.

Memory: Tie Liu's Cafe

Huang Zerong is in exile, living in the mountains, where he runs a small inn for travelers. That description might conjure up a dreamy Chinese ink brush painting, with a few tiny figures making their way up a steep path, dominated by pine-clad peaks, billowing clouds, and rushing rivers.

Huang's reality is a bit different. He lives in the middle of a tourist trap: the "ancient town" of Jiezi. It lies 50 kilometers west of Chengdu. To its north is one of the most sacred mountains in China, Mt. Qingcheng, credited as a birthplace of China's only indigenous religion, Taoism. The hills nearby are covered in pine forests and dotted with small temples. But whatever historical structures Jiezi once had are overwhelmed by cookie-cutter features of Chinese tourist spots: newly paved brick streets, Chinese-style lanterns made of plastic and steel, a remnant temple with a bedraggled cleric selling entry tickets and incense, and an occupying army of merchants running snack shops, bars, and lodges.

One of those inns belongs to Huang. He bought it in 2015 when he was released from jail, age 82, for running an illegal business. That operation was publishing one of the best-known unofficial history magazines in China: *Small Scars of the Past*, or *wangshi weihen*. Every month for a decade he and a team of volunteers published reminiscences of the Mao era. Copies of *Small Scars* were sent out at no charge to subscribers via courier because the post office wouldn't handle the publication. He estimates he spent more than 1 million yuan, or about $150,000, of his own money on delivery fees. When the axe inevitably came down, it was for running a magazine without a *kanhao*, or publication number, which the government grants to books and periodicals; without it, they are illegal.

Huang's downfall was preordained. It had nothing of *Remembrance*'s academic veneer, the digital savvy of Ai Xiaoming's movies, or the cat-and-mouse reporting of Jiang Xue's journalism. It was as forthright as any of the younger people's works, but without the protections and subterfuges possible with digital publications. Printed on A4-sized paper and stapled together, it was mailed off to the four corners of China, each issue an indictment of the founding father of the People's Republic, Mao Zedong. It was as subtle as Huang's pen name: Tie Liu, or "molten iron." The magazine's motto was emblazoned on each issue: "Refuse to forget. Face history. Uphold reform. Promote democracy."

Huang often focused on the Anti-Rightist Campaign and the chain-reaction of disasters that followed, but he included events up to the Xi Jinping era. Huang had been a journalist at *Sichuan Daily*, which, like all newspapers in China, is state run. For speaking out on a fairly innocuous topic he was declared a Rightist in 1957 and sent to a labor camp. Like others from that era, his name was cleared in 1980, when the reformist party secretary Hu Yaobang tried to right some of the Mao era's wrongs.

Huang left the newspaper age 52, in 1985, and became an entrepreneur. He invested in companies and ran magazines about private enterprise, profiling some of the country's first tycoons. Like Tiger Temple, he moved to Beijing, where he became part of a vibrant scene of skeptical thinkers, artists, writers, journalists, and scholars. This was still pre-Tiananmen, when many people inside the system hadn't completely lost faith in it, so his choice was unusual—especially as retirement for him was on the horizon. But it was a smart move. His *Business Week*–style magazines sold well, and he became wealthy. He himself was celebrated as someone who had "jumped into the sea" of private enterprise.

But he never forgot his lost youth and followed politics closely. In 1987, the great Chinese journalist Liu Binyan called for the 30th anniversary of the Anti-Rightist Campaign to be commemorated. Huang was eager to support this, but Deng was at the peak of his power—and it was Deng who had implemented Mao's plan to crush intellectuals. In 1997, there was a 40th commemoration, but it was small-scale.

In 2007, the 50th anniversary also came under attack. Huang decided he had waited long enough. He talked to a friend, Xie Tao, a former rightist and university lecturer. According to Huang, Xie gave him principles that would help the magazine survive political opposition.

"He suggested that we not deny the leadership of the Communist Party, not mention the military, not mention national defense and diplomacy, not mention sensitive topics. This is our principle. We only talked about history. That's why it lasted quite long. The police read it; it was not reactionary. Our thing doesn't sell (so no licenses needed). Tax bureau—we don't sell so we don't have to pay taxes. That's how we survived seven years."

That's not to say that the authorities didn't try to ban the publication. Huang said that the Central Propaganda Department issued two official documents declaring it to be an illegal publication, but they couldn't act. And so Huang continued to publish. Each issue was a kaleidoscope of articles: detailed analyses of the Cultural Revolution, reminiscences of the past, portraits of a person or place, and Huang's own recollections of that era.

By 2012, Huang's caution began to fade. Before Xi's assumption of power late that year, Huang wrote articles denouncing Mao and calling for his mausoleum in the heart of Beijing to be dismantled. He also launched a petition calling for Mao to be judged for crimes against humanity.

Huang, like so many others, misjudged Xi. He knew that Xi's father had suffered for being labeled a Rightist. Surely Xi would be sympathetic. Huang was wrong. He supported Xi's call for "rule of law," not realizing that Xi meant "rule by law." He wrote to Xi's anti-corruption czar, Wang Qishan, encouraging him in his campaign against graft, not realizing that anti-corruption was also a tool to crack down on dissenting voices.

Starting in 2011, with issue 65, Huang decided to cut costs and publish only electronically. By mid-2014, *Small Scars of the Past* had published its 113th issue, when Huang was detained for "stirring quarrels and creating trouble," a catch-all charge used to silence anyone the party doesn't like. After a month, the charge was changed to "engaging in illegal economic activities." In February 2015, he was fined 30,000 yuan, or about $5,000, and sentenced to 30 months in jail with a four-year reprieve if he pledged not to write about politics.

That's when he moved back to Sichuan for the first time in 40 years. He keeps an apartment in Chengdu but spends most of the time in Jiezi. He still had money, so he bought the lodge, which faces a river that runs through the edge of town. The ground floor is open-air and spotless, with tea and food for visitors. It is adorned with calligraphy by admirers and articles about his illustrious past. Upstairs is the bedroom he still shares with his wife of fifty years, a study, and a majestic balcony where he entertains private guests. He looks out over the trees and watches the river flow.

A team of eight men share the duties of watching over him. He estimates that it costs the state 1 million yuan, or about $150,000 a year, to fund the team.

"I'm more precious than the pandas," he jokes. "Now I'm more low key and they don't follow me everywhere. Mostly they come in to talk and drink tea."

His neighbors thought he must have been a top official ensnared in Xi's anti-corruption campaign. "They were afraid to ask. I was a mystery. Later they found out I was just a political prisoner," he said with a laugh.

I spent two days with him, walking through town to buy breakfast noodles at his favorite stall and discussing his past on his balcony. He was lively, sharp, and vigorous, but somewhat worn out by a lifetime of beating his head against the party's wall.

"I lost twenty-seven years of my life to them, more than a quarter of it," he said. "I don't think there's too much more they can do to me."

The Anti-Rightist Campaign and Mao continue to bother him. I asked him if this wasn't a bit dated—after it was now nearly 70 years in the past. Did that matter?

He had thought about it a lot and explained his views in detail. The Anti-Rightist Campaign meant silencing critical thinking inside and outside the party. That allowed Mao a free hand to pursue his disastrous policies, resulting in tens of millions of deaths. He also saw the parallels to Xi Jinping's rule after he abolished term limits.

"Without the Anti-Rightist Campaign there would have been no Great Leap Forward; without the Great Leap Forward, people would not have starved to death. If people didn't starve to death, there would not have been the Cultural Revolution. Without the Cultural Revolution, there would not have been Tiananmen."

Tiananmen? I wondered if that was right. But then he reminded me that it was Hu Yaobang's exoneration of the victims of the Anti-Rightist Campaign, such as himself, that caused Deng to get rid of him. His firing had incensed people so that when Hu died in 1989, they came out onto the streets, launching the protests.

What he misses most, besides the lost time, are his books. When he got out of prison in 2015, he found that all of his back copies of *Small Scars of the Past* had been confiscated, as well as a huge library of works on the past. Some had been published legally in past decades when intellectual life was more open. Others he had mailed up from Hong Kong. Now, all are gone. What should be his study is a dusty, empty room.

All that is left is his mobile phone. He uses the handwriting function to pen 500-word microblogs that he publishes daily on WeChat. As usual, he can't avoid some comments on politics, including protests in Hong Kong (he thought the 2019 demonstrators had gone too far and would make it easier for the government to crack down, a prescient analysis).

Mostly, he meets friends, who come out to Jiezi for the fresh air. Then he writes little essays about the flowers, the river, the friends. But in his heart is nothing but dread for the political system created by Mao.

"To settle the Anti-Rightist Campaign, we must fundamentally denounce Mao Zedong. We need to remove his portrait from Tiananmen. As long as Mao Zedong's portrait is hanging on Tiananmen, China will never have freedom or democracy. The day the portrait is gone is the day when China's progresses toward freedom and democracy, and the rule of law begins. As long as we hang a Mao portrait there, China will remain a tragedy."

I asked him what the link was to today. Surely this was something remote, something esoteric, only of interest to historians.

"Mao's body died but his ideas haven't. The Communist Party still upholds his ideas, regarding him as a great leader. But all the crimes of the Communist Party come from Mao Zedong, including those committed by Xi Jinping, Jiang Zemin, and Hu Jintao. Also Deng Xiaoping. This is how China's disasters came about."

11

Lay Down Your Butcher's Knife

The Xiao River rushes deep and clear out of the mountains of southern China into a narrow plain of paddies and villages. At first little more than an angry stream, it begins to meander and grow as the basin's sixty-three other creeks and brooks flow into it. By the time it re-enters the mountains 50 miles to the north, it is big and powerful enough to carry barges and ferries.

Fifty years ago, these currents transported another cargo: bloated corpses. For several weeks in August 1967, more than nine thousand people were murdered in this region. Its epicenter was Dao County, which the Xiao River bisects on its way north toward the Xiang and then the Yangtze. About half the victims were killed in this county of 400,000 people, some clubbed to death and thrown into limestone pits, others tossed into sweet potato cellars to suffocate. Many were tied together in bundles around a charge of quarry explosives. These victims were called "homemade airplanes" because their body parts flew over the fields. But most victims were simply bludgeoned to death with agricultural tools—hoes, carrying poles, and rakes—and then tossed into the waterways that flow into the Xiao.

In the county seat of Daozhou, observers on the shoreline counted 100 corpses flowing past per hour. Children ran along the banks, competing to spot the most bodies. Some were bound together with wire strung through their collarbones, their swollen carcasses swirling in daisy chains downstream, their eyes and lips already eaten away by fish. Eventually the cadavers' progress was halted by the Shuangpai dam, where they clogged the hydropower generators. It took half a year to clear the turbines and two years before locals would eat fish again.

For decades, this murder has been a little-known event in China. When mentioned at all, it has tended to be explained away as individual actions that spun out of control during the heat of the Cultural Revolution. Dao County was portrayed as remote, backward, and poor. The presence of the non-Chinese Yao minority was sometimes mentioned as a racist way of explaining what happened: minorities are only half civilized anyway, and who knows what they did when authorities weren't looking.

All of these explanations are wrong. Dao County is a bulwark of Chinese civilization, the birthplace of great philosophers and calligraphers. The perpetrators were almost all Chinese, who killed other Chinese. And the killings were not random. Instead, they were acts of genocide aimed at eliminating a class of people declared to be subhuman: make-believe landlords, non-existent spies, and invented insurrectionists—the "five black elements" who formed an underclass in Mao's China. Far from being the work of frenzied peasants, the killings were organized by committees of Communist Party cadres in the region's towns, who ordered that the murders be carried out and then sent underlings to those mountain towns and villages to make sure the killings took place. To make sure revenge would be difficult, officials ordered the slaughter of entire families, including infants.

The fact that we know the truth about Dao County is due to one person: a garrulous, stubborn, and emotional editor who stumbled over the story in the 1980s and has spent the past forty years researching and writing about it, finally publishing his findings in 2011 and updating them in 2016. His name is Tan Hecheng, and over the course of several years I accompanied him as he continued his lifelong quest in the lush, rugged mountains of southern China.

Traveling through Dao County requires a car and a driver, and Tan Hecheng never lacks for either. He splits his time between Beijing, where his daughter lives, and Changsha, his hometown. But when he comes to do research in Dao County, he is an underground celebrity and outlaw rolled into one. He put down in writing something that any local person over 50 has heard about but which few dare speak. Some hate him for exposing their families' murderous background, while the government tries to block his work. But many others view him with awe as someone who described an outrageous crime that was enabled by China's political system—the same one that runs the country today.

And so Tan doesn't lack for volunteers to help him get around. Which is probably a good thing, because you'll be hard-pressed to meet anyone who is more confused about geography than Tan. He was born in 1948, an age that doesn't preclude many people, even older people like Huang "molten steel" Zerong, from using mapping software to guide visitors through windy roads. But Tan doesn't just fumble with his phone; he can't figure out how to read a paper map, which way is north, or which way the Xiao River flows. Instead, his mind is overloaded with horrific images. As he gets older, they overwhelm him, becoming more real than ever: the woman buried alive with her children, the teacher executed at a bridge, the people lashed to stones and tossed into the rivers. They consume him, leaving no space for trivial details. And so, thankfully, we had local guides who knew the places he meant and could bring us there.

This isn't to say that Tan is not methodical. He documented the killings carefully in a 600-page magnum opus called Blood Myths. The 2016 revised edition, published in Hong Kong, has more than 700,000 Chinese characters, or about the equivalent of 1 million words. Like Yang Jisheng's epic work on the Great Famine, Tombstone, Tan's book is more a database of official documents, interviews, and descriptions rather than narrative history. Like Tombstone, it was edited and translated into English by the veteran team of Stacy Mosher and Guo Jian. They published it at a more manageable 500 pages as The Killing Wind.

Now that the difficult work of documenting the murders has been accomplished, Tan is still beset by the images and the implications for today's China. Some of his thoughts are subtle reflections, such as the abuses of unbridled state power or the misuses of history. But his thoughts return time and again to one graphic emblem from Buddhism: the bloody butcher knife that a killer cannot put down. Early on I asked him to explain, but he insisted that we first travel to Dao County.

Like most people, Tan had to experience the party's arbitrary nature before he could understand it. Born in 1948, the year before the People's Republic was founded, his was the first generation to have known nothing but the People's Republic and to have no access to outside information. That meant he grew up in the party's embrace and was educated in its version of history.

Like Ai Xiaoming and Jiang Xue, his family background hung over his upbringing. He grew up in Changsha, the capital of Hunan province, which lies on the southern edge of the great lake district that starts in Wuhan. His father had been a general in the government army, which was a problem, but he had fought heroically against the Japanese. His mother, however, was the family's real problem. She was born of parents who had participated in the 1911 revolution, and she had been a delegate to the Republic of China's national parliament. From early on, she was targeted as a counter-revolutionary. Red Guards gave her a "yinyang" haircut—shaving one side of the head—and beat her so badly that she couldn't move. When Tan found her immobilized in bed, her only advice was for him to get out of town as fast as he could.

"She said that if I were to argue, they would beat her worse. She just said to go, go quickly, get out."

Tan joined a group of Red Guards traveling around China. Later he trained as a carpenter and seemed to have a future as a craftsman. "My hands were quick and nimble!" he says of his youth. "And I liked working."

In 1978, when university exams reopened, Tan tested into Changsha's University of Science and Technology, where he developed an interest in writing. Back then, all college graduates were assigned jobs, and he was sent to a factory. He had a knack for what back then was called *baogao wenxue*, or "reportage literature," a kind of non-fiction that used real-life stories to make social criticism. He won a prize and drew the attention of the editors at *Furong*, or *Hibiscus*, a Changsha literary magazine looking for new talent.

His new job coincided with an effort by the party's reformist leader, Hu Yaobang, to account for the past. Besides rehabilitating millions of unjustly accused people, such as his parents, Hu decided in 1986 to send 1,300 officials to Dao County to investigate the killings. Their findings: 9,093 people were killed, including 4,519 in Dao County. Most shocking: 15,050 people were involved in the killing, mostly government officials. In fact, 37 percent of all local Communist Party members had participated in the killings.

Tan was seen as a reliable writer. He had enthusiastically supported Deng Xiaoping's reform policies. Many people had had difficult backgrounds in the Mao period but were now rehabilitated. Tan was no different. And because the media in China is essentially state-controlled, his presence wasn't unusual—he was part of the system. Down in Dao County, people spoke openly to him about the events. He had complete access to tens of thousands of pages of documents that the officials unearthed. But by the end of 1986, the political tide had turned against accounting for the past.

"When the first round of interviews was over, the political atmosphere was already darkening. Forces in the Party opposed what was called 'bourgeois liberalization.' So my article couldn't be published. And the more time went on, the more impossible it became. It got tighter and tighter."

The smart thing to do would have been to drop the project. Tan had a family and needed to think of them, too. But something about

Dao County wouldn't let him rest. He was meant to portray the massacre there as a mistake—as a few bad apples who let things get out of control, which is the way the party usually explains its mistakes. If he had been allowed to publish some of his findings, maybe this is what he would have written. But now that he couldn't publish anything, he was freed of this need to compromise and was faced with a stark choice: drop it or pursue it fully. He chose the latter, because of one horrible realization: not one of the roughly nine thousand people killed had been planning a counter-revolutionary event. It wasn't that some had been killed unjustly; all of them had.

"When I understood this, I was heartbroken. I began to realize that the Party had a history of violence. Already in 1928 it organized violent peasant revolts that killed masses of people. And land reform [shortly after the Party took power in 1949] was incredibly violent. It was one mass killing after another. All of a sudden it became clear. There was no justification for what happened. It was just terror."

That was when Tan felt his calling. He thought of the survivors, the family members, and the reform-minded officials who had given him information. He had pledged to them that he wasn't doing this for personal gain but for their—for all Chinese people's—descendants, so that this kind of state-led violence would not happen again.

He went back to his editors. They were nice people. One suggested he wait twenty or thirty years. Maybe around 2000 or 2010 it would be possible to publish it, he told Tan, never imagining that things would be even tougher later on. Tan thanked him, but it was clear that he didn't agree.

Word began to get around that he was traveling down to Dao County on his own to do follow-up interviews. By then, Tan had been identified as a troublemaker. He wasn't fired but was marginalized. Promotions, conferences, and prizes never came his way. He didn't care.

"You know, I can kiss ass as well as anyone," Tan said. "I'm really good at it. In fact, I'm an excellent ass-kisser! I can tell people what they want to hear. And I can write an article any way you want it. But I have a minimum moral standard: I can't turn black into white. Somehow, I just can't do that.

"So when they said they wouldn't publish it, I thought, 'okay, that's your problem,' but my life had changed. And so I thought, 'this is it. One way or another I will publish this.'"

When I traveled around Dao County with Tan it was like being on a slightly manic roller coaster. A boisterous man with soft features, an unruly cowlick, and an irrepressible gallows humor, Tan was constantly erupting with facts, figures, curses, and comments about places and people. When we drove by a village, he might begin to recount the details of who was bludgeoned or shot, but then cut himself short by shouting out: "Fuck, this place killed a lot of people!" In spite of ourselves we would start laughing and then decide, should we pass by this scene of a massacre? Or should we stop. Because there were so many, we often drove on but at a few places Tan insisted we stop.

One of those places was Widow's Bridge. In the 18th century, a wealthy widow decided to help people by donating money for the bridge over the Fushi River, a tributary of the Xiao. We arrived at dusk one early winter's day, the bridge peaceful and quiet, with stands of camphor trees and willows along the banks.

Tan had a similarly peaceful feeling when he arrived here in 1986. But then he was shown marks in the balustrade where sabers had bit into the stone after chopping off the victims' heads. As he recounts in his book: "Rubbing the knife marks made everything around recede into a blur; this shouldn't have been the place where people died. I couldn't keep tears from flowing down my face."

His tears were also shed for one of the most notable victims executed here, He Pinzhi, a local teacher whose family had owned a small amount of land before the Communist takeover. The family's landholdings had been absurdly small—less than half an acre, with no hired labor, and no land rented out—but Mao had mandated that every county have "landlords." And so people like the teacher's family were declared members of the exploitive landowning class.

But this wasn't the only reason that Tan cried at the bridge. The teacher had spent two decades trying to toe the line, writing obsequious paeans to Communist Party rule, and going to his death shouting out his fealty to Chairman Mao.

"China's literati," Tan wrote, "have always aspired to self-improvement and to guiding their country toward peace and prosperity, but ultimately they've never been anything more than subjects, commoners, and slaves."

Now, thirty years after his first visit, we stood there on the bridge talking to one of Teacher He's descendants, Zhou Shenliang. He was born three years after the killings and had mixed feelings about discussing the events. His side of the family is related to Zhou Dunyi, an

11th-century neo-Confucian philosopher who achieved enlightenment while fishing in one of the local rivers.

Zhou met us at the bridge because Tan wanted to go over some facts about the killings that day. He asks about his grandmother's pension. Because his grandfather was never reckoned to have been unjustly killed, the grandmother never got a proper pension. It was as if her husband had committed suicide. This is typical for most of the victims, who often received small payments and no recognition of what had happened. Meanwhile, only a handful of perpetrators were punished, and their children ran the county until the early 2000s, when they retired.

Zhou is a pudgy 40-year-old who runs a computer store in the county seat. The government appointed him to a commission to mark the 1,000th anniversary of Zhou Dunyi's birth. He answered all of Tan's questions politely but seemed ambivalent. I asked him if he felt uncomfortable talking about his family's suffering.

"It's not just that it's an unfortunate issue, it's that the party hasn't come to a clear decision on this issue," he says. "It's still very sensitive."

I understood Mr. Zhou's dilemma. Of course he wanted to clarify the events. But he also wanted to live a life. He had ambitions. He had a family. It wasn't as simple as the usual clichés one sometimes hears, such as life must go on, or people should forget the past. He had to deal with the reality that the same party was still in power. They had appointed him to the commission. They issued business licenses. They decided if your child went to university.

As we talked, Tan stood off to the side, beginning a monologue. After having spent a few days with him, I had come to expect these outbursts, which usually occurred when he was extremely agitated. They were a kind of therapy. He would wind himself into a near-frenzy, talking about how the party killed so many people, but also about how China's educated class was partially responsible because it went along with the system. When writing, he used very measured language, but out here on the bridge he couldn't contain himself.

Intellectuals were cowardly. They didn't stand up. They deserved it. The teacher had written a play lauding the party and still had been persecuted.

"He wrote an ass-kissing script but was still killed!" Tan said with a loud laugh. "He didn't believe any of what he wrote but he still kissed the party's ass! And even so they killed him! Ha!"

Zhou stood next to me, looking glum. To him, Tan was a marvel and a mystery. Zhou's family had suffered and Tan could explain it all so clearly and loudly, right in front of you. He had all the facts and figures. He had documents. He had written it down and published it abroad. He had brought a foreigner to learn about it. You had to re-spect all of this.

But Zhou was also concerned that Tan could be arrested. This drive, this passion, it's not normal, he thought. It's not what the system encourages. But Zhou respected it. It moved him. And so he listened and then after a while, he put his hand on Tan's shoulder and, using an honorific as a sign of genuine respect, said:

"Thank you, teacher Tan. Coming out here isn't easy. We appreciate it. Our ancestors appreciate it. Our future generations will appreciate this too."

Tan stops talking, his eyes wet with tears. He turned to the water and stared at it with incomprehension. Thirty years after coming here he still couldn't understand what had happened.

Maple Wood Mountain is a tribute to the development dictatorship that runs China. When Tan first visited this village thirty years ago, it had no roads. A car had driven him to a nearby town, and he had been forced to hike the remaining three miles up the mountain. The area was so poor that even a simple wristwatch was an unimaginable luxury, let alone electricity or running water.

Now the path has been widened and surfaced with concrete slabs. As we picked our way up the mountain in our SUV, we passed a team of laborers expanding it into a proper paved road with guardrails.

Electricity, water, and 4G data coverage were now givens. Many families sent their children to boarding schools in the nearby township, but for the very poor the state had provided a single-room schoolhouse. When we arrived, eleven children aged 5 to 10 sat under Communist Party propaganda posters, learning math.

Behind the school was another monument to this overly powerful state: a stone stele with a couplet that translated to this:

Father and Children, Rest in Peace
Those in this World, a Life of Peace

Several other lines explained its meaning. They listed the names of the dead father and three children, and the person who erected the stele—the person still in this world who needed peace—their wife and mother, Zhou Qun.

As we stood there examining the tombstone, a change came over Tan. During the previous two days, we had traveled maniacally through the county as he conducted new interviews while also, for my benefit trying to show me every major killing field and to talk to as many survivors as possible. But on this ridge, in front of this tombstone, he suddenly slowed down, as the memories of the past overcame him. He shook his head at me, not able to recount the story. He looked at me apologetically, closed his eyes, and looked down at the grave of Zhou Qun's family.

On 26 August 1967, Zhou Qun and her three children were dragged out of bed by village leaders. She had been working there for several years as a primary schoolteacher but had always lived under a cloud. Her father had been a traffic policeman during the time the Nationalist government had ruled China, enough to make her a counter-revolutionary offspring. That meant her family had been categorized as a black element.

For the previous eighteen years, the state had stripped black elements like Zhou of their property. It had assigned them bad jobs with low pay or rocky plots of land to farm. And it had inundated Chinese people with a barrage of propaganda that brainwashed many into believing that black elements were dangerous, violent criminals.

In the Cultural Revolution, Mao whipped up the propaganda another notch, declaring that these enemies were now readying a counter-revolution. In Dao County, stories began to fly that the black elements had seized weapons. The county government decided to strike pre-emptively and kill them. When village-level officials objected—as in many parts of China, many were related to their victims—higher-ups set out "battle-hardened" squads of killers, often former criminals and hoodlums, to push local officials to action.

The killings radiated out of the cities and towns at foot speed. Tan described it as an old-fashioned pestilence, which carriers spread from one place to the next by foot. At that time, transportation wasn't developed, and telecommunications were almost non-existent. The massacre's spread relied on officials walking to a locale and delivering the message. When an official arrived with the orders, the killing started. After the first deaths, locals were freed from moral constraints and usually acted spontaneously, even against family members.

This was not exceptional. Most accounts of the Cultural Revolution have focused on the Red Guards and urban violence. But a growing number of studies show that genocidal killings were widespread. Recent research, as well as in-depth case studies like Tan's, show that the killings were systematic instead of being sensational one-off events. One survey of local gazetteers shows that between four hundred thousand and 1.5 million people perished in similar incidents, meaning there were perhaps another one hundred Dao County massacres around this time.

Zhou was tied up and frog-marched to a threshing yard next to the storehouse. Thirteen others were there too, including her husband, who had been seized a day earlier. The group was ordered to set off on a march. At the last moment, one of the leaders remembered that Zhou and her husband had three children at home. They were rounded up and joined the rest on a five-mile midnight trek through the mountains.

Exhausted, the group ended up at Maple Wood Mountain at the very spot where we now stood. A self-proclaimed "Supreme People's Court of the Poor and Lower-Middle Peasants" was formed out of the mob and immediately issued a death sentence to the entire group. The adults were clubbed in the head with a hoe and kicked into a limestone pit. Zhou's children wailed, running from adult to adult, promising to be good. Instead, the adults tossed them into the pit too.

Some fell down 20 feet to a ledge. Zhou and one of her children landed alive on a pile of corpses on a higher ledge. When the gang heard their cries and sobs, they tossed big rocks on the ledge until it collapsed, sending them down onto the others. Somehow, all the family members initially survived. But as the days passed, each of them died, until Zhou was the last person in the pit with thirty-one corpses around her.

After a week, when an order had gone out to cease the killings, a few villagers from her hometown snuck to the cave at night and rescued Zhou. The village leadership from the town where she lived then recaptured her and debated killing her. Instead they locked her in a pigsty and forbade the wardens from feeding her. But a few courageous villagers tossed sweet potatoes in her cell at night, and she survived another two weeks until a posse of villagers from her hometown freed her again.

The next day we visited Zhou. She had remarried after the killings and had a daughter who refuses to let her mother talk about the past. But on this day, we caught her alone and asked her about those events.

Most of the people we talked to during our visit had been reticent to discuss those days. They often described it as pointless—the Communist Party still rules China, and the topic was off-limits. One woman, a victim of a gang rape by the killers of her family, even bluntly told Mr. Tan that his quest to write this history was pointless. As for the next generation, they were ambivalent. Some welcomed Tan as a bringer of truth, but many others wanted to forget the past—they had lives to live and hopes of their children going to university, buying a home, or traveling abroad. The suffering somehow cheapened this world of newfound prosperity, a reminder that it was built on violence. Few wanted to hear about it.

But Zhou was different. Now 81, she was still slender and walked with an erect bearing, her face finely chiseled and her eyes sunken. She talked lucidly about the events of the past. When she became emotional, Mr. Tan stood by nervously, not wanting to retraumatize her. But she insisted so that others would know what happened.

"Every time I see a child on the television, or see my grandchildren, I think of the three precious ones who died in the cave. Every single day I think of it."

"But fifty years have passed, and you have a family. There must be some consolation in what happened since?"

"No, never."

We visited so many other places in Dao County that after four days my head was spinning. We drove up to the dam that had been clogged with corpses. We visited two brothers who survived being tossed into the waters. We talked about the lack of justice. Hadn't the party's investigations yielded anything? They had, Tan told me, but the results had been grossly inadequate.

"According to the commission, 15,050 people were directly implicated in the killings, including one half of the Party's cadres and members in the county. But only fifty-four people were sentenced for their crimes and another 948 Party members were disciplined. In addition, families only received 150 yuan for each person killed. This was equivalent to about 5,000 or 6,000 yuan [about $1,000] in today's currency."

We talked about how a true reckoning with the past was less likely than ever. The government under Xi Jinping is nostalgic about the past. Criticizing the Mao era is impossible. But in Tan's view this is temporary. The system was rotten, and the government knows it— hence the endless, pointless campaigns to whitewash the past. One day the real story would come out, a simple fact he knew to be true from reading the histories of Sima Qian, Su Dongpo, and other ancient truth-tellers. Documenting this wasn't quixotic. It was a hard-nosed calculation that it would pay off—not for Tan personally but for his country.

We were near the end of our stay and so I asked him again what he had meant about the butcher sword. It was an idiomatic expression: *fang xia tu dao, di li cheng fo*. It literally means "lay down your butcher's knife and immediately become a Buddha." In Buddhist theology it can be read as an admonition to stop your ill deeds immediately and become a better person. What did he mean?

"I have three intentions. One is as the Buddha says, that people should put down their killing swords. Only then can they be absolved of their sins. Second, I wish the Communist Party would really put down its killing sword—to reform. And third, it's not about the knife in your hand. It's the knife in your heart. Wang Yangming [the neo-Confucian philosopher who lived from 1472 to 1529] said it is easy to defeat the bandits in the mountains but hard to defeat the bandits in the heart. This applies to the entire population. It's not aimed at the Communist Party but all of us: we have to lay down the knives in our hearts. Only then can we move toward a democratic path. So in the future if we have troubles, we won't have to solve it through massacres and murders or clashing of fists, or whoever is stronger wins."

But surely the state is no longer as violent as it was in the past?

"State power is still based on the barrel of a gun. Right now the Communist Party can't really cheat anyone anymore because they are [ideologically] bankrupt. In the past they relied on deception and violence. Right now it's entirely on violence. Think of all the arrests and detentions. This is the only way it rules. Lay down your knife and repent!"

Memory: Videoing China's Village

The Communication University of China in Beijing is the country's version of the Columbia Journalism School—an elite training ground for future journalists. The sprawling campus in eastern Beijing used to be miles out of town (all the better to keep pesky writers at bay) but has long been swallowed up by Beijing's urban sprawl and is easily reached by subway or highway.

One of its schools is the Cui Yongyuan Center for Oral History, named after a famous China Central Television host who joined the faculty in 2012. Cui Yongyuan was one of the best-loved personalities on CCTV, a humorous, self-deprecating host of several shows, especially a talk show "Tell It Like It Is" that he ran from 1996 to 2002. Cui left the show after a bout of depression, returned for another show, and then a popular series on China's battle with Japan in World War II. He eventually quit television to teach at the school.

From the party's perspective, Cui must have initially seemed a safe figurehead to run the center. His series on World War II gave him impeccable credentials—who could find fault in a journalist who wanted to chronicle China's life-and-death battle against Japan? And his reasons for teaching oral history were also unimpeachably patriotic: during his research for the show, he discovered that Japanese scholars had actually conducted more oral history interviews with Chinese veterans than Chinese scholars had. Oral history had to be taken seriously, he decided, and the party agreed, especially if it was to glorify the Chinese nation. The Cui Yongyuan Oral History Center was born, centered around workshops designed to train ordinary people in the craft of interviewing older members of their communities.

Cui, though, is a complex person. Born in 1963, he was not satisfied with a top job at China's state broadcaster nor heading the research center. Instead, he took to social media to call out problems in Chinese society, often landing in hot water. He questioned the country's headlong embrace of genetically modified corn, asking why research had not been conducted into its long-term effects on humans and the ecology. He had initially tried to make a television series about this topic and traveled to Western countries to learn about its debates over genetically modified organisms (GMO). The show, however, was nixed before it got into production and so Cui took to social media. There he engaged in a prolonged debate with Fang Zhouzi, a US-based debunker of superstitious thought who was a full-throated advocate of GMO crops. The debate was unpopular with the government, earning Cui a temporary ban from social media.

He also posted about Chinese actors not paying taxes, causing one of the biggest Chinese movie stars, Fang Binbin, to be banned from the screen. That was more in line with government priorities but also exposed double standards for rich and poor Chinese. Every couple of years he would come out with a new crusade, sometimes tolerated by the government, other times earning him warnings.

Likewise, Cui's center became something more than the government envisioned. Its workshops aimed to help ordinary people record oral histories in the population. The expectation was that these would be positive stories—how much better things were now than in the past, or how the party had led the country from strength to strength. But the state couldn't control what people would do with these news skills—what would they find when they began doing their own interviews about the last seven decades of Communist rule?

In 2016, I participated in one of these workshops, spending a week with eighty-one people from almost every province or region of China. The number was double the plan and reflected the topic's surging popularity.

Cui himself didn't lecture. Instead, the highlight of our three-day workshop was an afternoon with Wu Wenguang, one of China's most famous documentary filmmakers. While people like Tan Hecheng or Hu Jie worked almost entirely outside the system, Wu had managed to keep a foot inside it. He did that by positioning himself as an artist instead of a political documentary filmmaker, giving him more leeway to explore China's troubled history.

Born in 1956 in southern China's Yunnan province, Wu studied literature at Yunnan University in the late 1970s, before working for a local television station. At that time, documentaries were known as *zhuanti pian*, or "special-topic films," and involved carefully scripted and controlled pieces. In 1988 he quit his job and moved to Beijing, where he began to follow the country's budding underground art scene.

This was the time of the Tiananmen Massacre, but Wu's film didn't directly touch on the political events of the time. Instead, he caught a deeper social trend: the ability of people in Reform-era China to drop out. Previously, people had jobs assigned to them by the state, but reforms allowed for free enterprise. That unshackled people—like Wu himself—to pursue their own interests.

The result was the 1990 film *Bumming in Beijing: The Last Dreamers* (*Liulang Beijing*), pioneering what became the trademark style of independent films in China ever since then. Unlike the state's carefully organized "special-topic films," Wu's work featured handheld cameras and unscripted interviews. The result was often meandering, long, and almost purposefully jerky—as if to say that this isn't a state product.

He called the style *jishi pian*, which can be translated simply as "documentary" but literally means "recording-reality films." The term is a bit different from the standard term for documentary film, *jilu pian*, which is more akin to "making a record," perhaps implying that reality was messier than a didactic recording of the past.

After making a dozen documentary films on topics as varied as Red Guards, farm workers, and the freewheeling 1990s, Wu felt that even his independent films were running into a wall. In his 2005 film "Fuck Cinema," he talks to a director who points out that even if you can film something, the processing companies are too worried about government censorship to make prints.

What saved him and other documentary filmmakers was the spread of cheap digital technology. This bypassed the need for expensive equipment and outside production people like film printers. You filmed and that was that—you could replay it immediately on your camera or on your computer.

That same year, he launched the Village Documentary Project. He recruited ten migrant workers in Beijing, trained them to use digital video cameras, and sent them back to their villages to tell the stories of their hometowns.

Five years later, in 2010, he launched his most influential work, the Folk Memory Project, which has sent dozens of young people back to their hometowns to investigate the Great Famine, and to erect memorials to those who died. Over the project's ten years, his students have visited 246 villages, interviewed more than 1,300 people and made dozens of films. The films are held by Duke University, which lists 657 films, from full-length features to shorter interviews.

Wu's project was centered at Beijing's Caochangdi artist village, where the participants often ate, slept, and even danced together under the guidance of his then-partner, the choreographer Wen Hui. That made it an art project, helping to insulate Wu from charges that he was exposing China's hidden past.

In person, Wu looked the part of the monk-like auteur: the 60-year-old sported a shaved head, a scruffy beard, tortoise-shell glasses, cargo pants, traditional black cotton shoes, and a black t-shirt that read:

100% Life
Zero% Art

He was physically compact and self-possessed, his energy building as the afternoon went on. Speaking in a low urgent voice, he caused us to lean forward in our cramped plastic chairs to hear him. He engaged the students as they described their projects, cajoling them, and always asking them one central question: what were their intentions?

A chubby fellow from Xi'an with silver temples and glam-rock glasses wanted to record the death of his village.

A jittery man from Shandong said he wanted to describe mental illness in the countryside.

A woman showed a clip of her mother talking about violence in the Cultural Revolution.

Wu gave advice to each, adding a refrain that was pounded into our heads:

"You have to know why you're doing this. Why do you want to make this film? What are your goals? There's no such thing as just recording history. You need a goal."

Another point that Wu hammered home was the need to take time. He showed a film by Zhang Mengqi, one of his star students, who had come to the class with him. It was shot in southern China, and the people spoke a dialect that was incomprehensible to Mandarin speakers. One man asked if Zhang had grown up speaking the dialect. Wu cut him off and answered sharply.

"You learn the dialect. You think the students could speak their dialect? They couldn't. But they learned it after going back for a few years."

The man gulped. "Oh, ok, I didn't realize . . . "

Another asked the difference between this and journalism.

"Time. We spend time. We spend weeks and months. We go back again and again."

He mixed up his tough message with humor, too.

"You have to talk and talk and talk! Do you like talking?"

Everyone laughed and applauded.

"Ok, so you've got it. Talk and listen, talk and listen, but mostly listen."

Wu set up his camera, putting it on a tripod in front of his face.

"It's a conversation based on equality. We're equal. We're not better than the people we're interviewing. The camera is an extension of your face, or your gut."

Wu's assistant took the camera and put it behind him, streaming the image on the big screen. It showed Wu talking to students, critiquing their work. Someone asked what camera to buy, and Wu recommended a popular, inexpensive digital camera. "Get external microphones. You have to have good sound quality."

One person asked him about Yang Kuisong and his interviews of people at the Jiabiangou labor camp.

"You need files. You need preparation. Do your homework. Don't just accept what people tell you. This isn't a series of random conversations. It can look like that but it's not."

Politics hovered in the background. Wu handled it deftly. He asked his 25-year-old assistant why her film touched on the famine.

"It made my father who he was. He grew up in the aftermath of it. And so it made me who I am."

"That's why the past matters. It might have happened before you were born but it still affected you. You just didn't realize it because you didn't know about it."

To show his point, Wu played a scene from a movie. It shows an old man. He's deaf. It could be any old man who can't understand us and who we can't understand—the sort of person we might brush off. The interviewer is asking him what he ate in 1960.

"I can't hear you. I'm deaf."

"What did you eat?"

"I can't hear you."

"What did you eat?"

The audience laughed.

"WHAT DID YOU EAT?"

The old man finally heard the question. His answer silenced the crowd.

"We didn't eat anything. My brother starved to death."

The clip ended. People fidgeted. Then someone asked if these sorts of questions are wrong. Aren't they bothering people who might want to forget the past?

Wu responded ferociously.

"You're not bothering people. You're in a project. They're part of it. You're not the leader, you're just a participant. They are telling their stories. They are telling China's stories."

PART III

The Future

The reason I have continued to live is that I grieve to think that I have things in my heart that I have not been able to fully express, and am ashamed to think that after I am gone my writing will not be known to posterity.

Sima Qian, "Letter to Ren An," ca. 90 BCE

12

Virus

Like the verdant forests of northern Europe, the wetlands of China have long been refuges of mystery and memory. Surrounded by farmlands and town, these areas were known as the *jianghu*—literally "river and lakes" that hid bandits and brigands but were also home to a mythic world of knights-errant fighting for righteousness and justice—the deep values of Chinese culture that are still reservoirs of resilience in times of suffering.

In the region around Wuhan, this political battle was underpinned by an ecological crisis. In ancient times, people observed that rice thrived in the soggy fields created by springtime floods. They tried to re-create this ecosystem in a more predictable manner: they settled permanently—and precariously—next to the writhing waters of the Yangtze and its tributaries, using dams and dikes to limit floods, and creating miniature wetlands in the form of rice paddies. States encouraged this sedentary lifestyle because it created wealthy populations that were easily controlled, conscripted, and taxed—unless of course they escaped to live as *jianghu*.

But as China's population exploded over the past 250 years, this fragile balance tipped. People moved closer to the rivers in greater numbers, building over wetlands that acted as natural sponges, spurring greater floods, flows of refugees, and cholera outbreaks—a cycle that the historian of Chinese hydrology Chris Courtney calls the "modern disaster regime." The economy boomed, but so too did underclasses who lived according to *jianghu* rules.

Modern engineering has limited these floods, but humans continue to find new ways to overrun nature. The best example is how one of the world's recent public health crises originated in Wuhan—a contemporary version of the political-ecological disaster regime.

This time, the trigger occurred when a corona virus prevalent in animals jumped to humans in 2019. The exact cause is unclear—it could have been humans consuming wild animals, which were sold in dirty and poorly regulated markets. Or it might have been when efforts to research a coronavirus went astray and leaked from a lab. In any case, the crisis was made worse by China's political system. If it once encouraged sedentary lifestyles near dangerous waterways, it now ignored best practices in public health. Nearly two decades earlier, similar conditions had caused a coronavirus to spread from animals to humans. That disease, Severe Acute Respiratory Syndrome, or SARS, had highlighted a series of solvable problems, such as limiting the wildlife trade, improving hygiene at markets, and improving public health structures.

In the end, however, only a few of the lessons had been learned. The state had built new bureaucracies to monitor public health and had constructed labs with high-tech equipment. But at heart, the state remained focused on a narrow set of goals, primarily economic growth and political control. And so it lacked the capacity to take on hygiene at the markets (or for that matter at China's often filthy hospitals). It also lacked the courage to discourage the consumption of exotic animals, which remained a popular practice of the middle and upper classes. When the disease emerged, the government not only froze; it made the situation worse by arresting whistleblowers and issuing misleading statements. When it finally reacted, four weeks had passed, giving the virus time to gain a foothold.

The government mishandling of Covid-19 was paralleled by a resurgence of the *jianghu*. This time, it was counter-historians, journalists, and filmmakers who defied the state's iron hand, documenting how it had created another crisis. They forced the government to acknowledge missteps and showed that, reports of their demise to the contrary, they continue to exist in contemporary China's backwaters, ready to spring to action when the state's guard is down.

On 16 January 2020, Ai Xiaoming returned to Wuhan after a short trip to visit old friends in Guangzhou. The next day, she heard about a viral cold that was going around but shrugged it off: it was winter, and viruses were not unusual. Her main focus was her father, who was now 95 years old and bedridden. He needed a new caregiver because the old one was moving away, so she visited several hospitals to find one. Nothing struck her as unusual. On the 19th she again heard rumors of a new kind of pneumonia but didn't think much of it. Suddenly, the next day, everyone was talking about the strange illness spreading through the population. But state media offered only an information vacuum. Panic began to grip Wuhan.

Three days later, on January 23, the government suddenly implemented a draconian lockdown. Roughly 57 million people in Wuhan and fifteen surrounding cities would stay locked in their homes until April 8, something the World Health Organization called "unprecedented in public health history." People had received no warning and many lacked food or other necessities. Wuhan quickly turned into a ghost town. Many people were consumed by panic and dread—when would it end? What was the plan?

Like millions of other people in Wuhan, Ai's first concern was for her family. She went to pharmacies to buy basics for her father's care, such as cotton swabs, disinfectants, and laxatives. Already, disinfectants were in short supply as people thought (incorrectly, as it later turned out) that the virus might be easily transmitted on surfaces. Just as in other parts of the world, masks sold out quickly and pharmacies jacked up prices. Chinese New Year was just two days away, on the 25th, but the huge flow of people traveling for family reunions ground to a halt. For the first time since it opened more than a century earlier, the main train station in Wuhan's business district of Hankou closed.

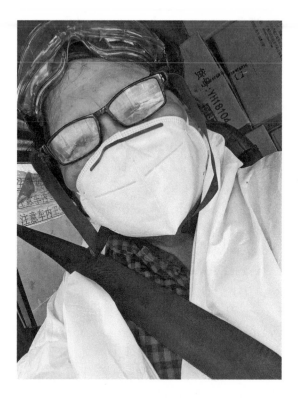

Ai quickly plugged into local volunteer organizations. On the 29th, she joined a team to deliver sixty-five hundred sets of personal protective equipment to hospitals and community centers. They also gathered 600,000 yuan (nearly $100,000) in donations. Ai suited up in a white protective gown, double-masked, and joined the crew to see the situation for herself.

What she saw shocked her. Her team handed over equipment to community center staff members who had no protection except for cotton masks. The sets of protective clothing were welcome, but inadequate; Ai was told that the disposable gowns would be reused.

Ai wasn't sure what to do with the information. In years past, she would have brought along her digital camera and tried to film the disaster as it unfolded. But she would need at least one assistant and didn't want to risk infecting them. Also, she had her father to think of. If she were to investigate further, she risked bringing the virus home.

So Ai did what thousands of other Chinese did: she published her unfiltered thoughts online. And to her surprise, this article was not censored. Ai began to write more, joining a flood of criticism against the government.

Ai's first article was about the fate of a fairly obscure ophthalmologist named Li Wenliang. He was an unlikely focal point for Chinese anger at the government, but maybe that was the point. He had been an ordinary, apolitical person. But in late December 2019, a friend at the Wuhan Central Hospital handed him charts of patients who were suffering from what seemed like a new kind of SARS. They were quarantined, but the illness seemed to be spreading.

Li did what many Chinese would do: he didn't issue a clarion call on his public social media feed. He didn't unfurl a banner in downtown Wuhan or write an open letter to authorities. That's what a dissident would have done. Instead, he used his WeChat app to contact a group of friends and warn them about the new illness. To prove what he said was true, he included the charts and a CT scan of a patient's chest.

"Quarantined in the emergency department," he wrote about seven patients stricken with the mysterious ailment. "Family members and relatives should take precautions."

That was enough to trigger public security, who monitor even private WeChat discussion groups. That same day, December 29, police hauled him in for questioning. Three days later they compelled him to sign a statement that his behavior was "illegal." He was forced to write *ming bai le,* or "I understand," and affix a thumbprint in red ink.

The government then misled the public on December 31, saying in a statement that there was a pneumonia outbreak centered on the wildlife market but that it was "preventable and treatable." The statement was later deleted (but can be found on the internet archive).

Li's warning was one of many that were leaking out at that time. Seven other people were detained, and all were charged with spreading rumors. In one of the most widely reproduced internet memes, television news broadcasts across China on January 3 repeated the same story: that rumor-mongers were misleading the population and would be dealt with severely.

The exact sequence of events will be debated for years to come, but it is clear that local leaders covered up the virus's existence for about a month. They probably were worried that admitting to such an outbreak would derail their careers. An important government meeting was scheduled for January and the holidays were just around the corner. And so authorities put a lid on the news, hoping that it wasn't really so severe and would go away.

But censorship has limits when everyone knows the truth. This was the case in Wuhan, where thousands were becoming infected, and hundreds were dying. Wuhan is big, but learning about ill people or hearing about overcrowded hospitals was not difficult. Once the lockdown was implemented, the government had to admit that something was up. So for weeks and even months, government censorship became uneven and erratic. That gave *jianghu* historians a chance to publish video and print investigations.

Dr. Li surfaced as a key person because *jianghu* journalists uncovered that he—a doctor with concrete proof—had been one of those convicted of spreading rumors. Not only that but on February 1 he wrote on his Weibo public feed that he was ill with Covid. He had been hospitalized since January with a fever, a lung infection, and other symptoms. By the third day, he was on oxygen. Despite these symptoms, on January 27 he gave an anonymous interview with Chinese media describing how he had been reprimanded for raising the alarm. Now he had decided to reveal his identity. Here was a whistleblower who was dying of the disease about which he had been prevented from warning the public. He became a rallying point for popular unrest.

Realizing that his death would be a public relations debacle, the hospital treating him began issuing bulletins about his progress. But his condition deteriorated. He began accepting interviews with Chinese and foreign media. He posted a picture of himself on social media, his brow and hair doused in sweat, an oxygen masked strapped to his face, and his eyes staring into the camera. Suddenly, the government was facing the greatest public relations debacle since the 2008 earthquake in Sichuan province.

When Dr. Li died on February 7, social media erupted. Prominent public intellectuals like Ai reacted with online tributes. She wrote a piece of calligraphy with one character repeated four times: *xun xun xun xun*. "Xun" means to teach, train, or admonish. Ai had two meanings in mind: she was referring to the *xun jie shu*, or "letter of admonishment," or confession, that he had been forced to sign, and also to Li as someone who had offered the country a *jiao xun*, or moral guidance for speaking the truth.

She added in red the now infamous characters *ming bai le*, or "I understand," that Li had written at the bottom of the confession. When she posted the calligraphy online, she explained that the three characters refer to more than just Dr. Li's humiliating confession. For a politically conscious person, being *ming bai* means understanding the truth of China's political situation and being willing to speak plainly about it.

Many others reacted by posting on Li's account on Weibo. This is a social media platform similar to Twitter, in that anyone can follow anyone else and respond to their post. Millions posted comments, especially on his February 1 post announcing that he was ill. Hashtags, such as "Wuhan government owes Dr. Li an apology" and "we want freedom of speech," went viral. His Weibo account became a safe space where people could vent or mention their anxiety. Some came to wish him good morning or good evening. As spring arrived in the weeks after his death, they told him that the cherry blossoms were opening. Others whispered that they missed him.

One political cartoonist took the best-known picture of him, wearing a surgical mask, and turned it into a mask of barbed wire. Some commentators thanked him for his bravery, while others apologized for his treatment by the authorities. Many repeated a quote he had given in an interview with Chinese media: "A healthy society should have more than one voice."

For Ai, the crisis hit home in late January when her father developed a fever. In normal times, she would have called an ambulance and taken him straight to a hospital. But the hospitals were dangerous places, with the virus spreading rapidly through patients and staff alike. She made a rational but painful decision to keep him home. She realized that this meant he would die, but decided it was better that he pass away surrounded by family and friends than alone in a room with beeping lights.

She kept him cool, turned him every two hours, fed him through a nose tube, and washed his body. Three days later, on February 2, he stopped breathing. The next day his body was transported to a crematorium and the family held a small farewell ceremony led by a Buddhist monk. In hindsight they felt lucky; on February 5 the city announced that funerals were banned. According to official figures, by around this time 1,770 people had died of Covid-19. People like her father were collateral damage.

Caring for her father was just one of her tasks in running the extended family's affairs. As a feminist scholar, she knew that some people might see this as unfair, but she didn't look at it that way. If she ran the household, then her beloved younger brother could spend his time turning his company's resources toward helping the public. Her son was working for him as well, and for these months the conglomerate redeployed its personnel to help restock hospitals, resupply community centers, and deliver food to the needy. She felt it was a fair division of labor, even as she struggled with the daily chores. She had to hope that she would be allowed out to shop for food. She had to wait in line. She saw how these small problems multiplied across the vast metropolis, leading to a breakdown in public spirit. With her father's passing, she now had time to publish her thoughts.

Panic is leading to problems and crises more horrendous than the epidemic itself, because it is resulting in isolation between individuals and aggravated selfishness, arising rapidly and on a massive scale. We have seen meanness, self-protection and treating neighbors as enemies. This barbaric behavior triggered by panic amounts to a humanitarian crisis, which is a more harmful virus.

Like many people who experienced the events of early 2020, Ai realized immediately that government malfeasance had played a big role. She didn't explore the question of whether a faster government response could have stopped the virus's spread. That was for future generations to debate. But it was clear to her and millions of other Chinese that the government had covered up the virus's existence for about a month. It had only locked down the city after the disease had started to spread uncontrollably, and then it did so with a ferocity that scared people almost as much as the virus.

"The initial strict control of information made the spread of the virus inevitable," she wrote. "Many of the measures taken afterwards were not subject to sufficient public debate but were imposed."

Others came to the same realization, flooding the public sphere with criticisms and reportage on the crisis. Some turned to underground historians from half a century ago to understand the crisis. One was Yu Luoke, whom we read about earlier in the book. He was the young man who was not allowed to enter university because of his bloodlines—his parents had served the Kuomintang government in a minor capacity, turning the entire family into untouchables in Mao's China. When the Cultural Revolution started, he penned a classic essay called "Bloodlines," tens of thousands of which were sold on street corners as a pamphlet. In 1970, he was executed.

The Wuhan lockdown coincided with the 50th anniversary of his death by firing squad. Ai and others posted about him on WeChat. His brother's 2016 essay on the 50th anniversary of his detention went viral. This story of arbitrary state power resonated in what was to become the start of three years of lockdowns.

Others duplicated the long-established methods of underground historians by publishing outside the Chinese firewall on sites such as YouTube and Twitter. Like many people, they found ways to obtain VPNs necessary to do this, showing that the ability had always been there. This linking of dissent inside and outside China would become a hallmark for future protests.

The most daring and short-lived was by a videographer named Chen Qiushi. Chen had already reported on the 2019 Hong Kong protests, traveling there on his own and making videos about the protesters. He challenged state media descriptions of the protests as violent with the peaceful reality that he witnessed, posting his reports on his Weibo account.

On January 23, Chen arrived in Wuhan and began filming. By then, his Weibo and WeChat accounts had been blocked so he posted to YouTube and Twitter. On January 30, he went to a Wuhan hospital that was overflowing with ill people. In one of the most famous broadcasts from the lockdown, Chen said: "I am afraid. In front of me is disease. Behind me is China's legal and administrative power. But as long as I am alive, I will speak about what I have seen and what I have heard. I am not afraid of dying. Why should I be afraid of you, Communist Party?"

Even though most Chinese couldn't see these reports, they were so damning that he worked for only two weeks before being detained. His detention also showed that YouTube and Twitter are easily accessed by more Chinese intellectuals than is generally realized. This meant the images could be reposted on Chinese social media. Of course, they could be blocked but they could also be formatted in ways that were harder to censor.

Even more influential than Chen was a 36-year-old former lawyer and citizen journalist named Zhang Zhan, who published for two months before being detained. Zhang was a trained lawyer who had been disbarred for handling human rights cases. Like Chen, she had been detained in 2019 for protesting on behalf of Hong Kong's pro-democracy movement.

On February 1, she traveled from her hometown of Shanghai to Wuhan. Her first stop was to see Ai Xiaoming. Ai had heard of Zhang because of her work as a human rights lawyer. Just like the old days, Ai took Zhang in and let her stay in her small apartment outside the family's compound. She gave her an orientation to the city's layout, and then Zhang moved into a hotel. She borrowed a bicycle and began riding around Wuhan, carrying a shaky camera to some of the key scenes of the outbreak.

Her videos documented empty shops, belching crematoria, overflowing hospitals, and the Wuhan Institute of Virology, a place that some people speculated might have been where the virus originated. She filmed a community health center, reporting that a man had been charged for a Covid test even though the government claimed they would be free. She accused the government of covering up the true number of deaths and of censoring the news. She also showed how many people who had lost loved ones were not allowed to mourn—any public gathering was banned.

"It's 12:40 AM. The sound of the funeral home's crematorium," she said in one of her trademark jumpy videos. "They work day and night."

None of these reports were masterpieces of investigative journalism. All of the journalists made clear that they could only describe what they saw. Interestingly, most of them bent over backward to represent the government's viewpoint, as if they hoped that these reports might be allowed on Chinese social media. Chen, for example, addressed a common criticism that the government should have opened up the city's empty hotels to house the patients, explaining that their air circulation systems would have spread the disease. Instead, the power of these chroniclers lay in showing the reality on the ground, which contrasted sharply with the government portrayal of events.

This was journalism from the front lines. While the official media served up interviews with officials and images of well-ordered hospitals, these journalists showed the reality. These reports would soon be censored, but they recalled days in the recent past when people like Jiang Xue had worked for state media. And they showed that during this national crisis, voices other than the government's bullhorn were being heard.

Perhaps even more shocking was how social media inside the firewall was awash with complaints and reports. One of the most popular ways to spread ideas was to publish diaries. By nature they are personal and thus can be portrayed as simply thoughts and feelings. And yet they were posted online, making them public. The US-based academic Yang Guobin has tallied more than two hundred online diaries that chronicled the panicky fear that gripped Wuhan in early 2020. "Keenly aware of the unprecedented nature of the Wuhan lockdown, diarists saw themselves as witnesses to history and were determined to leave personal records through diary writing," Yang noted in a study of these diaries.

Ai was one of the most prominent and popular online diarists, but the most famous was the Wuhan writer Wang Fang, better known by her pen name Fang Fang. She was a novelist best known for gritty works about Wuhan's dockworkers, hooligans, and factory workers. This kind of socialist realism carried with it implied criticisms but was acceptable to the government. Fang Fang was a member of the state writer's association and had carved out a comfortable existence.

But the 64-year-old had recently begun staking out more controversial positions. In 2016, she had published a novel called *Soft Burial* that described the land reform campaign of the 1940s and '50s, using the main character's lifelong amnesia as an allegory for how Chinese people had forgotten the violent founding years of the People's Republic. Now, in her own measured and folksy way, she described her shock at how the virus came to spread.

Part of the power of Fang Fang's diary was that she reflected the lives of many Chinese who lived within the system. She was no dissident or outspoken voice, such as Ai Xiaoming. She had an apartment provided by the state. Communist Party officials came to visit her before Chinese New Year's with gifts because she was a local celebrity. No one could accuse her of being radical.

So her portrayal of Wuhan in these days carried weight. She described five days of "utter panic" in Wuhan: three days before the lockdown when everyone knew that a terrifying virus was on the loose, but nothing was being done, and two days afterward when the local government was unable to explain what it was doing. Were they to be on their own? Would anyone help Wuhan? Her diary entries began receiving tens of thousands of views and comments.

She described how it was only on January 25, when a team of specialists arrived from Shanghai, that people finally knew that the country was behind them. But why did it end up like this? On her diary entry for January 26, she wrote that it wasn't so much that officials in Wuhan were incompetent. Instead, the virus outbreak was a typical result of China's authoritarian system of government.

> *Prohibiting people from speaking the truth and the media from reporting the truth leads to disaster; and now we are tasting the fruits of these disasters, one by one. Wuhan is always vying to be first at everything, but now it is first in line to taste this suffering.*

Fang Fang used her prominence to help make people aware of Dr. Ai Fen, who headed the emergency ward at the Central Hospital of Wuhan. She had been censured for leaking information about the virus and accused of trying to destroy Wuhan's development. That caused her to keep quiet until March, when she finally spoke out and gave an interview with a state-run magazine called *Renwu*, or *People*. Dr. Ai revealed that it was she who had given Dr. Li the information that he had posted on social media. The interview was titled "The Whistle-giver."

The article reflected Dr. Ai's pent-up anger, and she shocked readers by using expletive-laden language: "If I had known it would come to this, I wouldn't have cared about any censure. I'd fucking talk about it everywhere, right?"

The article was immediately censored but Fang Fang reposted it. Others joined in, using emojis, Morse code, and Romanized Chinese characters to bypass censors. Readers engaged in what they called an "online relay" to keep the article alive ahead of the authorities. In a March 11 post that received more than ten thousand comments, Fang Fang wrote:

> *Over the course of this process of resistance, posts get deleted, then reposted, over and over again. Preserving these deleted posts gradually becomes a sacred duty of those netizens. This sacred duty comes from an almost subconscious realization that keeps telling them: Protect those posts, for protecting them is the only way to protect yourself. Once things get to this point, I have to ask my dear internet censors, do you think you can really delete it all?*

On one level, the answer to Fang Fang's rhetorical question is yes, of course it can. And it did so in many different ways. One especially effective way to silence people like Fang Fang was to rely on home-grown nationalists. The day after her post on Ai Fen, Fang Fang noted that she was now under attack by "ultra-leftists" and nationalists.

Her critics noted that many other countries had botched handling the virus. By contrast, if the Chinese government had been a bit heavy-handed, hadn't it at least saved many lives? In China, official figures show that at that time only 5,226 people died of the virus. Even if twice as many died, it was far fewer per capita than almost any other country. After the lockdown, Chinese children went to school, restaurants and bars largely reopened, and life mostly returned to normal. At least for the first year or so after the outbreak, this was a defensible position.

For the next year or so, that became the prime takeaway for most people: the government was firm, even severe, but people stayed safe. The issue of allowing the wild-animal markets to exist and of not responding in December were buried in the avalanche of bad news from the rest of the world—the overflowing morgues in Italy, the 1 million who would eventually die in the United States, the classrooms around the world that lay empty for an academic year.

In this context, the initial support for critiquing the government slowly diminished. People like Fang Fang became harmless cranks or Western stooges. Many of the diarists' works were slowly erased.

As for the more outspoken, the government rounded them up. Chen Qiushi was already detained—he would only emerge 600 days later to post an enigmatic but telling comment on his Twitter feed: "Over the past year and eight months, I have experienced a lot of things. Some of it can be talked about, some of it can't, I believe you understand."

In May, Zhang Zhan was detained, went on a hunger strike, and in December 2020 was sentenced to four years in jail for "picking quarrels." Ai Xiaoming did not forget her friend. Taking now to Twitter because her WeChat feed was again blocked, she photographed herself wearing a mask with the characters "Zhang Zhan is innocent and must be released!"

She also wrote a letter in calligraphy to the Shanghai courts that were hearing Zhang's case. Drawing a parallel to Lin Zhao, the Shanghai poet who was jailed and executed in 1968 for contributing to the magazine *Spark*, Ai reproduced a letter that Lin had written:

> To you,
> My Prosecutor, your excellency
> I respectfully offer a rose.
> This is the politest protest.
> Without a sound,
> Gentle and civil.

In an accompanying letter she wrote:

> Human Blood is not Water/ Flowing into a River

> With the posthumous poem of Lin Zhao in prison, to the prosecutor of the Zhang Zhan case in the Shanghai Pudong New Area's Procurator and the presiding judge of the Shanghai Pudong New Area Court:

> Zhang Zhan is not guilty and should be released!

> Scholar, Independent Documentary Filmmaker
> Citizen of Wuhan: Ai Xiaoming
> Night of 27 December 2020

All of this can be seen as evidence that China's authoritarianism is endlessly powerful. Citizens might briefly force open a space, but ultimately they fail. And yet it also shows the enduring power of China's counter-historians. Looking more closely at the sequence of events, it is clear that the government lost control of how the history of the virus outbreak was being written—and even now seems unlikely ever to recover it fully.

Consider the whistle-blower Dr. Li Wenliang. After his death, the government countered his fame by trying to coopt him. It made the doctor a national martyr, portraying him as a valiant fighter against the virus. In reality, of course, Li was an ophthalmologist who died after an eye patient gave him the virus. His fame had nothing to do with fighting the virus. Instead, he was famous because he had been silenced for warning against the virus.

This is so obvious that even China's most popular online encyclopedia, *Baidu Baike*, acknowledges the government's bungling of Li's case. Li's entry accurately reports that the government later withdrew the charges against Li and penalized the local police precinct for inaccurately charging Li with spreading rumors. The censorship was portrayed as having been caused by a few bad apples—the government's standard way of dealing with errors that can't be covered up—but it clearly shows that Li was victimized. That is a victory for China's citizen journalists, who brought all of this to light.

Li remains such a potent symbol that the government has not taken down his Weibo page. Two years later, the comments hadn't stopped, with people writing on it as if Li were a salve for the problems of modern China.

"The construction industry is having mass layoffs," wrote a man who said he worried about his career prospects. Other posts were more explicitly political. Several commenters quoted the written apology that police forced Dr. Li to sign after he was reprimanded. Others mentioned recent news events that have stoked public anger, including officials' tepid response to the case of a mentally ill woman who was found chained in a shed. "They're ignoring people's anger," one user wrote.

Perhaps most important, the events in Wuhan show the potential anger, dissatisfaction, and critical thinking that lies beneath the surface. People like Ai Xiaoming, Jiang Xue, Tiger Temple, and Tan Hecheng represent a minority of Chinese. But their well-articulated critiques resonate when people are shaken from their lethargy. This is why one way to look at the Wuhan outbreak is as an example of government power. But a more convincing explanation is that it was a classic example of the repeated eruptions against unchecked government authority.

Memory: Soft Burial

It is 2015 and an old woman begins to recover her memory. She is 85, but for the past sixty-five years has not been able to remember what happened before she was 20, when she washed up half-drowned on a riverbank. Since then, she has constructed a life for herself but has always been slightly anxious, worrying about some sort of impending disaster.

The woman is widowed, and her son has gone to one of China's coastal boomtowns to earn his fortune. But now he has returned to work in their hometown, Wuhan. He is successful and buys a bungalow in an upscale subdivision so they can live together. She is ecstatic that after so many years apart she can be with her son. And yetut the new house unsettles her: the spaciousness, the landscape paintings, the color of the quilts, the wealth that it represents. Finally prosperous, she finds that her past begins to return.

"They will come and take it away," she murmurs to her son, who assures her that he earned it all fair and square. They have nothing to worry about. But names begin to float up and she utters them, not sure what they mean.

Slowly, she withdraws into herself. In her mind's eye she sees eighteen steps and realizes that they represent the eighteen levels of hell in Buddhism. She begins to descend the steps, recovering one piece of her past after another: the drowning of her first child, the murder of her family, and her burying them with her own hands—a hasty "soft" burial where the bodies are tossed in a pit without a coffin and covered in soil.

This is the rough outline of Fang Fang's 2016 novel *Soft Burial*, a compelling, eerily calm book that unfolds like a series of interlocking mysteries. The memories of the woman, Ding Zitao, parallel efforts by her son, Qing Lin, to investigate her buried life.

An architect by training, Qing Lin travels to the western regions of Hubei with a friend who is studying the lost manor houses of rural China, once populated by a class of landed gentry that from his naïve perspective mysteriously vanished in the middle of the last century. Slowly, Qing Lin realizes that his family stems from this class of people, and he learns that the Communists slaughtered them around the time of the Communist takeover in 1949.

Fang Fang's novel was published by the People's Literature Publishing House, one of the country's largest and most commercially oriented presses. Censors—and in China most censors are in-house—probably thought the events were far enough in the past not to matter. And, besides, Fang Fang, is one of China's best-known state-approved writers. And initially, the publisher's instincts seemed spot on: *Soft Burial* became a bestseller. In April 2017, it won an independent Chinese literary award, named after a deceased author, Lu Yao.

That's when for the first time in her life she realized the price of challenging government history. The same day that she won the Lu Yao prize, a group called the Wuhan Workers and Peasants Reading Group denounced *Soft Burial* as a "poisonous anti-Communist plant." By early 2017, retired senior Communist officials were attacking it. On May 25, the publisher halted production and online bookstores stopped sales. Since then, it has been banned. A year later, Fang Fang resigned as head of the Hubei branch of the writers association and in 2021 was removed from the group's national leadership.

Fang Fang's transgression was to expose the original sin of the People's Republic of China: the violent land reform campaign of the late 1940s to early 1950s, when millions of farmers were killed for owning what usually amounted to small plots of land. They were called landlords, portrayed as evil, and destroyed.

Few doubt that some sort of land reform was necessary in China— tens of millions of farmers lacked land while some had huge landholdings. Many international observers, including those sent by the United Nations, said land reform was urgently needed to modernize China's agriculture. And indeed when the Kuomintang Party retreated to Taiwan in 1949, one of its first acts was to implement land reform there.

But the Communist Party's chief goal was not social justice. Instead it wanted to obliterate the people who had constituted the backbone of China's pre-Communist society: the small-scale landowners who built schools and roads, managed religious life, raised militias to fight bandits, and paid taxes. Destroying them, as Guo Yuhua discovered in her investigation of the Ma Family Mansion, was necessary for the party to install its totalitarian control over Chinese society.

This is clear from the many examples of land reform where farmers were happy to have the land but didn't harbor grudges against the landlords. Many had been benevolent or at least harmless. Some had a social conscience and even supported the revolution. That's why the party had to send in activists to whip up peasants so they would denounce the landlords and violently punish them. That led to the millions of deaths, often by being buried alive in the ground that they were accused of unjustly owning. This is captured in *Soft Burial*, where the heroine's family supported the revolution and local farmers only turned on them after being incited by activists.

Land reform remains a taboo topic in China. In 2021, the Cyberspace Administration of China issued a list of ten "historically nihilist" rumors that cannot be accepted. One was that many landlords were actually good people and that land reform—at least the violent way it was carried out—was a mistake.

One reason it remains a hot topic is that the party's own efforts to justify it are so ham-handed. The party relied on official authors, such as Ding Ling and Zhou Libo, to write simplistic novels portraying good farmers versus bad landlords. They were aided by left-wing foreign writers, most notably William Hinton, whose widely read account, *Fanshen*, whitewashed the campaign into a case of stern-but-fair wealth redistribution.

The novel was a departure for Fang Fang. Most of her novels had been hyperrealist depictions of life in reform-era Wuhan. But she couldn't forget a story she had heard when growing up. Her mother's friend kept worrying that her family would give her a "soft burial," like her relatives, who had been classified as landlords. Without a coffin, the body would be twisted and broken by the earth and the dead could never reincarnate. As she grew older, Fang Fang decided she had to tackle this topic. She began to read extensively on the campaign, traveling to western Hubei and Sichuan to research the book. Archives were off-limits, but she conducted interviews and consulted books by unofficial historians, such as Gao Hua. Using these sources as a foundation, she used her imagination to fill in the blanks.

The novel is remarkable for its beautiful descriptions of the countryside and the modest, refined courtyard houses where the more prosperous farmers once lived. Unlike her other novels, this one is written in a slow, even voice, with the reader drawn in by the heroine's mystery—who is she and what is her terrible secret?

Like Hu Jie's woodblock prints and oil paintings, the novel is a way of giving a voice to the dispossessed—of using art to fill a hole in the archive. But instead of illuminating the Great Famine like Hu Jie, Fang Fang ventures into the even more fraught territory of land reform.

Of course, the novel is also an allegory for China's own soft burial of the past. Although the heroine is too old and senile to confront the past, her son has a choice. In his travels to the countryside with his friend, he comes upon more clues about the family home. His friend urges him to follow those clues and learn more. But the young man refuses. He has to live in this society. He is afraid of knowing too much.

Later, his friend calls him and says that he is pushing ahead with his project to document the old manor homes. He will write what really happened to their inhabitants. He has chosen to remember. As he talks to his friend, the young man realizes that the path he thought he could choose—to forget—is no longer an option. If someone remembers, then others can no longer forget. One memory is enough to challenge amnesia.

He thought to himself, I chose to forget, and you chose to re-member. But because of your choice to record these cases, then how can I now forget them?

13

Empire

The Qing dynasty was arguably the most powerful in the long history of kingdoms and states that have sprung up on the lands that now comprise the People's Republic of China. Established in 1636 by a nomadic people, the Manchus, the Qing conquered the Chinese Ming dynasty eight years later. Harnessing the Manchus' military prowess with China's economic and cultural might, the Qing ballooned into a mega-dynasty with territory twice the size of the Ming and larger than any other dynasty that now, in the way that historical shorthand works, we think of as being Chinese.

The Qing were so successful that it absorbed lands that rarely (if ever) had been under Chinese control—including Tibet, Xinjiang, Mongolia, and Manchuria—and certainly not all at the same time. When the Qing collapsed in 1911, the new nation-state that was built on its foundations, the Republic of China, inherited most of its territory. Its most significant loss was Outer Mongolia, or what today is the independent country of Mongolia, and parts of Siberia. Otherwise, the Qing's blown-out borders are what the People's Republic of China inherited when it was established in 1949.

This legacy leads some people to describe today's China as a modern-day empire. But this misses a key difference. Empires are made up of a center (the metropole, as it is known in colonial studies) and colonies that are usually ruled through a colonial administration—think of Great Britain as the metropole and India as a colony. The colonies were almost never considered part of the empire's homeland. China, by contrast, does not distinguish between an ethnic Chinese state and colonies populated by conquered peoples. Instead, it incorporates the Qing conquest lands inside the borders of a modern nation-state, making them part and parcel of the Chinese nation.

That matters because modern nation-states view their borders as hard, fixed, and eternal. They are sacred and inviolable. And if a piece of territory is lost through war or another cataclysm, then the country's identity is gravely wounded. For China, this means that the Qing conquest lands can never be surrendered and that they must be mythologized as having been always part of the Chinese nation, as if Chinese people (however one wants to define this term) have lived on these lands forever—and that all of these peoples who ever lived there were always Chinese. Thus the Mongolian monarch Genghis Khan is lionized as a "a great man of the Chinese people," while minority schoolchildren learn classical Chinese poetry as if it were their cultural heritage rather than a neighboring land's.

The upshot today is that entire regions and peoples have been appropriated as Chinese. Since 2011, the government has claimed that Tibet has been part of China "since ancient times," even though this defies any historical understanding of the two lands' interactions over the centuries. Likewise it claims Taiwan or Hong Kong as having always been an inviolable part of the motherland, even though these territories have floated in and out of Chinese control. Most importantly, these claims make no concession to what people living there today want for themselves--the idea of self-determination never applies to territories that China claims as its own.

Instead, the state regards these as non-negotiable core interests. It does so not by democratic means—for example, holding a poll to see if Uighur or Tibetan or Hong Kong people want to be part of the People's Republic—but, as the religious studies professor Michael J. Walsh writes, by establishing "a link between territory and sacredness, thereby invoking the inviolate." Chinese territory is hallowed; it cannot be challenged on any grounds or under any circumstances. It is and always has been Chinese.

Even though the Qing collapsed more than a century ago, its conquest lands still vex China's leaders. They pay lip service to international norms, hence many of the territories are called "autonomous regions" or are promised some sort of self-rule. But they are in fact run from Beijing. The result is that nearly half the lands of China's territory, including most of its border regions, are minority areas but are heavily militarized and run by a core of ethnic Chinese officials. Some of these places, such as Xinjiang, Tibet, and Hong Kong, have been in a state of unrest for decades, culminating in crackdowns. For Tibet and Xinjiang, that has meant forced assimilation, so their peoples adopt Chinese culture and norms. For Hong Kong it means reneging on the fifty years of autonomy it was supposed to enjoy until 2047.

All of these regions are flashpoints that will continue to plague China in the decades to come. And all of them are focal points for China's counter-historians, including many ethnic minorities who otherwise do not have a voice in today's China.

The Tibetan writer Tsering Woeser was educated in Chinese schools, writes in Chinese, and lives in Beijing; her works have been translated into English via a foreign-based website, High Peaks Pure Earth. That's made her a go-to person for foreign media and led some people to think of her as somehow inauthentic, the product of cultural assimilation and foreign fascination.

And yet hers is a classic story of internal exile and resistance. She lives under house arrest in Beijing but still manages to pen trenchant critiques of the system. Her fate is familiar to many minorities in an unreflexively dominant culture; she has had to compromise to survive but still maintains integrity and dignity.

Unknown to many people familiar mainly with her online work, Woeser has also produced one of the most important counter-histories on Tibetan history. Banned in China, it documents how Tibet was devastated during the Cultural Revolution, helping to explain the region's enduring unrest.

I talked to her on several occasions but over the course of the 2010s it became increasingly difficult to get into her home in eastern Beijing, which she shares with her husband, the writer Wang Lixiong. Their apartment was under 24-hour surveillance, an absurd state of affairs captured in the 2014 film *The Dossier* by the independent film-maker Zhu Rikun. He tells Woeser's story in her own voice as she reads from her police file.

On one occasion I got in to see her only by taking a couple of back entrances that the Public Security Bureau didn't bother to guard (Woeser keeps a close eye on the police and gave me last-minute directions for which door to enter). That gave me a long afternoon in the couple's richly decorated apartment, learning about her work challenging the party's history of Tibet, as well as Wang's work to re-think policy in Tibet and Xinjiang.

Woeser's unusual status stems from her family history. Her father, Tsering Dorje, was recruited into the People's Liberation Army in 1950 when he was just 13 years old. He stayed in the army and rose in the ranks, creating a privileged life for his family. That gave Woeser the mixed-blessing of a Chinese-language education. The family lived near an army base in the Tibetan city of Darzedo (also known by the Chinese name Kangding). She attended a Chinese-only high school aimed at the children of China's occupying forces and Tibetans like her father.

"When I went to school, the first thing we said was 'Long Live the Communist Party!' and things like that. So I had no knowledge of Tibetan history. I knew nothing. The school wouldn't mention anything—that we had a history or were a people. But I knew about Chinese history and people like Qu Yuan [the 3rd-century BCE poet who has been adopted as a national patriot]."

Her awareness grew after she moved to Chengdu, the western Chinese metropolis in neighboring Sichuan province. There she studied Chinese literature at the Southwest University for Nationalities. That was set up in the 1950s as a school to train minorities to serve in the Chinese civil service—people like her father who were coopted into the country's modern-day empire. But it was also a place where she got to know many of China's other fifty-five minorities. One point all had in common was discrimination. "So suddenly, there it was . . . this consciousness of being a minority."

After graduation, she moved back to Tibet, living for a year in Kangding to work as a journalist. At that time she received a samizdat copy of *In Exile from the Land of Snows* by John F. Avedon, a 1984 account of the Dalai Lama's flight from Tibet. Woeser said she believes it had been translated into Chinese with the goal of criticizing it. But realizing how explosive the material was, authorities quickly withdrew the book—too late, however, because Tibetans had photocopied it and were passing it around.

The book challenged everything she knew about Tibet. It explained how the People's Liberation Army had invaded Tibet in the 1950s, violating an agreement with the Dalai Lama. Thousands had been killed and many fled to India, including the Dalai Lama. Unable to believe what she had read, she gave it to her father.

"My father was very laconic. He doesn't like to say much. But he said that 70 percent of it was accurate. So then I realized that it basically was correct, and I thought, gosh, they killed so many Tibetans! I read that book several times."

After Kangding, she moved to Lhasa, her family's hometown, to work as an editor and writer at *Tibetan Literature*, a government-run magazine. There she witnessed the discrimination faced even by those who tried to fit in. She was living with her mother's brother, who had joined the Communist Party at a young age. But every time he stepped outside his front door, even he had to carry his identity card and present it at checkpoints. "This touched him deeply. Here he was a middle-aged man being harassed by teenage soldiers."

Woeser was left alone because she had lighter skin and looked more Chinese. But her life changed when her father moved back to Lhasa in 1990, dying a year later, aged 54.

"I already was realizing I was a Tibetan but when he died, I went to monasteries to seek solace. There I met monks. After they trusted me, they began to tell me what had really happened. They told me about the violence against Tibetans in March of 1989 [during an uprising]. I began to think I had to write that down. That's when I started writing essays. I wrote their stories."

The more apolitical of these articles—slices of life in monasteries, for example—were published in Chinese literature magazines. She also wrote poetry in Chinese, slowly exploring Tibetan symbols and imagery. As a writer, Woeser was becoming more and more Tibetan, but at the time her shift could be accepted as a kind of exoticism that Chinese readers found appealing.

But her father also left her something unambiguously political. He had been a passionate photographer and she remembers him spending many of his free hours organizing boxes of negatives. After he died, he left her these files. She had thought his photography had been a hobby and that he had left her nothing more than amateur snaps. But when she held them up to the light, she found that they were actually brutal images of the Cultural Revolution—people being humiliated and beaten, or of zealots destroying Tibetan temples. He had used a Zeiss Ikon, a top-end camera at that time, and the photos were clearly the work of a professional. Few people had cameras back then. And who would have been allowed to take these photos, and then annotate them with notes? She began to realize that he must have been an official photographer documenting Tibet's destruction.

What to do with them? She couldn't publish them in China and was slightly intimidated by them. They sat in her Lhasa apartment for several years until she read Wang Lixiong's *Sky Burial: The Fate of Tibet*. At the time, the two did not know each other but she was immediately impressed. Here was an ethnic Chinese person who had spent a decade studying Tibet. The book had been praised by the Dalai Lama as a fair account of the region and its prospects under Chinese rule. It had been published in 1998, when an accommodation with the Dalai Lama still seemed to be an option for some of Beijing's leaders. Wang would be wise enough to know what to do with her father's photos. She mailed him the boxes. As Wang later wrote:

"I put my gloves on and went over the negatives under a light.

"Almost immediately I realized that I could not accept her gift. The negatives were too precious."

Wang wrote back telling her that he was willing to help, but as an outsider to her people he shouldn't do the main work. She must. That was the start of Woeser's new life as an underground historian.

The boxes contained more than four hundred photos, making them the largest known cache of images about the Cultural Revolution in Tibet. Government archives may hold more, but if they exist, they are off limits. In an era when few people owned cameras, they radically increase the number of images about this crucial decade.

More important, the photos deepen our understanding of the destruction wrought on Tibet. Because of their number and her father's careful notes, they yield concrete data as to when attacks took place. This is rare because so little documentation of any kind exists on the Cultural Revolution in Tibet. For example, "The Cultural Revolution Database," a digital archive edited by the California-based historian Song Yongyi, has more than ten thousand entries but only eight on Tibet. Likewise, of the more than three thousand letters published in *A New Collection of Red Guard Publications*, only four are from Tibet.

And yet it is obvious from the destruction of thousands of temples and tens of thousands of manuscripts during the Cultural Revolution that the violence was even greater in Tibet than in ethnic Chinese parts of the country—something that holds true in Xinjiang and Inner Mongolia, too. This was because the campaign was also a racial one, with ethnic Chinese unleashing their prejudices: if the Communist Party cast doubt on Chinese culture, then how much worse were the inherently backward cultures of the half-civilized peoples of these borderlands? Hence the destruction of traditional culture and elites was more systematic and thorough here than elsewhere—something that counter-historians such as Wu Di, whom we met in chapter 10, noticed in Inner Mongolia.

From 1999 to 2006, Woeser devoted herself to filling in some of the gaps that the photos still left. She conducted seventy oral history interviews, incorporating them in a book published in Taiwan called *Shajie*, a Tibetan word that means "revolution" but in Chinese sounds like the words "killing and looting." That book contained three hundred of her father's photos, with the oral histories helping to explain them. She also published an accompanying volume, *Tibet Remembers* (*Xizang jiyi*), which had the complete oral history transcripts.

These are unique resources. When her books appeared, the only academic study of the Cultural Revolution in Tibet was one chapter of Tsering Shakya's *The Dragon in the Land of Snows*, the definitive account in English of the first four decades after 1950 in Tibet. Later, a monograph on the Cultural Revolution in Tibet was published in English by the overseas-based scholars Melvyn Goldstein, Ban Jiao, and Tanzen Lhundup.

In 2020, Woeser's book was expanded and translated into English, with the title *Forbidden Memory*. It includes new interviews and pictures that Woeser took of the same sites that her father had photographed. The contrasts are sometimes striking: young Chinese Red Guards pose in front of a Tibetan monastery in her father's picture. In Woeser's, Chinese tourists stand at the same sites, staring down at their phones.

Another photo shows a young Tibetan woman wielding a hoe to destroy the golden eaves of the Jokhang Palace in Lhasa. Woeser identifies the woman and writes:

> *In the photograph, she looks young, as if she had been taken over by a huge passion of some sort that led her to take the action that today shocks Tibetans. What drove that passion? Why were these places—the monasteries and temples saturated with religious energy, historical meaning, and artistic inspiration for the Tibetan nation—in her mind seemingly only a pile of rubbish composed of the Four Olds that therefore should be erased without hesitation? Why did she seemingly believe that turning the past to ruins would give birth to a bright new world?*

The photos raise many questions, such as why her father took them. The authorities probably thought that he was documenting positive actions—smashing a despicable form of government and backward cultural practices. That may also have been his intention, although he may also have just been a soldier doing his duty. His works are without comment, although his acknowledgment to her of Chinese atrocities and the hours he spent cataloguing the negatives point to more complex emotions.

For today's viewer these cool frames refract absolute horror. For some family members, they are cathartic experiences. Woeser writes in the text that in 2012 she showed the son a picture of his father being humiliated and beaten. The son, now middle-aged, stared at it for a long time. Then he began to cry silently, gripping the person next to him for support. His body shook. Woeser began crying too.

> But finally he said, choking, "My father told me that he had seen someone taking photographs when he was struggled against," he said. "I wasn't in Lhasa then. I never thought that I would one day see what it was like."

Woeser had intended to publish the book in Taiwan anonymously. In 2003, however, she had published a collection of her essays in China called *Notes on Tibet* (*Xizang biji*). The book was quickly banned—what had been acceptable to publish in earlier years was now too sensitive. Woeser suddenly became a dissident. At times, she felt that the entire Lhasa security apparatus was focused on her.

So that year she moved to Beijing, where she was in a bigger pond and so attracted less attention. She and Wang married the next year and moved into their apartment. She began writing online on Tibetan issues, mainly for foreign websites. The decision cut her off from Tibet. As the director Zhu documented in *The Dossier*, she is banned from even entering Tibet. During a drive there with Chinese friends, their two cars were stopped at the border. The seven Chinese, including her husband, were allowed to enter Tibet. Woeser, the only Tibetan, was denied entry.

In his book *The Whisperers*, about Soviet citizens living in the Stalin era, the scholar Orlando Figes made popular the idea that all people can do in a tightly controlled society is to "whisper" memories of the past. That's not true in most parts of China—digital technologies make possible some sort of conversation—but it does capture the reality in China's borderlands. Even well-educated and privileged people like Woeser found out about her land's cataclysms only thanks to fortune and persistence. This near-lack of historical memory means that what we think of today as a revival of memory about the Communist takeover is more like a "postmemory," where traditional forms of first-generation witnesses (books, testimonies, documents) are lacking. This leaves fiction as an important way to remember the past traumas.

One of the most popular themes of these works were the events of 1958 to 1959. In the eastern borderlands of Amdo, an uprising that began in 1958 spread to Lhasa the next year. That led to China's full-scale invasion, the slaughter of tens of thousands of Tibetans, and the Dalai Lama's flight to India. In ethnic Chinese parts of the country, events from that era, such as the Great Leap Forward and the Cultural Revolution, can be discussed (albeit with evermore circumspection). But on the Tibetan plateau, what is simply known as "58"— *nga brgyad* in Tibetan—is almost completely taboo. Until now, it remains a blank spot in the historical record.

The ability to speak about this era is so limited that it is often only through foreign-based scholars and publications that Tibetan voices are preserved. One example is a hugely ambitious book called *Conflicting Memories: Tibetan History under Mao Retold*. This is edited by three Western scholars—Robert Barnett, Benno Weiner, and Françoise Robin—who draw together new scholarship on Tibet as well as original texts translated into English for the first time, all of them banned in China.

One example is a short story by Alo Rinchen Gyalpo called "The Traveling Path." He was born in the 1960s to what had been a wealthy family. He trained at the Shanghai School of Drama and Art in the early 1980s, specializing in scenography for traditional Tibetan opera. The story switches between a trial in the 1980s, the 1958 uprising, and the years that follow it, including the Cultural Revolution.

Maybe the most significant work of fiction is *The Red Howling Wind* by Tsering Dondru. It is an sprawling work with huge historical scope that perhaps one day will be translated fully into English. It starts with "the dreadful day" in 1958 when most of the males in the community were killed or captured and ends with Mao's death in 1976. In compensation for their suffering, the government gave each resident two bricks of dried tea, which they "abandoned like rocks to wipe one's ass"(432).

Some might argue that the borders of the Qing are only problematic when the lands are dominated by non-Chinese peoples, such as Tibetans, Uighurs, or Mongolians. In fact, ethnic Chinese borderlands are often just as troubled. In Hong Kong, China's one-size-fits-all approach to governing spurred two decades of protests that were only suppressed with violence in 2019 and then extinguished by passing a draconian national security law the next year. In the words of Hong Kong scholar Ching Kwan Lee, Chinese rule transformed "a shoppers' and capitalists' paradise into a city of protests at the frontline of a global backlash against China."

When negotiations with Britain started in the early 1980s, China promised Hong Kong autonomy. In what seemed like a novel way of managing a territory that had not been under Chinese control for nearly one hundred and fifty years, it offered a deal called "one country–two systems." Hong Kong was to keep its laws and its way of life from the 1997 handover until 2047. That seemed to refute the idea that anything inside China's borders had to be identical with core territories. In other words, the colonies could be autonomous of the metropole.

In fact, the concept of one country–two systems was not new. It was exactly the same term—*yiguo liangzhi*—used by Chinese negotiators in the 1950s as a way to bring Tibet into the national fold. This agreement, implemented in 1951, allowed Tibet to keep its institutions, including the Dalai Lama, but left issues such as defense and foreign affairs to China. The person in charge of those negotiations was Deng Xiaoping. He had run the party's southwestern China bureau, which negotiated with the Tibetans, and during negotiations with the British he was China's paramount leader.

The main difference was the leeway given Hong Kong. Tibet's autonomy lasted only eight years before it was crushed, while Hong Kong's lasted more than twenty. This might stem from its being populated by ethnic Chinese or because it was temporarily protected by the treaty signed with the United Kingdom. More likely, Hong Kong was for a while too important as a global financial center, which (at least until about 2020) was crucial for China's strategy of listing companies on international capital markets. In any case, Hong Kong existed in a gray area for two decades. That allowed a combative protest culture to arise, demanding more democracy (which China had promised under the agreement with the UK) and better protection of citizens' rights.

The British had never conferred full democracy on Hong Kong but had left it with a partially elected legislative council, a fairly free press, and an independent judiciary. Without these institutions, many Hong Kongers feared that they would become just another Chinese region where residents suffer from censorship, arbitrary arrest, and other symptoms of unbridled government power. Businesses also worried that the loss of rights would undermine prosperity by politicizing business disputes and hurting the city's world-class financial industry.

These fears explain why support for the protesters was so broad. In 2019, most detainees were young people, but frontline protesters also included doctors, airline pilots, and accountants. Opinion polls showed that residents consistently blamed the government for escalating the conflict, despite a propaganda barrage blaming the protesters.

Beijing's biggest error in trying to subjugate Hong Kong was to use what the sociologist Ho-Fung Hung calls "racialist nationalism." This is essentially what the Qing Empire used to control the vast territories it acquired in the 18th century. Qing authorities encouraged Han Chinese emigration and introduced Chinese culture in these regions, making Chineseness the benchmark for correct assimilation. Hong Kong would seem to be different from these areas because, according to modern racial discourse, it is "Chinese" in the sense that its residents were historically part of the same cultural world as Beijing or Shanghai.

But areas such as Hong Kong have long been on the margins of mainstream Chinese culture, zones of refuge and resistance closer in spirit to the *jianghu* world of outlaws than the established, stable centers of Chinese civilization. They speak a language different from the North Chinese dialect that the People's Republic adopted as standard Chinese. And, of course, they were under British rule for more than one hundred and fifty years, creating different cultural and political expectations. These are among the key reasons that many people there have not felt themselves to be part of the sacred project of rejoining the motherland.

That leaves Beijing with only one way to explain Hong Kong's skeptics: they are un-Chinese. One of Hong Kong's best-known public figures, the civil servant and later politician Anson Chan Fang On-sang, was attacked as a "traitor to the Han race" (*hanjian*) and for "forgetting about your ancestors" (*shudian wangzu*). Being un-Chinese means you cannot be part of the motherland and thus must be removed from power. And so, systematically, Beijing gutted the Hong Kong elite that tried to keep some sort of autonomy.

Until the mid-2010s, Hong Kong's special position made it a bastion of China's counter-history movement. Many of the people we have met in this book knew that if their works were banned in China, they could publish in Hong Kong. That is where Tan Hecheng, whom we met in chapter 11, published his account of the genocidal campaign in Hunan, or Tan Chanxue published her memoirs of the magazine *Spark* that we read about in chapter 4. It is also where Jiang Xue published her lengthy magazine article on *Sparks*, and where Ai Xiaoming had won a prize for her documentary film on the Jiabiangou labor camp.

Hong Kong was also the home of the Universities Service Center, a onetime hub of scholarship on mainland China. Founded in 1963, its scholars began their work by interviewing the huge flows of refugees trying to escape the Communist takeover of China. The next year, it opened to scholars from around the world seeking a window into China. From the 1980s onward, however, many foreign scholars simply went to the mainland and used the libraries at their home institutions.

The center remained important because of a reverse flow of scholars from China seeking access to an uncensored archive of their country's past. This was where Gao Hua found material and respite from professional harassment in Nanjing, allowing him to finish *How the Red Sun Rose*. So, too, He Shu, who co-founded the magazine *Remembrance*. All wrote recollections of their stays there, which were published on the center's "Folk History Archive" that includes roughly five hundred recollections of the Communist era, often by counter-historians and liberal thinkers.

The flow of scholars and material to Hong Kong began soon after the Communist takeover of China in 1949. One of the most prominent was Sima Lu, a library director at the Communists' war-time base in Yan'an and later director of the local branch of the Xinhua Daily newspaper. After leaving Yan'an, he ran pro-democracy publications in Chongqing and Hong Kong. His most important work, however, is his fourteen-volume *Chinese Communist Party History and Selected Documents* (*Zhonggong dangshi ji wenxian xuecui*), published in Hong Kong in 1973.

It was in Hong Kong that the deposed party secretary Zhao Ziyang was able to publish his memoirs while under house arrest. Even his successor, Li Peng (or members of his family), published his diary in Hong Kong. Other memoirists recounted their days serving at the top of government, political scientists tried to analyze why Communist China kept regressing back to authoritarianism, and literary scholars wrote about the personal side of the Communist era's traumas. One book told love stories of couples who doggedly refused to be destroyed by labor camps and exile.

This vibrant publishing world began to decline after 2010. A key reason was the government's realization that Chinese people were being poisoned by counter-histories.

That worry began soon after ordinary Chinese people were permitted to travel to Hong Kong in 2003. By 2010, 36 million mainlanders were visiting the territory annually. Many began bringing back books inside China. That year, authorities launched a campaign called "Southern Hill," referring to an imaginary watch post overlooking its troubled southern territory. Chinese nationals returning from Hong Kong were subject to X-ray searches of their luggage. Books were confiscated and people fined. Tour guides were put on notice and instructed to warn visitors not to buy books in the bookstores. Local governments across China began reporting how they were targeting Hong Kong books.

The campaign moved to a new level in the mid-2010s when publishers and booksellers living in Hong Kong began disappearing. The first to vanish was the 72-year-old publisher Yiu Mantin, after making a short visit across the border in 2013. Yiu's Morning Bell Press had published liberal thinkers and writers and was about to release a critical biography of Xi Jinping by the essayist Yu Jie. The next year, Yiu was given a ten-year sentence.

That draconian punishment was followed by a series of detentions and kidnappings. In 2014, two Hong Kong journalists who ran political affairs magazines and had questioned Xi's rise to power were arrested on a visit to Shenzhen. After being detained for more than a year, both men pleaded guilty to operating an illegal business and distributing magazines to relations in the mainland.

Most notorious was the case of five men who were associated with Mighty Current Publishing and its bookstore, Causeway Bay Books.

Chinese agents abducted them, took them across the border, and forced them to confess. All five gave nationally televised confessions. One was Gui Minhai, a Swedish citizen taken from his apartment in Thailand. In 2020, Gui was sentenced to 10 years in prison after he was tried for "providing intelligence overseas."

The government's thinking can be seen in the way Chinese media described the bookstore as a threat to national security. One official party paper said the store "survives by causing trouble in mainland society. It took advantage of the large number of mainlanders entering and leaving Hong Kong after the handover and made itself a prominent source of 'prohibited books' to the mainland. It must be said that it has interfered in the affairs of the mainland in disguise and damaged the major interests of the mainland to maintain harmony and stability."

Until 2020, the effect of these measures was largely self-censorship. Publishing was risky, but legal. But the new national security law meant that it was now illegal.

Universities came under pressure, too. Especially thorny was the Chinese University of Hong Kong's Universities Service Center— the mecca for mainland underground historians. The university essentially eliminated the center but left its books as a separate collection inside the library. Speakers, forums, and independent research projects were terminated. The Folk History Archive was an especially vexing problem. Its collection of hundreds of interviews and articles included memoirs and reminiscences by some of China's best-known public intellectuals. In 2022, the university announced it would no longer service the site, raising the prospect that it could pull the plug at any moment.

Publishers were faced with a more concrete issue: what to do with thousands of books they had published. Even if the booksellers had been closed, many were still in warehouses, being sold quietly or hoping for a change in government policy. Suddenly, it seemed that these books would have to be pulped.

Memory: The Lost Warehouses

In February 2022, a friend sent me an urgent notice on an encrypted messaging app. It was Bao Pu, one of the city's better-known publishers of unofficial histories. His New Century Press once regularly published memoirs by some of China's most important dissidents, thinkers, and activists, as well as photobooks and collections of official documents that challenged the government's account of key events. Since 2019, it had been difficult for him to publish, in part because printers were too afraid to touch his manuscripts. He had tried printing in Taiwan and shipping the books back to Hong Kong, but customs made trouble. After the new National Security Law had been passed in 2020, he had all but given up and was thinking of new projects, and possibly even of moving abroad.

Now there was a more pressing matter: the warehouses where he and other publishers kept their books wanted them to clear out their stock. The titles were so sensitive that even storing them had become a potential violation of the law. The warehouse owners issued an ultimatum: get them out immediately or they would all be pulped. Bao Pu sent me a picture to show the scope of the problem. Long metal bookshelves held thousands of books. All of them had to go.

His request was simple but urgent: would I take a shipment of the books—immediately? A local entrepreneur would pay for the shipments, so cost wasn't a factor. The key was that they would find a worthy home. I had contacts with research libraries; would I help?

I immediately agreed. Six weeks later, my office was filled with 380 banned books--roughly five copies each of seventy-nine books on everything from political reform and memoirs to accounts of famine and love stories about politically persecuted families. My colleague Kathy and I quickly unpacked them and put them on new shelves we had ordered for the occasion.

Sitting there, row on row, the books were an eloquent testament to untold hours spent by Chinese people trying to figure out their country for themselves. These were written by people mostly working on their own time, at night, after years in prison, sometimes in exile, and other times holed up in an apartment under 24-hour surveillance. They had documented, speculated, pondered, and written as best they could. There was no money in this, but they felt compelled to set in words the problems that their country faced.

When people talk about Hong Kong political books, some focus on the handful of racy titles about Xi Jinping's wife or Jiang Zemin's lovers, but these were always outliers. The majority have always been valuable memoirs, efforts to analyze China or to recount forbidden histories. Some were written by former high-ranking political advisors. Others were by relatively ordinary teachers or students caught up in political upheavals. They were what in any open society is part of the normal political discourse—the sorts of books that ought to have been featured in a weekend book review or on a television talk show.

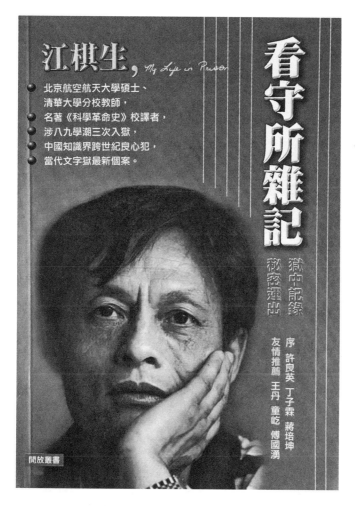

Some were poignant, such as *My Life in Prison* by Jiang Qisheng, an account by a prominent member of the 1989 student demonstrations and later a veteran activist. Like many of these memoirs, it starts out with a photo section: grainy pictures of Jiang's youth, his friendships, the people he met, and a shot of him, older and gaunt. The last chapter is called "My Last Day in Prison," a terrifying account of the uncertainty that his jailers created for him before he finally was released.

Some of these books had covers like small tabloid newspapers, urging readers to look inside with exclamatory headlines and key take-aways. Jiang's book, for example, stated "Records from inside prison" and "Secretly carried out." It featured prefaces written by mothers who had lost their children to the 1989 massacre and blurbs by some of China's best-known activists, including Wang Dan.

As I held it in my hand, I wondered, how on earth could a book like this be pulped? These fragile works had been consigned to the fringes of the empire, and now they were in retreat once again.

I flipped through a book by the late Phuntsog Wangyal Goranangpa, a Tibetan communist who broke with the government and had submitted open letters calling for a fairer policy toward China's minorities. His book, *A Long Way to Equality and Unity*, was published by Bao Pu in Chinese, and in Tibetan by the Khawa Karpo Tibet Culture Centre.

Sometimes, the titles and a blurb were enough to capture the color and verve the authors felt. Explaining the title of his book, *Thick and Black in Zhongnanhai*, Chen Pokong writes, "The Chinese Communists have mastered the traditional dark and secret arts of traditional China." Or Gao Yaojie's *China's AIDS Plague: 10,000 Letters*, in which the Chinese AIDS whistle-blower reflects on the avalanche of letters she received after publishing China's first book on the virus. Another was Dong Fu's *Withered Seedlings and Flowers*, a richly documented account of the Great Famine in western Sichuan by a writer who grew up there. Others included a biography of Mao's third wife, Jiang Qing, and her husbands; an edited volume about people's experience with Chinese security services called *Close Encounters with the Chinese PSB*; and a Festschrift for one of the most influential economic reformers of the 1980s, Chen Yizi, who later was marginalized for opposing the military crackdown on students in 1989.

Eager to ship the books to libraries, I rushed through many of them, but spent a day entranced with *Emotional Traces of the Rightists*, a book that told seventy-two love stories about couples torn apart during the 1950s Anti-Rightist Campaign. I thought of Ai Xiaoming's film *Jiabiangou Elegy*, and how women often traveled thousands of miles to try to save their husbands, or at least give them a proper burial. The book was edited by Zhou Suzi, a scholar of classical Chinese whose husband was sent to a labor camp for twenty years.

Zhou's own story was typical of the other couples' accounts. She and her three daughters traveled by foot from southern China to the Hexi Corridor in hopes of being near him. Later, the four were driven out of the region and walked to the Loess Plateau, where they had prospects of a plot of land. When that didn't work out, they trudged to Hangzhou, the city in south-central China near where she grew up and lived with a relative. Then police drove them out, forcing them to walk more than 1,000 miles back again to the labor camp. The family was eventually reunited after twenty years.

Given the quality of the books, it didn't take long to find them a home. I called up my doctoral advisor at Leipzig University and a professor who ran a program on the legacy of Maoism at Freiburg University. They agreed to take a set each. A few other universities quickly stepped in, too. One set was left, and I decided selfishly to keep it.

Then we began packing up the books and sending them out into the world for more people to discover, until perhaps one day they could be sent back to where they belonged: China.

14

The Land of Hermits

The Zhongnan Mountains once marked the end of the known Chinese world. The name means "southern-most," and its verdant peaks were once the *axis mundi* for Chinese civilization, a pillar linking heaven and earth. That is why for millennia they have been home to Buddhist and Taoist hermits seeking refuge from court intrigues, a place to seek the intersection of eternal and temporal values. But located just south of the imperial capital, Xi'an, they were also close enough to allow the recluses living there to re-enter the secular world at the right moment.

Like underground historians, hermits are often misunderstood as being lone wolves. Many people imagine that they are isolated, each one living atop a mountain, shunning human interaction. Hermits do live apart but are usually within walking distance of each other so they can get help in an emergency. And they do interact with the outside world to buy grains, oil, and other staples that are hard to grow in the mountains. They are alone but networked, and in Chinese society they have always represented one of the most important counterpoints to the world of government politics.

One day I set off to explore these mountains with Jiang Xue. I volunteered to rent a car and drive, but she said an acquaintance wanted to drive us. As I got to know her, I realized that her blunt writing had attracted supporters from China's middle class who try to help her in many small ways. One patron was the man who would be our driver: a senior engineer in the national railway company, and also a devout Buddhist. So one morning at 7:00 AM we set off from Xi'an in his SUV, his stereo playing Miles Davis's "Kind of Blue," and Buddhist prayer beads swinging from his rearview mirror.

Independent thinking has many wellsprings, but in China it is rarely fostered at school. Instead, it usually comes from firsthand experiences—an encounter or event that opens one's eyes. Jiang's awakening involved her grandfather's death. We discussed his story again and then sat quietly in the back seat, watching the mountains rise to meet us as we sped south. Soon we were surrounded by green-clad mountains and rushing streams. The temperature dropped and the clouds gathered overhead as we began to leave the highway for winding back roads.

Our driver was visibly moved by her family story and said he wanted to add something about modern-day utopianism. His job involves building a high-speed version of the mountainous rail lines that cost Tiger Temple and his generation so much. China's bullet train network of twenty-three thousand miles might amaze the world, he said, but most of it operates at a huge loss. He wondered if the money couldn't have been better spent simply improving regular rail service.

"If only journalists like Jiang Xue had more of a voice," he said, "then we could openly discuss what our country needs."

In late 2021, Xi'an became the biggest Chinese city after Wuhan to suffer a lockdown. After allowing the virus to spread unchecked in Wuhan in early 2020, the party had gone to the other extreme by locking down any Chinese city that had even a tiny virus outbreak. Initially this was not so unusual; other countries that could, such as New Zealand and Australia, did the same thing. The fear was that once transmission started, it was hard to stop. Better to slam on the brakes than risk mass outbreaks, jammed hospitals, and serious fatalities among the elderly and immune-compromised. But as effective vaccines became common in 2021, most countries abandoned this policy.

China refused, for reasons that initially made sense. By locking down in 2020 and early 2021, it avoided the mass deaths that had accompanied lax policies in other countries, such as the United States. But as vaccines became available and the rest of the world opened, people began to get frustrated. Known as "zero-Covid," the policy was closely identified with Xi, making it hard for the government to abandon. Through late 2021 and 2022, the message of staying the course continued: the rest of the world was slack, while China was tough but caring.

A problem for Beijing was that variants of the virus were harder to control with lockdowns and border closures, and so they kept recurring. By late 2022, China's 1.4 billion people had been under a collective lockdown for nearly two years, with foreign travel essentially banned; most major flight routes canceled; and business, cultural, and educational ties curtailed. Many outsiders noticed Shanghai's lockdown, which lasted from March to June 2022. That was partly because of its length but also because of Shanghai's stature as China's most cosmopolitan city. Xi'an's lockdown was a few months earlier, starting on 22 December 2021, but in some ways, it was more typical: there were no foreign media in the city to report on it and the 13 million affected suffered in silence—except for the voices of China's underground historians.

As often is the case, the government was good at the military-style side of things: stationing guards in front of compounds, setting up testing sites (in Xi'an's case, a staggering twelves thousand testing stations erected for a one-month lockdown), and spraying neighborhoods with huge clouds of disinfectant—a pointless (and potentially harmful) exercise because the virus is not spread on surfaces.

But as often was the case, Chinese officialdom failed to deal with human-oriented problems—perhaps because these were secondary to the political concern of smashing the virus. Many people reported difficulty finding food and accessing essential medical services. Some people began bicycling or walking toward the Zhongnan Mountains, hoping to break the blockade by walking over them to Wuhan.

Jiang Xue did what she did best: write. In a long essay of about five thousand characters (or roughly six to seven thousand words in English) she described the first ten days of the lockdown. She told of being warned of a lockdown a few hours ahead of time, rushing out to the store, only to find that it was crammed with others who had heard the same rumors. She described the breakdown of online ordering, leaving people dependent on friends and connections to buy food. She spent much time interviewing migrant laborers who live in shacks and dorms, which were now closed. Once, they had depended on cheap takeout meals for food, but these were no longer available.

Just as Ai Xiaoming's father died a collateral death in Wuhan, Jiang Xue wrote about the people with heart attacks who were turned away from hospitals. "In this absurd city, as long as you don't die from the virus, it's not a death."

The section that garnered the most approval—and probably caused her the most political problems—was the description of a friend who had sent her a note repeating a government slogan "Xi'an can only win!" She sent him a note about the man who had the heart attack and left it at that. But then she felt she had to add something more blunt:

"'Xi'an can only win' is typical boastful, clichéd, and empty talk. Another one is 'we must spare no cost.' These kinds of words sound good but in reality, every ordinary person has to ask themselves if they are the 'we" (making the decision to spare no cost) or if they are the cost that has to be paid."

The piece had a huge impact. It was posted on 3 January 2022, and lasted five days before censors took it down. In that time, I watched the piece gain two hundred thousand readers. It was compared to Fang Fang's *Wuhan Diary*, in part because of its moderate tone. Her empathy is with the people and their suffering. She only indirectly called out the government.

When it was pulled, the nationalist blogger Hu Xijin, who once edited the government-run tabloid *Global Times*, said that he didn't agree with all of her points but it should have been allowed to stand. Its impact was big enough to merit an entry in the Chinese-language edition of Wikipedia (which is banned in China). Jiang Xue told me that she was later called in to public security for three meetings because of it. She began to wonder how much longer she could hold on as an independent journalist. Her daughter was attending high school in Canada. She began to plan to visit her to get a break from China.

Jiang Xue had posted her piece on the WeChat public account called *mocun gewu*, or "Silent Observer." The name itself is a small expression of dissent. *Mocun* can be translated as "silent" but it is best known as meaning the soul leaving an immobile body and wandering to other lands. It stems from the Taoist classic *Liezi*, where a king sits at a banquet. A magician takes him to other realms. After what seems like ages have passed, the king returns to the banquet, wakes up, and asks his retainers what has happened. They say he has simply sat there silently (*mocun*) for a few moments. And so the term has been glossed to mean sitting silently while one's spirit travels far—a metaphor for Chinese society.

Immediately after Jiang Xue's article was posted, the "Silent Observer" account was closed for violating internet regulations. Shortly after, the account was relaunched as "New Silence" and resumed with an article by the well-known writer Zhang Shiping, who goes by the pen name Ye Fu. He has written numerous essays and short stories about the brutal early years of Communist rule in western Hunan province and now lives in exile in the Thai city of Chiangmai. His essay was a meditation on the *jianghu*—the honorable bandits and rogues of the backwoods who had become a symbol for Chinese people with a conscience.

Ye Fu noted how hard it is to translate *jianghu* into English and made his own suggestion: "where there are brothers." Ye Fu meant it in a broader sense of any people, male or female, who band together against the establishment. Such people do not talk too much about their work; they just do it. And when they need help, they call on allies, who give aid without asking a question. Think of Zhang Zhan arriving in Wuhan at the start of the virus. Whom did she call? Ai Xiaoming, who put her up until she could get her bearings. That is the *jianghu*.

Ye Fu added that the *jianghu* in today's China are under siege. In the past, it was compromised or organizations, such as temples' self-help associations that helped people band together—in other words, the *jianghu* was part of civil society.

"In today's mainland China, what the imperial court wants is that all corners of the land revere its orthodoxy, and for that it must crush civil society. The tangible *jianghu* has long ceased to exist, but in the hearts of the people the *jianghu* continues unbroken."

We stopped at a temple in the mountains. It is dominated by a fourteen hundred -year-old gingko tree that each autumn covers the courtyard in a cloak of golden leaves. We had lunch with the abbot, a gregarious host who served us a ten-course vegetarian meal along with locally grown tea.

Across the Zhongnan Mountains, the government had been on a demolition campaign. It had torn down illegal villas, hermit huts, and extensions to temples. The demolitions were part of a move against corrupt building practices but also in line with efforts to bring all religions more firmly under government control. The campaign is aimed primarily at Islam and Christianity, which the government sees as troublingly political. And yet all faiths have a social or political component. Over the past century, for example, a movement called "humanistic Buddhism" has encouraged followers to address problems in society rather than retreating into pietism.

The abbot confirmed the demolitions. As a show of good faith, he had ordered that newly built toilets in his temple be torn down. The abbot was friendly but smooth and practiced. His was a government temple and he was not about to pick a quarrel with the government—what was the point? Were his toilets really illegal? No; he had applied for permission and obtained most of them, but as is often the case in China some were missing. So he admitted them to authorities and offered the toilets as a sacrifice. Better to be safe and make a token effort to appease the higher-ups.

Normally, no one would have cared about hermit huts and temple toilets, but high politics were involved. The tear-down campaign was meant to implicate the provincial party secretary, who was about to be deposed. In this context, it made good sense for the abbot to show

that he was a team player. He could later reapply for more permits and
have the toilets rebuilt. None of us could blame him.

There were other ways of dealing with the state. After lunch we drove
two hours to a small rushing river. We crossed over a simple steel
bridge to what looked like an abandoned logging camp. The entrance
was guarded by an enormous boulder emblazoned with a six-foot-
high character *wu*—"realize," or "awaken"—painted in red. Next to
it were four smaller characters, *fo huo mao peng*, "Buddha protects the
Thatched Hut," referring to a hermit's home. Across the street was
another boulder with four characters, *a mi tuo fu*, or Amitabha, the
great savior Buddha. This was the work of someone who had the
means—or, more likely, the devoted followers—to mark the entrance
to his refuge in grand style.

Inside, the hermit's limited resources were more apparent. We drove
down a small road of broken-down sheds and simple brick buildings.

One of the few in working order was inhabited by the hermit, who was dressed in dark yellow padded cotton clothes against the chill and damp. His feet were clad in Chinese army surplus boots made of padded cotton with rubber-capped toes against the mud. He was 70 years old, his head shaven, his smile calm and permanent. . He had lived in the Zhongnan Mountains for ten years and in this hut for five.

His formal education had ended in middle school, but he was widely read and enjoyed discussing philosophy. The week before, a group of students from the country's two most famous universities, Peking and Tsinghua, had come to stay for a week, to hear him talk and to climb in the mountains.

The American translator, writer, and Buddhist scholar Bill Porter—whose book on the hermits of the Zhongnan Mountains was translated into Chinese, turning him into a celebrity in China—makes an important point about hermits. He calls being a hermit "spiritual graduate school." It only makes sense for people who have already served time in a temple and who know the basics. Only then is it possible to gain the savvy, and the spiritual sustenance, to survive the winter.

Jiang Xue led most of the conversation, sometimes translating the hermit's heavy Shaanxi accent into more standard Mandarin. We talked about his choices in life.

"There are a lot of rules and regulations in a temple: what to do, when to pray. That's fine, but it's also noisy. There are too many people, even when there are no tourists. When you have to find your own food, and kindling, it's different. That's a kind of spiritual cultivation too. After you've taken your vows, you should live in a temple to learn everything. You need to know rules and ceremonies. After you've learned that you can go out to the mountains."

He said people always want to know what it's like to be a hermit, which reminded me of how people often ask underground historians like Jiang Xue or Ai Xiaoming what it's like to be on the outside of society. What is it like to run the risk of angering people and alienating family and friends? Ai's brother was supportive but distant. I thought of Jiang Xue's father, who was proud of her but begged her to avoid overtly political themes. Another similar question that hermits get is how to survive financially, a worry Jiang Xue faces all the time.

"If you want to understand hermits it's not easy," the old man said, as Jiang Xue nodded gravely. "You can meet people. That's easy. But you have to live with monks and nuns to understand them. Superficially you can learn, but it's like you're looking at a closed door. Only when you open it can you get inside the circle."

Earlier in the day, I had asked Jiang Xue what it was about Buddhism that inspired her. She took my notebook and wrote out a verse :

> The great wish of the Dizang Bodhisattva
> Is if hell isn't empty
> It won't become a Buddha
> Only when all beings are liberated
> Will it realize Enlightenment.

"The meaning," she said, "is that this Bodhisattva won't achieve Buddhahood until hell is empty, but hell will never be empty. But it persists in trying, even though it's impossible. It's a bit like the myth of Sisyphus."

Was her life so hopeless? She took a breath and thought of the people she had worked with in Xi'an.

"It's like [Chen] Hongguo. What hope is there of succeeding? It won't have an immediate impact on society. He can be detained or thrown out, like Tiger Temple was in Beijing. But they still go out and do it. In my eyes, whether it's Liu Xiaobo [the deceased Chinese Nobel Prize Laureate] or the 709 lawyers [the civil rights activists named after the month and day they were detained in 2015], their spirit is a Bodhisattva's spirit. They know what the outcome will be, but they still do it."

Our visit to the temples had forced us to leave the bridges and tunnels that slice through the Zhongnan Mountains, turning them from a cosmological center point of the Chinese world to another of China's endless mountain ranges that had to be blasted into submission. Packed with cars heading to and from Xi'an, the highways rumbled above us while we crawled along the byways below. It felt as if we were lost, with China racing ahead and people like Jiang Xue left behind.

She told me she hears this all the time: what she is doing is romantic or interesting but pointless. She heard it again recently from a friend who had been a prominent journalist in southern China. In his day, he had been an outspoken advocate of civil society. He had penned fiery editorials calling for its establishment. He had set up conferences promoting it.

Then he was hauled in for questioning and sent to jail. His cellmates were drug dealers and hardened criminals. That had been his *wu*—his spiritual awakening. It had been a scare tactic and it had worked. After his release a few months later, he fled to Hong Kong and then made his way to the United States. He was now trying to make ends meet running a restaurant.

Jiang Xue met him on a trip to New York. He was polite but questioned her work. He told her that it might have a moral value but practically it was irrelevant. The best one can do is survive and fight another day. She told me this quietly, her voice trailing off. Then she stopped. She gathered herself and spoke with surprising finality:

"But I disagree," she said. "It matters if you try. I want to be a normal person in an abnormal society.

"I want to be able to say truthful things and express what's in my heart."

15

Conclusion

Learning to Walk Underground

This book starts with a quote by Hannah Arendt, which might seem odd for a work on 21st-century China—except that it was used in an article by Jiang Xue. She was profiling wives of human rights lawyers and started the piece with Arendt's question. I was struck by how the lines applied to anyone working for change in China today: is their work pointless, or trailblazing? The light of a candle, or a blazing sun?

Arendt's quote is especially apt because it is open-ended. It doesn't imply that people working for change in dark times are bound to win because good always trumps evil, or some other dubious cliché. It doesn't give us the easy answer. But the implication is clear: in dark times, light is precious; it always matters.

For people who see China as hopelessly authoritarian—and this is by far the dominant view in many countries today—they will note the troubles faced by the individuals I profile. They will point out that Ai Xiaoming is barred from leaving China, while Jiang Xue, as of writing this conclusion in 2023, had left the country to visit her daughter in Canada and possibly to work abroad. The Hong Kong publishers have been shut down and their books scattered across the globe. And during the Covid lockdowns, people rose up in more than twenty cities across China—Wuhan, Xi'an, Shanghai, Beijing—including young people, workers, and the elderly. They helped hasten the end of the government's draconian policies. But at the end of it all, Xi still ruled China with an iron fist and many demonstrators were detained. It is easy to argue that the leviathan has won.

And yet this would be a selective reading of these people's lives or the history of this seventy-five-year movement. Ai Xiaoming is under close watch but still works on projects. So does Tiger Temple. Chen Hongguo from the Xi'an debating space I Know I Know Nothing offers online lectures. The journal *Remembrance* still publishes regularly and circulates broadly. Jiang Xue still writes, and her articles are still widely read in China. People repeatedly find opportunities to bypass censors and publish trenchant critiques of China's authoritarian system. They write diaries and articles that attract large audiences. They are shut down. But they return, again and again, just as they and their forebears have for seventy-five years.

I do not mean to offer false optimism but the realism of someone who has spent more than twenty years inside China since the mid-1980s, including all of the 2010s, when Xi took power and implemented his vision of a strong state. Control has never been this tight for so long since at least the 1970s. These *are* dark times.

What this book shows, however, is a movement that is not defeated. China's new, more muscular authoritarianism has given these groups its best shot. It has launched its broadsides. It has shut down journals, closed publishers, hounded filmmakers, jailed freethinkers, and put countless others under mind-numbing house arrest.

But now it sits there, as its leader ages and its economy slows, facing people who are conditioned to see defeat as merely temporary. Ai Xiaoming, Jiang Xue, Chen Hongguo, Tan Hecheng, Wu Di: they see themselves as heirs to the unofficial "wild" historians of past ages, the sworn brothers and sisters of the *jianghu* who know that many will fall but that their ranks will be replenished. They *know* they will win, not individually and not immediately, but someday. In essence, the Chinese Communist Party's enemies are not these individuals but the lasting values of Chinese civilization: righteousness, loyalty, freedom of thought. As strong as the party is, is it stronger than these deep reservoirs of resilience?

This applies not just to the Xi era but also to the nearly seventy-five-year history of the People's Republic of China. The fact that people still resist and do so in a more coordinated form than at any time in the past, seems more significant than the banal point that an authoritarian regime is authoritarian. The fact is that independent thought lives in China. It has not been crushed.

This raises two fundamental questions: what does this say about China's trajectory, and what does it mean for how outsiders approach the country?

For China's future, the clearest implication is that state control does have limits. China's surveillance state is real, but it is not able to completely crush independent activists who avail themselves of digital technology. This is not because the state is constrained by laws or a conscience but that it lacks the ability to eliminate this movement.

This is not for lack of trying. Control of history has been one of Xi Jinping's top priorities since taking power in 2012. Think of the visit to the National Museum of History immediately upon taking power, his statement a year later on the need to abide by the Communist Party's version of history, and his repeated pronouncements identifying history with the party's very existence. There is also his 2021 resolution on party history, a hugely significant recounting of the Chinese Communist Party's myth-like history—only the third time in the party's history that it has felt a need to assert itself in this fashion. And after Xi's apogee at the Twentieth Party Congress in 2022, his first visit was to the Communists' mythic base area of Yan'an.

These are clear statements of concern which have been followed up with concrete measures. As an example, consider the great counter-history journal *China Through the Ages*. This was one of the most influential publications in writing the true history of the People's Republic. It was founded in 1991 with the support of a liberal general in the People's Liberation Army, and publicly supported by one of Mao's personal secretaries, as well as by Xi Jinping's father. And yet it was shuttered in 2016. If the state did not feel threatened, why would it take the remarkable step of closing a publication endorsed by Xi's own father?

But desire does not mean ability. *China Through the Ages* could be closed because it was, to use a cliché from the world of business, a legacy bricks-and-mortar organization. It had a staff, an office, files, and it was sold through legal channels. You could subscribe to it through the post office or buy it at a newsstand in even a provincial city. That gave it huge reach, but also made it vulnerable. Once its license was pulled and its offices occupied, it died. Similarly, the state could close the Hong Kong publishers because they also were traditional businesses.

Such measures do not work as well for most of China's underground historians. It is possible on an individual basis to harass people to the point that they can't work. If someone had tailed Tan Hecheng day and night for three decades, he never could have researched the party's genocidal policies in Hunan. Likewise, Hu Jie, Ai Xiaoming, Jiang Xue, and others. But if they are even just a little bit free, they start interviewing, and then all they need is a computer and a data connection to mount their challenge. The cyber revolution that is meant to make China a digital superpower also enables resistance to persist.

Stopping these people from working requires an inordinate commitment of resources. It is not the same as an operation to close down a magazine. It means deploying scores of agents 24/7 for *each person* who has to be stopped. That can be done during sensitive periods, such as around a party congress. And it can be done indefinitely to a few hundred people. But China has thousands of people contributing to this movement. It can't be done to all of them all the time. And when dissatisfaction grows, and a wider population is mobilized, the state can become overwhelmed.

This battle is already exacting a steep toll on the state. Most estimates are that the money spent on China's domestic intelligence services rivals the national defense budget, with each accounting for 10 percent of government expenditures. With most of the budget—as with most countries—tied up in non-discretionary spending, the huge outlay on domestic intelligence prevents the government from investing in other priorities that are critical to people's well-being and to China's rise on the global stage.

And this is just the financial cost. Cracking down on dissent and rewriting history is a priority for every government official at every level, from Xi to a county boss. They hold countless meetings on the topic and instruct personnel across the bureaucracy—not just the security apparatus—to mobilize in its service. This colossal waste of time diverts the state from more pressing tasks.

One example is the Covid-19 pandemic. It demonstrated that China lacks hospital beds, rural clinics, and stocks of medication. Other underfunded priorities include rural education, unemployment insurance, and elderly care. Instead of an unstoppable juggernaut, the Chinese state begins to resemble East Germany, which was hobbled by huge outlays on its Stasi security apparatus.

Some people ask if this movement is analogous to the Soviet-era historical group Memorial, which won a Nobel Peace Prize for uncovering the abuses of the Stalin era and undermining Soviet rule. For now, I would say no, because we are not at the same phase in China's development—or, better, in the regime's decay—as the USSR was in the 1980s. The Chinese Communist Party is still vigorous and the economy strong enough that the state can still shout down China's underground historians.

But prosperity is not inevitable. For any country, it requires constant self-reflection and an ability to think up new solutions to new problems. The Chinese Communist Party's ability to do so is open to question, especially when we consider its decade-long aversion to meaningful economic reform and its failure to build a top-ranked education system for non-elites.

As these tensions begin to affect ordinary people—by limiting job growth, wage increases, and their country's standing in the world— they could create conditions where alternative viewpoints are more welcome. This would make the unrest during the Covid lockdowns less an outlier than a harbinger for future decades. And so, while China is not the 1980s Soviet Union, in some very broad sense it might be closer to the 1960s Soviet Union, a period when it seemed stable and powerful but when the seeds of the regime's sclerosis were planted. If so, the kinds of people we have met in this book will play ever-larger roles in China's future.

In terms of how outsiders should approach China, the vibrancy of China's counter-history movement should force us to retire certain clichéd ways of seeing China. One is the tendency to see it as nothing more than an example of out-of-control authoritarianism. That might be accurate for describing the Chinese Communist Party, but China's counter-historians are in fact part of global conversations over how we approach our past and create our future.

In the United States, for example, the descendants of enslaved Africans have confronted the fact that the historical record offers little about the horrors of slavery. In the archives, the enslaved person's voice is absent. People such as the Columbia University professor Saidiya Hartman have become academic superstars by filling in these gaps. Hartman's method is to use facts as a foundation for fictionalized stories that try to tell this erased past. This allows her to reach hugely different groups in society, from rappers to politicians.

In China the fundamental issue is similar: huge gaps exist that make it hard to *feel* the crises of years past. We have few biographies of the landholders killed in the early 1950s. And likewise, we have few images of famine in 1950s China. To make the situation in China even more extreme, the archive isn't just sparse; it is off limits.

That's forced writers and artists such as Fang Fang and Hu Jie to fill in the gap through deeply researched novels and artworks. What

Hartman calls "critical fabulation" can be seen in Fang Fang's *Soft Burial*: a recovery of memory based on historical research and leaps of imagination.

Another way to deal with erasure is found in the work of Gao Hua, who created his own personal counter-archive of papers, dossiers, and documents. Based on this immense trove of material, Gao was able to write a definitive history of the Chinese Communist Party's first major purge, challenging the party's mythic founding years in Yan'an.

Another trend in China that has echoes elsewhere is the need for what the Vietnamese-American writer Việt Thanh Nguyen calls "just memory." This means a history that includes multiple perspectives—and not just the victor's. This desire to include multiple voices is exactly what Chinese counter-historians achieve in their works.

Finally, Chinese underground historians share another realization that has gained great currency around the world. This is the idea that trauma exists even when memories are suppressed. The German-British writer W. G. Sebald calls this "secondhand memories," a concept similar to Marianne Hirsch's "postmemory." This comes to the fore especially in China's ethnic minority areas.

The only major difference between the concerns of China's underground historians and their better-known overseas counterparts is that China's largely avoid jargon. People like Ai Xiaoming and Guo Yuhua are familiar with the Western writings on their fields, and in Guo's case her ethnographic work is informed by academic discourses on suffering. But by and large they are more blunt and more concrete than the writings of those who operate mainly in the academy.

One reason might be that the stakes are higher in China. Some Western academics—Hartman and Nguyen, for example—have broad readerships. But by and large most write for other specialists and their ideas circulate only narrowly. China's underground historians consciously aim for the masses. They add to the historical record with new information and accounts, but their goal is action—they are, unapologetically, activists who seek to change society. Western academics might see themselves in the same light, too, but for Chinese public intellectuals it is an existential question. If Western academics fail, they are ignored. If Chinese thinkers fail, they go to jail and sometimes die there.

Thinking of Chinese underground historians as part of our intellectual world also helps us think of ways to include them in our lives. One of the great debates in many countries is with whom in China should we talk? One answer would be to meet the sorts of people described in this book. They should be invited to speak at our film festivals, think tanks, universities, libraries, bookstores, and other public forums. They should be shoo-ins for fellowships and scholarships.

This happens too infrequently. Part of it is ignorance, part of it is language, and part of it is politics. The first two are related: the fact that China's underground historians rarely speak English means that only the most atypical or exceptional Chinese thinkers are known abroad. For most, their books and articles are rarely published overseas, and many have trouble communicating in English. That means they are underrepresented as visiting fellows at prestigious universities and think tanks, and rarely speak at book fairs.

Commercially, it is hard to make an argument that these works will find wide audiences. Some works, such as those by Tan Hecheng and Yang Jisheng, have been commercially published but only because the translation costs were picked up by foundations. Others, such as the works of Hu Fayun and Ye Fu, have been translated by A. E. Clark of Ragged Banner Press in what only can be described as a labor of love. And then there is the admirable work of David Ownby of the University of Montréal, whose "Reading the China Dream" website translates the work of many public intellectuals—most of it translated by Ownby on his own time and only after he received tenure, allowing him to devote time to a task that gets little academic recognition. Unfortunately, these efforts remain exceptions.

One solution would be to encourage more private foundations to translate Chinese nonfiction. Foundations, however, are driven by a market-style ethos requiring them to have a measurable "output" that will effect some sort of measurable change—in other words, they want to fund projects that will train a certain number of civil society leaders or lawyers, establish non-governmental organizations, and so on. A Chinese book translated into English is rarely regarded as adequate output. Perhaps it is time to question these self-defeating priorities.

Films are even trickier. Most of them are subtitled, but many of China's underground documentaries are not released in a conventional manner—for example, during a specific year or season timed to attract film festival awards. Hu Jie, for instance, often uploads his films to YouTube and then continues to rework them over several years. That makes it hard to determine exactly when the film was released and whether a film festival can consider it as current. He and other Chinese filmmakers want their films to be freely available for Chinese people to download, further complicatingthe aim of festivals to sell tickets. Despite these problems, it strikes me as remarkable that people like Ai Xiaoming and Hu Jie have made dozens of documentary films and yet are not the subject of retrospectives.

One reason might have to do with aesthetics. The director Wang Bing, who made a film on Jiabiangou, is represented by a French art gallery and is considered an arthouse director. The others I have discussed in this book, however, have not made it into this rarefied circle. This might be simply due to bad luck but possibly also because their work is seen as too "journalistic," whereas most foreign film festivals prefer aestheticized works.

And then of course there is the issue of politics. In years past, foreign film festivals were venues in which non-mainstream Chinese filmmakers could obtain an audience. But those opportunities have rarely existed for underground films and have shrunk in recent years. As some studies have shown, some foreign festivals are unwilling to invite independent Chinese documentarians because the festivals depend on films made in or financed by China.

Cumulatively, this lack of engagement with Chinese critical think-ers hurts our own priorities. We often bemoan the lack of interest in China among young people. Fewer and fewer study Chinese or go there to study. Having these sorts of inspiring people come for resi-dencies, to mentor, and to lecture—rather than as refugees when they are at the end of their rope—would expose our societies to the living traditions of Chinese civilization.

I structured this book as moving from past to present to future. The last chapters (on the virus, borderlands, and hermit-like strategies of survival) indicate ways that this movement is likely to develop. Let me discuss these shifts in a bit more detail, especially because they point to future changes in the movement

One important shift is that its center of gravity has partially moved abroad. With the destruction of Hong Kong as a safe haven, Taiwan seemed like the next logical base for Chinese public intellectuals. The island is predominantly ethnic Chinese, and most people speak Mandarin Chinese. It is also a bastion of traditional Chinese culture and values, and features thriving religious communities, a vibrant press, and an independent publishing scene.

But Taiwan's importance is limited. Although Kuomintang of-ficials from the mainland once ruled Taiwan, several generations have now passed. As China has become more authoritarian, many young Taiwanese want to cut ties with China and are uninterested in its battles. They look inward for their identity and not across the Taiwan Straits. Some dream of formal independence from the main-land. Others see themselves as having more in common with island nations in the region, such as Japan, the Philippines, and Indonesia. And some Taiwanese politicians seem wary of antagonizing China by offering visas or refuge to Chinese intellectuals. This could change, but so far Taiwan has not been central to Chinese thinkers and dissidents seeking an overseas base. Many visit, but most end up elsewhere.

Instead, opposition has centered in North America and Europe, where local Chinese communities, foundations, and universities are more likely to support their work. In the past, this sort of exile meant irrelevancy. Few things were more sobering than to see how important dissidents, such as Wei Jingsheng, became marginalized once they left China. Some latched onto extremist ideas and became cranks.

Some of this might be an inevitable form of culture shock for people who lived their lives battling authoritarianism and suddenly found themselves cast into societies with few boundaries. But some previous generations of exiles might not have been able to plug back into China. The new generation of critical thinkers is better able to use digital technologies to stay in conversation with people inside China. We saw this in the Covid lockdowns, when people in China posted videos to Twitter or YouTube as a way to preserve the material they had created, allowing others in China to download it, repackage it, and post it on Chinese social media.

This reached a high point during the "blank paper" protests in late 2022, when protesters held up blank sheets of paper as a way of protesting censorship. During this remarkable outpouring of anger and grief, Twitter and Instagram became a marshaling yard for digital resistance, with people in China simultaneously posting to it and drawing from it. It showed once again how even though relatively few people in China have VPN technology, only a small percentage needs to access the uncensored internet for this action to have an impact back inside China.

This is how Jiang Xue has continued to find an audience. Her article on New Year's Day 2023 was posted on a site banned in China (www.ngocn2.org), but readers simply converted it to a photographic image known by its file-name suffix, .jpeg. These can more easily be posted on Chinese social media because they are the equivalent of posting an image, making it harder for blocking software to read the file and pick out sensitive words and phrases. These techniques will probably become dated and should not be romanticized as a panacea for avoiding censorship. But it is hard to ignore how underground historians keep finding ways to reach Chinese audiences during critical times of national debate.

In a way, underground historians can be seen as pioneers for techniques used by broader parts of the population during crises. Just as the underground historians have used VPNs to post videos or publish abroad, so too did a surprising number of the 2022 protests opposing Covid lockdowns. Their ability to do so shows that bypassing the firewall isn't something limited to just a few people with special means but is easily done—if there is a perceived need to do so.

A parallel change in the movement is a more inward orientation, with many counter-historians treating their work as time capsules. People like Tiger Temple and Ai Xiaoming know that their works will probably never be freely aired in China in their lifetimes. But they continue in the belief that their work will matter in the future. They want future Chinese to know that in the 2020s, when things had never been darker, Chinese people inside China did not yield to comfort or fear. They kept interviewing, at the very least to get on the record the victims of Chinese Communist Party rule before these people passed away. But also so that Chinese people in the future would see that in this era there were Sima Qians and Su Dongpos. Not everyone had given in.

Stepping back a moment, it is useful to put this in a broader historical context. When the Chinese Communist Party took over China, it ruled with an awesome totalitarian terror. Think of the students in Tianshui in 1960. They thought of themselves as a single spark that could light a prairie fire. That became the name of their magazine, but over the next decades that spark almost went out as it lay buried in a vault.

Forty years later, *Spark* was rediscovered by counter-historians, digitized, and put online. That made it, as we saw in chapter 7, move from "stored memory" to "functional memory." In other words, it moved from being an artifact in a storage room to an object on display where it can inspire people living today.

Of course, the people profiled in these pages will grow old, die, possibly be arrested, or fade away. But if the history of this movement has taught us anything, it is that it has grown with time, despite setbacks. We can look at individual battles and see defeat. But we can also see an endless cycle of creation, of new sparks that leap off the flint of history every time it is struck.

It seems fitting to end this book with the story of how one of the most influential underground history journals has survived the Xi Jinping era. I first met the editors of *Remembrance* in 2013, just after Xi took power. Since then, important journals have been closed down. But *Remembrance* has continued to publish. Some of that is due to moving some editing work overseas. The journal now has a print version with an ISBN number so it can be sold to libraries and interested people. But the writers and some of the editors are still based in China. This makes *Remembrance* another example of the cross-fertilization apparent in the 2022 Covid protests: material is collected in China and given a platform overseas where it is safe from censorship but still can be accessed by a significant number of people inside China.

I wondered what the editing staff thought. By this time, I was no longer living in China and couldn't just take the subway up to Tiantongyuan to see Wu Di. I was also concerned about writing him directly, so I wrote the publishers in the United States.

A few weeks later I received a reply with a PDF titled *fanjiao Jiaozi Zhang*: "Please deliver to Dumpling Zhang." I smiled: my Chinese family name is Zhang and during my visits to the magazine's offices we would often make dumplings, with Wu Di acting as my instructor. The letter was unsigned but written in Wu's typically humorous style and dated 20 February 2022.

Over the past few years, the statement said, historical work has become difficult. So the magazine has a policy: "In order to grow far and long, do not become big and strong." In other words, in order to survive, the journal does not try to become too large-scale. Specifically, the journal has rededicated itself to studies of the Cultural Revolution and avoided more current research. Second, articles must be edited to avoid straying into unwanted territory. Third, the journal never charges so as to avoid the claim of "illegal business operations," which was used to close down other underground historians.

The rest of the statement is a colorful parody of a classic Chinese novel, where chapters often end with a promise of more to come. It seems fitting to leave the last word to these true underground historians:

> *After more than ten years of experience,* Remembrance *has learned a few things. First, it knows how to shrink its body like Swallow Li San.** *Over the past decade it has been able to disappear, to grow and to shrink. When in danger, it becomes tiny and runs away by pretending to stop publishing and distributing only to a few hard-core fans. When the crisis is over, it makes a comeback and publishes widely.*
>
> *Later, it learned "earth walking skills" from [the god] Nazha in* The Investiture of the Gods.† *With this spell, no firewall can hold it, for it can walk underground.*
>
> *This causes headaches for officials, but they have no way to catch it because it is based overseas. Even cultural agents and red spies can't grab it. And its editors are good at keeping secrets (something they learned from the party's own underground work).*
>
> *If you want to know what happens next, please await the next installment.*

---

* Swallow Li San is a Chinese folk hero who robbed from the rich and gave to the poor. He could shrink in size to escape, leaving behind only a small paper swallow.

† *The Investiture of the Gods* is a collection of myths and stories about Chinese deities. Nazha is one of its main heroes. He learned to walk under the earth's surface and appear in different places to confuse his enemies.

Appendix: Exploring China's Underground History

For those looking to read original sources, I recommend the China Unofficial Archives, a Chinese-English online resources set up by people interested in preserving the remarkable output of Chinese historians over the past seventy-five years. Its URL is www.minjian-danganguan.org. It includes articles, open-source books, movies, and short videos. I have included English-language introductions to many of these works and, when possible, links to English translations.

For English speakers, I offer below a selective list of other books, articles, videos, and movies that you might want to read or watch yourself. None of this is by any means complete and I'd welcome any feedback, which you can send to me via the contact page of my personal website, www.ian-johnson.com.

A. Films and Videos

There are two main sources to see many of the films discussed in this book. One is through commercial distribution companies and the other is through YouTube, which Chinese directors often use as a way to make their films public.

1. dGenerate and Icarus Films

dGenerate Films is the most prominent distributor of independent Chinese cinema. Most easily accessible are those that its distribution partner, Icarus Films, has made available. Most relevant to this book are the films of Hu Jie, a full list of which are found in this book's bibliography. I would start with his classic trilogy: *Searching for Lin Zhao's Soul, Though I Am Gone,* and *Spark.*

2. YouTube

Many other filmmakers use YouTube. The bibliography lists several films of Ai Xiaoming and Tiger Temple (Zhang Shihe) found on that platform. Sometimes films are taken down or the URL changes. In that case, I would suggest searching for the film by title. If I find that films are disappearing, I will consider hosting some of the films on minjian-danganguan.com.

To get a start, I recommend Ai Xiaoming's "Central Plains" and "Jiabiangou Elegy" and Zhang Shihe's short film "Pursuing One of the Sparks."

In addition, to get an idea of the stories and scope of this movement, I strongly recommend visiting the site of the Chinese Independent Film archive, https://www.chinaindiefilm.org/, which describes what is probably the most important collection of Chinese independent films at Newcastle University.

B. Books

1. *Wuhan Diary: Dispatches from a Quarantined City* by Fang Fang. A classic account of the Wuhan lockdown.
2. *How the Red Sun Rose: The Origins and Development of the Yan'an Rectification Movement* by Gao Hua. A challenging work because of its length and detail, but a standard reference work detailing Mao's violent use of history. Gao's introduction explains how he came to write the book.
3. *In Search of My Homeland* by Gao Ertai. A very readable account of life in the Jiabiangou labor camp and life in the World Heritage Site Dunhuang caves during Mao's China.

4. *Blood Letters: The Untold Story of Lin Zhao, a Martyr in Mao's China* by Lian Xi. It's hard to recommend too strongly this classic account of one of the writers for the 1960 magazine *Spark*. Lin's life story is incredibly powerful, and Professor Lian tells it well.

5. *The Killing Wind: A Chinese County's Descent into Madness during the Cultural Revolution* by Tan Hecheng. Expertly translated and edited by Stacy Mosher and Guo Jian, this is a bit of a challenging work due to its length. But this or *How the Red Sun Rose* gives a sense of the ambition, scope, and professionalism of China's underground historians.

6. *The Silent Majority* by Wang Xiaobo. Translated by Eric Abrahamsen. An absolutely important essay that offers ideas that lie at the heart of the underground history movement. It is available online for free at https://media.paper-republic. org/files/09/04/The_Silent_Majority_Wang_Xiaobo.pdf.

7, *Golden Age* by Wang Xiaobo. A ribald, hilarious, great novel. Written by an outsider who challenges the political system and its cultural lackeys, it is a testament to the power of literature to test the state's narrative.

8. *Soft Burial* by Fang Fang. A deeply researched and very readable example of how historical fiction can be used to fill in the holes of China's censored archives. It has been translated and is due to be published in the coming years. Watch for it!

9. *Hard Road Home* by Ye Fu. This is a collection of short stories by a member of a Chinese ethnic minority, the Tujia. Published by Ragged Banner Press, a New York state–based publisher of underground fiction (http://www.raggedbanner. com/index.html). Ye Fu is a popular underground writer in China and lives in exile in Thailand. His works often touch on forgotten or erased histories in remote parts of the country, using them as meditation on larger issues, such as cruelty and justice.

10. *Such Is This World* by Hu Fayun. Likewise published by Ragged Banner Press, Hu's book was an online sensation for

its light fictionalization of the SARS epidemic. Its themes seem even more relevant now. Hu currently lives in Vienna with his second wife but keeps a home in Wuhan.

11. *Tombstone: The Great Chinese Famine, 1958–1962* and *The World Turned Upside Down: A History of the Cultural Revolution*, both by Yang Jisheng. Like Gao Hua's *Red Sun*, both of Yang's books are edited and translated by the duo of Mosher and Guo. Both also use primary archives and interviews to explain the two most notorious events in the history of the People's Republic. Unfortunately, these archives are now closed, and Yang (b. 1940) has largely retired from writing. Still, it would be amiss to omit them from this list as they are hugely ambitious and influential works.

3. Articles

Almost all the articles cited in this book are in Chinese. For a start, I recommend the articles by Jiang Xue listed in the bibliography. I use the Internet Archive addresses to avoid dead links. Machine translating the pieces in your browser (for example: Google Translate has a browser extension that allows this) is far from ideal, but it will give a flavor of the works.

Acknowledgments

This book was the result of more than twenty years of thinking and writing about China, making it impossible to do justice to everyone who contributed to it. Let me first, however, salute several benefactors.

First, thanks to the National Endowment for the Humanities for making me a Public Scholars grantee. This is a generous grant, and its application process helped me hone my ideas. It was also a lifesaver in 2020, when I was expelled from China and suddenly had to find new sources of income. Thanks also to the Robert B. Silvers Foundation for making me an inaugural grantee in 2019. This was extremely meaningful because Bob Silvers, who had been editor of the *New York Review of Books* before passing away in 2017, had been such a staunch supporter. I also want to thank the Pulitzer Center on Crisis Reporting, which gave me several travel grants.

As a freelance writer based in China, I could not have survived without regular outlets for my work. Thanks again to the *New York Review*, especially Bob, his successor Ian Buruma, and his successor Emily Greenhouse. Michael Shae was also a constantly inquisitive and thoughtful editor. Another editor there, Hugh Eakin, founded what was then quaintly known as the review's "blog," which he and his successor, Matt Seaton, developed into a vital part of the magazine. In 2010 Hugh gave me the green light to start what has now turned into a thirty-part series of Q&A interviews with Chinese thinkers (which still enjoys a dedicated page on the *Review*'s website). This series planted the seed of this book, helping me to realize the importance of history to China's public intellectuals and introducing me to some of China's most remarkable people.

I also benefited greatly from writing for the *New York Times*, which accredited me as a correspondent between 2010 and 2020. The colleagues and editors I worked with are too numerous to list, but I especially want to thank former foreign editor and now editor in chief Joseph Kahn, former Asia bureau chief and current foreign editor Philip Pan, bureau chiefs Edward Wong, Jane Perlez, and Steven Lee Myers, and the many correspondents who worked in China during that decade, most notably the fine political reporter Chris Buckley, editor and later columnist Li Yuan, Chinese site editor Ching Ching Ni, video meister Jonah Kessel, Shanghai bureau chief Keith Bradsher, journalist-turned-restaurateur Jonathan Ansfield, and Amy Qin. Thanks also to numerous news assistants and researchers who helped out on many stories. After the *Times* Beijing bureau was closed by Chinese authorities in 2020, all moved to other jobs or careers, but I want to mention Adam Wu, Grace Liu, Chen Jiehao, Adam Century, Becky Davis, and Helen Gao.

I also benefited from many discussions in Beijing. Besides the subjects of this book and the many people interviewed for the Q&A series, I learned much from former *Times* China bureau chief Ed Gargan; Charles Hutzler at the *Wall Street Journal*; Emily Feng, formerly with the *Times* and now with National Public Radio; former *Times* editor Jeanne Moore and her husband, the anthropologist Jing Jun. I also had discussions with many Chinese journalists. After consulting with them, we felt it better not to mention their names, but I appreciate their time and advice.

A special thank you also to Kiki Zhao, formerly with the *Times*, who helped with follow-up reporting inside China. Kiki generously visited a couple of sites to gather updated material.

I also want to thank universities for sponsoring talks I gave on the subject of hidden or underground history, especially Stephen F. Teiser at Princeton, Haun Saussy at the University of Chicago, and the Asian Studies Development Workshop at the East-West Center in Hawaii. I also benefited greatly from a workshop organized by curator Hsiaoting Lin of the Hoover Institution on the legacy of Li Rui, with panelists Li Nanyang, Orville Schell, and Aminda M. Smith. A workshop on the "Digitization of Memory in China" at the University of Bonn, organized by Maximilian Mayer and Frederik Schmitz, helped me think through the ideas of Aleida and Jan Assmann, which help inform key arguments of this book.

At that conference and at several other meetings I learned much from Professor Guobin Yang, a pioneer on the Internet in China. Thanks also to Professor Lian Xi of the Duke Divinity School and his work on Lin Zhao; the London-based researcher Jiang Shao and his work on unofficial publications; David Ownby of the University of Montreal for his "Reading the China Dream" website, which shows the richness of intellectual life in Xi's China; and Sebastian Veg of EHESS in Paris for his work on *minjian* intellectuals.

After my expulsion, Kenneth Dean at the Asia Research Institute in Singapore helped arrange a perch for me there in the 2020–2021 academic year, giving me a sane vantage point during the high point of the pandemic. As always, Philip Clart, who is my *Doktorvater* at Leipzig University, helped me think through certain aspects of civil society. Philip, I promise to finish my thesis, now!

In 2021, I was fortunate enough to join the Council on Foreign Relations as the Stephen A. Schwarzman senior fellow for China studies. CFR provided a stimulating home for the end phase of writing this book. The council's fellows hold regular brown bag lunches where we critique each other's work. This provided very important feedback, leading me to write the preface and think through my arguments more closely. I also got excellent advice from CFR's director of studies, James M. Lindsay, and the council's past president, Richard Haass, both of whom read drafts and offered important suggestions and critiques, as well as Patricia Lee Dorff of CFR's publications department, who helped shepherd this book. Special thanks to research associate Kathy Huang, who helped check facts, figures, and links—a very difficult task given the fluid nature of underground history.

My agent, Sarah Chalfant, of Wylie, gave wise counsel throughout. I especially remember meeting her in a deserted London in early 2020 shortly after my expulsion, when she gave me the confidence to carry on. Through her I got to know the excellent team at Oxford University Press, including David McBride, Sarah Ebel, and Niko Pfund, all of whom have been consummate professionals and highly supportive, despite a few busted deadlines. Sarah also helped arrange a reunion with Simon Winder of Penguin U.K., which has published most of my other books. Simon gave the book a thorough reading and made many excellent comments.

A special thanks is owed to the Nanjing-based researcher Russell Leigh Moses, former dean of academic affairs at the Beijing Center for Chinese Studies, where I taught for a decade. Russ read drafts of this book and was a constant source of good advice. He encouraged me to apply for the NEH grant and helped greatly with the application.

The biggest thank-you goes to my wife, Sim Chi Yin. In her previous incarnation as a photographer for the agencies VII and Magnum, Chi Yin accompanied me on several key reporting trips, especially to Wuhan to interview Ai Xiaoming and Hu Fayun; to Xi'an to interview Jiang Xue, Tiger Temple, Chen Hongguo, and the *Zhiwuzhi* crowd; and to Hunan to roam the hills with Tan Hecheng. Her photos grace this book, but it is her ideas that give it whatever deeper meaning it might have.

Notes

PREFACE

xiii **Solzhenitsyn, Kundera, or Forman**: Especially relevant is Alexander Solzhenitsyn's *Gulag Archipelago*, which chronicles the Soviet prison camps, Milan Kundera's *The Joke* and its satire of totalitarianism, and Milos Forman's film "The Firemen's Ball," which satirized Eastern European Communism. The parallels are imperfect because all three defected or emigrated to the West, giving them greater freedom and resources, but these earlier works were created in the home countries, suggesting similarities to those that I discuss in today's China.

xiv **Jiang Xue posted a widely circulated article**: "2022 jizhu qingnian dailaide guangliang," originally posted on NGOCN Telegram site, https://web.archive.org/web/20230118213333/https://ngocn2.org/article/2023-01-01-new-year-the-youth/.

CHAPTER I

3 **hard to travel two hundred miles in any direction**: Gregory Veeck, Clifton W. Pannell, Christopher J. Smith, and Youqin Huang, *China's Geography: Globalization and the Dynamics of Political, Economic, and Social Change* (Lanham, MD: Rowman and Littlefield, 2016), 30.

5 **"Do you really understand the water"**: *Inscribed Landscapes*, trans. Richard Strassberg (Berkeley: University of California Press, 1994), 187.

5 **"with so many painful and dangerous matters":** Jerome
Silbergeld, *Back to the Red Cliff: Reflection on the Narrative Mode
in Early Literati Landscape Painting* (Ann Arbor: Regents of the
University of Michigan, 1995), 29.

9 **perfect dictatorship**: Stein Ringen, *The Perfect Dictatorship:
China in the 21st Century* (Hong Kong: Hong Kong University
Press, 2016).

11 **Communist Party rule can be divided into two periods**:
"Xi Jinping: Zai fazhan zhongguo tese shehui zhuyi shijianzhong
buduan faxian, chuangzao, qianjing," 习近平：在发展中国
特色社会主义实践中不断发现、创造、前进 [Xi Jinping:
Continue to discover, innovate, and progress in the process of
developing socialist society with Chinese characteristics], *CPC
News*, accessed 1 December 2022, https://web.archive.org/web/
20221201210745/http://cpc.people.com.cn/n/2013/0106/c64
094-20101215-2.html.

11 **To destroy a country's people**: Cao Yaxin 曹雅欣, "Xi
Jinping: Mieren zhi guo, bi xuanqu qishi" 习近平：灭人之国，
必先去其史 [Xi Jinping: To destroy a country's people, start with
destroying their history], *China Daily*, accessed 1 December 2022,
https://web.archive.org/web/20221201204953/http://china.chi
nadaily.com.cn/2015-08/06/content_21520950.htm.

CHAPTER 2

17 The Ditch: scenes and quotes are taken from *Jiabiangou Elegy*,
an independent documentary film made by Ai Xiaoming and
released in five parts to YouTube in 2017. See "Jiabiangou jishi—
01 youpai nongchang" 夹边沟祭事—01右派农场 [Jiabiangou
Elegy—01 Rightist Farm], accessed 20 August 2022, https://
www.youtube.com/watch?v=M0NN1F_HegY&t=2182s.

18 **Ai Xiaoming biographical information**: Interviews with the
author in person on 29 June 2016, and by phone 4 January 2021,
as well as follow-up correspondence in 2022

19 **"The person punished does not know the reason"**: Milan
Kundera, *The Art of the Novel,* trans. Linda Asher (New York:
Harper Perennial, 2000), 102–103.

22 **Up to 2 million died in land reform**: For a discussion, see Brian DeMare, *Land Wars: The Story of China's Agrarian Revolution* (New York: Oxford University Press, 2019), 161–162.

27 **Up to 45 million died**: Frank Dikötter, *Mao's Great Famine: The History of China's Most Devastating Catastrophe, 1958–1962* (New York: Bloomsbury, 2011).

29 **Most people received roughly five hundred yuan**: As per interviews in Ai's film.

30 **Yang Xianhui**: *The Woman from Shanghai* (New York: Anchor Books, 2010).

30 **"As an author . . ."**: Translated by Sebastian Veg, "Testimony, History and Ethics: From the Memory of Jiabiangou Prison Camp to a Reappraisal of the Anti-Rightist Movement in Present-Day China," *China Quarterly* no. 218 (June 2014), 514–539.

34 **Xi statement that Mao era cannot be rejected**: Jiang Yu 江宇, "liangge bu neng foudingde lishi neihan he xianshi yiyi" "两个不能否定"的历史内涵和现实意义"The Historical Connotations and Practical Significance of 'Two Cannot Be Rejected'" *CPC News,* 12 October 2013, https://web.archive.org/web/2/http://cpc.people.com.cn/n/2013/1012/c69120-23179702.html.

35 **Ai's point is clear**: She makes this explicit in a 2019 interview with Zeng Jinyan. See "Jiabiangou Elegy: A Conversation with Ai Xiaoming," *Made in China Journal* 2 (2019), 132. Also available at https://press-files.anu.edu.au/downloads/press/n6874/pdf/jiabiangou_elegy.pdf.

35 **Ai was aided by Zhang Suiqing**: Ai Xiaoming 艾晓明, "women yiqi zouguo de lu: chentong daonian wode zuopin xiangdao Zhang Suiqing xiansheng" 我们一起走过的路：沉痛悼念我的作品向导张遂卿先生 [The Road We Walked Together: A Sorrowful Tribute to Mr. Zhang Suiqing, the Mentor of My Works], *NewCenturyNet*, 15 April 2017, https://web.archive.org/web/20190409221906/http://2newcenturynet.blogspot.com:80/2017/04/blog-post_15.html.

36 **"Stop listening to the rain . . ."**: Translated by Alice Poon, "More Poems by Su Shi (Su Dongpo)," *Blogger*, accessed 22 November 2022, accessible at https://alicewaihanpoon.blogspot.com/2016/10/more-poems-by-su-shi-su-dongpo.html. Used by permission.

MEMORY: FACING WALLS

37 **Facing Walls**: Details of Gao Ertai's experiences are drawn
from his memoir *In Search of My Homeland* (New York: Ecco,
2009), and email exchanges with the author in November and
December 2019.

40 **His writings circulate online**: Gao Ertai 高尔泰, *Huangshan
xizhao* 荒山夕照 [Sunset over the desolate mountain], Personal
History WeChat subscription channel, 13 April 2020, https://web.
archive.org/web/20221205020329/https://mp.weixin.qq.com/s/
9GzSZkioYcQ7XrZPgpkXZA, accessed 30 November 2022.

41 **"Writing In Search of My Homeland"**: Gao Ertai 高尔泰,
*Xunzhao Jiayuan*寻找家园 [In search of my homeland] (Taipei:
Yinke Wenxue Zazhi Chuban Youxian Gongsi, 2009), 9, cited in
Maciej Kurzynski, "In Defense of Beauty: Gao Ertai's Aesthetic
of Resistance," *Philosophy East and West* 69, no. 4 (2009), 1007.

CHAPTER 3

43 The Sacrifice: Details of Jiang Xue's life drawn from a series of
interviews with the author in 2016, 2019, 2022, and 2023.

48 **"A thousand mountains and not a bird flying . . ."**:
Translation by Bill Porter, in *Written in Exile: The Poetry of Liu
Tsung-yuan* (Port Washington, WA: Copper Canyon Press, 2019), 57.

MEMORY: BAMBOO STRIPS

60 **Details of Liu Guozhong's works**: Ian Johnson, "A
Revolutionary Discovery in China," *New York Review of Books*,
21 April 2016. https://www.nybooks.com/articles/2016/04/21/
revolutionary-discovery-in-china/.

60 **First Historical Archives of China**: In 2021, the archives
began to move to the Forbidden City.

61 **Three batches of bamboo slips**: A fourth, the Mawangdui
site in Hunan, which was excavated between 1972 and 1974, is
probably most famous, but its texts date from later era.

61 Twenty-five hundred **slips**: The exact number of slips is open
to debate. At least two thousand are full slips. The other five
hundred are fragments.

CHAPTER 4

65 Unless otherwise noted, details of the establishment of the
magazine *Spark*, biographical details of Zhang Chunyuan, Tan
Chanxue and the other students, as well as direct quotations
from the people involved are drawn from Tan's memoir *Qiusuo:
lanzhoudaxue "youpai fangeming ji'an" jishi* 求索：兰州大学
「右派反革命集团案」纪实 [Seeking: The Rightist Anti-
Revolutionary Group Case at Lanzhou University] (Hong Kong:
Hong Kong Tianma Publisher, 2017).

67 **"Grain production was supposedly sky high . . . "**: 谭
蝉雪，《求索：兰州大学「右派反革命集团案」纪实》:
Tan Chanxue 谭蝉雪, bianzhu *Qiusuo: lanzhoudaxue "youpai
fangeming ji'an" jishi* 求索：兰州大学「右派反革命集团
案」纪实 [Seeking: The Rightist Anti-Revolutionary Group
Case at Lanzhou University] (Hong Kong: Hong Kong Tianma
Publisher, 2017), 10.

68 **"The next day I heard that someone found a
fingernail..."**: Tan, *Qiusuo*, 11.

69 "He really opposed those who only thought . . . ": Hu Jie 胡杰,
director, *Spark* (dGenerate Films, 2020), 00:58:03. https://icarusfi
lms.com/df-spark.

70 **"If you do not break out of silence . . . "**: Tan, *Qiusuo*, 3.

74 "The power of truth . . ." and "Freedom, I cry out . . .":
Translation by Lian Xi, *Blood Letters: The Untold Story of Lin Zhao,
a Martyr in Mao's China* (New York: Basic Books, 2018), 75 and 93.

79 **Wushan population, and estimated deaths**: Du's estimate as
per Tan, *Qiusuo*, 44.

79 **"Now all these different voices are gone"**: Tan, *Qiusuo*, 255.

86 **"grand church worship"**: Lian Xi, *Blood Letters*, 140

86 **"the most selfish person"**: Lian Xi, *Blood Letters*, 193.

86 **"In the future they will make up another volume . . . "**: Lian Xi, *Blood Letters*, 195.

88 **Every Man Dies Alone**: Hans Fallada, *Every Man Dies Alone*, trans. Michael Hofmann (New York: Melville House, 2009). The book was also published in English as *Alone in Berlin*, and a film was made of it with the same name.

92 **"Redemption for my soul"**: Lian Xi, *Blood Letters*, 244.

92 **"a martyred saint"**: Lian Xi, *Blood Letters*, 220.

92 **"Now we have our genealogy"**: Lian Xi, *Blood Letters*, 246.

MEMORY: REBIRTH

93 **Etchings**: All quotations from this Memory vignette are taken from interviews conducted with Hu Jie in Nanjing, 26 March 2015. In addition, I conducted follow-up phone interviews with him on 9 June 2020 and on 8 March 2022 to fact-check and update the information.

CHAPTER 5

98 **Edgar Snow on Liu Zhidan**: Edgar Snow, *Red Star over China* (New York: Grove Press, 1968), 209.

98 **Purge of Liu Zhidan, Xi Zhongxun and Gao Gang**: For a complete account, see Joseph W. Esherick, *Accidental Holy Land: The Communist Revolution in Northwest China* (Berkeley: University of California Press, 2022), 117.

99 **"Halt the executions!"**: Esherick, *Accidental Holy Land*, 122.

99 **Mao's use of the base area's history**: Gao Hua, *How the Red Sun Rose* (New York: Columbia University Press, 2019), 743.

101 **"debased character . . . execrable"**: Gao Hua, *Red Sun*, 743.

101 **Mao wrote several essays against Wang**: Several of Mao's most important essays: "On Practice" and "On Contradiction" were penned in 1937 when Wang was sent back to China.

102 **The rectification campaign is portrayed in China as a great achievement**: See, for example, the entry in *Baidu Baike*,

which describes it as a "great pioneering work in the history of party building. "Yan'an zhengfeng yundong" 延安整风运动 [Yan'an rectification campaign], *Baidu Baike*, accessed 22 November 2022,https://baike.baidu.com/item/%E5%BB%B6 %E5%AE%89%E6%95%B4%E9%A3%8E%E8%BF%90%E5 %8A%A8/4416458.

102 **"thought reform"**: See, for example, Robert Jay Lifton, *Thought Reform and the Psychology of Totalism: A Study of "Brainwashing" in China* (New York: Norton, 1961).

103 **Wang Ming and Meng Qingshu crying before Mao**: Gao Hua, *Red Sun*, 633.

103 **Wife of one official died of "mental derangement."** Gao Hua, *Red Sun*, 728.

104 **Wording of 1945 history resolution**. "Resolution on Certain Questions in the History of Our Party," 20 April 1945. This is taken from the 1965 "First Edition" of vol. 3 of the *Selected Works of Mao Tse-tung* as the Appendix to "Our Study and the Current Situation." The 1965 text Romanizes Mao's name as Mao Tse-tung but, I have converted it to pinyin for consistency's sake. "Appendix: Resolution on Certain Questions in the History of Our Party," *Selected Works of Mao Tse-Tung*, vol. 3 (Beijing: Foreign Language Press, 1965), 178, http://www.marx2mao.com/PDFs/MaoSW3 App.pdf.

104 **"labored painstakingly"**: Gao Hua, *Red Sun*, 690.

104 **"magic incantation"**: Gao Hua, *Red Sun*, 749.

105 **Gao Gang's purge**: See Eric Shiraev and Zi Yang, "The Gao-Rao Affair: A Case of Character Assassination in Chinese Politics in the 1950s," in *Character Assassination throughout the Ages*, ed. Martijn Icks and Eric Shiraev (New York: Palgrave Macmillan, 2014). I also relied on Frederick Tewies, *Politics at Mao's Court* (London, Routledge, 1990).

108 **Documentary politics**: Wu Guoguang, *Anatomy of Political Power in China* (Singapore: National University of Singapore, 2005), 100.

108 **Deng's history resolution**: Deng's role is drawn in part from
       Robert Suettinger's essay: Robert Suettinger, "Negotiating
       History: The Chinese Communist Party's 1981," posted 17 July
       2017, https://project2049.net/wp-content/uploads/2017/07/
       P2049_Suettinger_Negotiating-History-CCP_071717.pdf.

109 **Oriana Fallaci interview**: "Answers to the Italian Journalist
       Oriana Fallaci," *Deng Xiaoping Collected Works*, vol. 2. The
       original webpage has been taken down. It is archived at https://
       web.archive.org/web/20220521071225/http://en.people.cn/den
       gxp/vol2/text/b1470.html.

110 **Deng on discrediting Mao**: Quote from *Selected Works of
       Deng Xiaoping*, as per Suettinger.

MEMORY: HOW THE RED SUN ROSE

112 **Biographical details and quotations**: Unless otherwise
       noted, postscript to *How the Red Sun Rose*, 707–718.

112 **Gao Hua's father as an underground radio operator**:
       David Cheng Chang, interview with the author 23 March 2021.

114 **Gao's use of the Universities Service Center**: 15 March
       2021 interview with former USC head Jean Hung. For a
       discussion on the center's fate see chapter 13.

CHAPTER 6

117 **Colonial Williamsburg**: For statistics, see "2020 Annual
       Report," Colonial Williamsburg, accessed 20 April 2022, https://
       www.colonialwilliamsburg.org/learn/about-colonial-williamsb
       urg/#annual-reports.

117 **Yan'an new theme park**: Sui-Lee Wee and Elsie Chen, "'Red
       Tourism Flourishes in China Ahead of Party Centennial," *New
       York Times*, 25 June 2021, https://www.nytimes.com/2021/06/
       25/business/china-centennial-red-tourism.html.

118 **Figures on Yan'an memorial sites, attendance, and revenues**:
       "China's 2019 'Red Tourism' Revenue Tops 400b Yuan," State

Council Information Service, accessed 15 March 2022, https://
web.archive.org/web/20221205204123/http://english.www.gov.
cn/statecouncil/ministries/202105/19/content_WS60a50610c
6d0df57f98d9bef.html#:~:text=BEIJING%20%E2%80%94%20
The%20revenue%20generated%20by,NCHA)%20said%20on%20
May%2019. See also "China's Yan'an to Be Revamped into "City
of Revolutionary Museums," *Xinhua News*, accessed 3 April 2021,
https://web.archive.org/web/20221205204418/http://www.xinhua
net.com/english/2021-04/03/c_139857078.htm.

118 **Critics of idealized places of memory**: In the United
States, for example, writers such as Ada Louise Huxtable
criticized Colonial Williamsburg in the 1960s. See her article
Ada Louise Huxtable, "Dissent at Colonial Williamsburg;
Errors of Restoration," *New York Times*, 22 September 1963, 131,
https://www.nytimes.com/1963/09/22/archives/dissent-at-
colonial-williamsburg-errors-of-restoration.html.

118 **Statistics on red tourism/education for 2021**: "Renmin
ribao: yonghao wenwu ziyuan, jianghao hongse gushi" 人民
日报：用好文物资源 讲好红色故事 [People's Daily: Make
good use of cultural resources, tell good red stories], *WeChat*,
29 March 2022, https://web.archive.org/web/20221205205423/
https://mp.weixin.qq.com/s?__biz=MzI5NzE4MDI4NQ==
&mid=2247494880&idx=5&sn=30dec863a79933e0f685888cc
ea84109&chksm=ecbb.a1f2dbcc28e4f4c6623112ffb9bb8950620d
322bda3390a1b63bd5e1751a12aad65f4796&scene=27. The article
is accompanied by a table of statistics. The source is not cited,
but given the authoritative nature of *People's Daily* it is safe to
say it reflects the central government's figures.

119 **Xi Jinping keynote speech in 2010**: "Hu Jintao huijian
quanguo dangshi gongzuo huiyi daibiao, Xi Jinping jianghua"
胡锦涛会见全国党史工作会议代表，习近平讲话 ["Hu
Jintao visits representatives of national working meeting on party
history, Xi Jinping gives a speech") *Xinhua news agency via Sina*,
21 July 2010, https://web.archive.org/web/20221202204512/
http://news.sina.com.cn/c/2010-07-21/175220728776.shtml.

119 **17,000 employees**: "Cong shenmin dao kao kaifang-zoujin dangzhongyang yanjiushi" 从神秘到开放-走进党中央研究室 [From Mystery to Openness–into the Party Central Research Office], *China News*, accessed 2 December 2022, https://web. archive.org/web/20221202205042/https://www.chinanews. com.cn/gn/2010/07-21/2415049.shtml.

120 **Xi Jinping speech at National Museum of China**: "Xi Jinping: chengqianqihou jiwangkailai jixu chaozhe zhonghuaminzu weidafuxing mubiao fenyongqianjin" 习近平：承前启后 继往开来 继续朝着中华民族伟大复兴目标奋勇前进 [Xi Jinping: Build on the past and open up the future; continue to advance toward the goal of the Great Nation Rejuvenation of China] *Xinhua News*, 29 November 2012, https://web.archive.org/web/20221205215653/http:// www.xinhuanet.com/politics/2012-11/29/c_113852724.htm.

120 **Their ideals and convictions wavered**: Chris Buckley, "Vows of Change in China Belie Private Warning," *New York Times,* 14 February 2013, https://www.nytimes.com/2013/02/ 15/world/asia/vowing-reform-chinas-leader-xi-jinping-airs- other-message-in-private.html.

120 **Later books and videos repeated concerns about the fall of the Soviet Union**: See, for example,"Lishi xuwuzhuyi yu sulian jieti 历史虚无主义与苏联解体" [Historical Nihilism and the Dissolution of the Soviet Union] *Youku Video*, accessed 28 April 2022, https://v.youku.com/v_show/id_XNTgoNDE wNTk2OA==.html.

121 **Document Number Nine**: For a reliable translation, see "Document 9: A China File Translation: How Much Is a Hardline Party Directive Shaping China's Current Political Climate?" *ChinaFile*, 8 November 2013, https://www.chinafile. com/document-9-chinafile-translation#start.

121 **Banking books from Hong Kong**: See, for example, Ian Johnson, "Lawsuit over Banned Memoir Asks China to Explain Censorship," *New York Times*, 25 April 2015, https://www.nyti

mes.com/2015/04/26/world/asia/china-lawsuit-over-banned-
li-rui-memoir-censorship.html.

122 *Seeking Truth* **on foreign forces**: "Jinfang 'lishi xuwu zhuyi'
liyong hulianwang qinglue zhongguo" 谨防"历史虚无主
义"利用互联网侵略中国, [Beware of "historical nihilism"
using the internet to invade China], *China Daily*, accessed 2
December 2022, https://web.archive.org/web/20221202211
521/http://china.chinadaily.com.cn/2015-10/28/content_22303
537.htm.

122 **The Five Heroes of Langya Mountain**: Josh Chin, "In
China, Xi Jinping's Crackdown Extends to Dissenting Versions
of History," *Wall Street Journal*, 1 August 2016, https://www.wsj.
com/articles/in-china-xi-jinpings-crackdown-extends-to-dis
senting-versions-of-history-1470087445?mod=article_inline.

122 **Illegal and Harmful Information Reporting Center**:
The center's main site is https://www.12377.cn/index.html.
On 9 April 2021, it announced that it had added historical
nihilism:
"Jubao wangshang lishi xuwuzhuyi cuowu yanlun qingdao
12377" 举报网上历史虚无主义错误言论请到12377 [Please
report online historical nihilism to 12377] *Illegal and Harmful
Information Reporting Center*, 9 April 2021, https://www.12377.
cn/wxxx/2021/fc6eb910_web.html.

122 **A list of other taboo topics**: Alexander Boyd, "The
Historical Nihil-List: Cyberspace Administration Targets Top
Ten Deviations from Approved History," *China Digital Times,* 16
August 2021, https://chinadigitaltimes.net/2021/08/the-histori
cal-nihil-list-cyberspace-administration-targets-top-ten-deviati
ons-from-approved-history/.

124 **Xi's explanation of resolution**: "Full Text: Xi's Explanation
of Resolution on Major Achievements and Historical
Experience of CPC over Past Century," *Xinhua Net*, 16
November 2021. http://www.news.cn/english/2021-11/16/c_
1310314613.htm. For the Chinese original, see https://web.arch

ive.org/web/20221205220844/http://cpc.people.com.cn/n1/
2021/1201/c64094-32296476.html.

124 **"In the late spring and early summer . . .":** "Resolution of the CPC Central Committee on the Major Achievements and Historical Experiences of the Party over the Past Century," *Xinhua Net*, 16 November 2021, http://www.news.cn/english/2021-11/16/c_1310314611.htm.

125 **Visit to Jurong:** I visited the archives on 3 November 2010.

127 **Red Guards burned temples to the ground and dug up foundation stones:** Unpublished oral history interviews from 2010, 2011, and 2012 in the author's collection. I personally saw the stones strewn at the bottom of two hills that contained major monasteries. In the 2010s, they were built anew in a completely different architectural style.

127 **The earlier gazetteer:** *Jurong Maoshan Zhi* 句容茅山志 [Jurong Maoshan Gazetteer], Jurong shi defangzhi bangongshi bian, 句容市地方志办公室编 (Hefei: Huangshashu Chuban, 1998), 82.

MEMORY: THE NATIONAL MUSEUM

129 **Zhou Enlai said museum did not emphasize "red line" as well as other details on the museum's early history:** Chang-tai Hung, "The Red Line: Creating a Museum of the Chinese Revolution," *China Quarterly* no. 184 (December 2005), 927.

129 **Deng on the lack of Li Dazhao photos being "totally unacceptable":** Chang-tai Hung, "The Red Line," 928.

129 **British think tank declares Beijing a third-tier city:** J. V. Beaverstock, R. G. Smith, and P. J. Taylor, *A Roster of World Cities* (Leicestershire, UK: GaWC, 1999), doi:10.1016/S0264-2751(99)00042-6.

129 **Largest museum under one roof:** For details on the renovation, see Ian Johnson, "At China's New Museum, History Toes Party Line," *New York Times*, 3 April 2011, https://www.nytimes.com/2011/04/04/world/asia/04museum.html.

130 The Enlightenment show avoided discussing human rights:
    Interview with German curators, Johnson, "At China's New
    Museum."

131 **Museum Director Wang Chunfa statement**: "Message from
    the director," accessed on 22 April 2022, http://en.chnmuseum.
    cn/about_the_nmc_593/message_from_nmc_director_595/201
    911/t20191122_173222.html.

131 **Items on display in new exhibition**: Personal observation.
    See also "Fuxing zhi lu·xinshidai bufen zhanlan mianxiang
    gongzhong kaifang" 复兴之路·新时代部分展览面向公众
    开放 [The Road to Rejuvenation· New Era Portion is Open
    to Public] Central Commission for Discipline Inspection
    China, archived at https://web.archive.org/web/20221208180
    116/https://www.ccdi.gov.cn/toutu/201807/t20180705_175
    124.html.

PART II

133 Part 2 "Defeating the bandits . . . ,": Cited in George L. Israel,
    *Doing Good and Ridding Evil in Ming China: The Political Career of
    Wang Yangming* (Leiden: Brill, 2014), 1.

CHAPTER 7

136 Fang Lizhi, "The Chinese Amnesia," *New York Review of Books*,
    27 September 1990, trans. Perry Link, https://www.nybooks.
    com/articles/1990/09/27/the-chinese-amnesia/.

137 Jan Assmann, *Cultural Memory and Early Civilization: Writing,
    Remembrance, and Political Imagination* (Cambridge: Cambridge
    University Press, 2011). First published as *Das kulturelle
    Gedächtnis: Schrift, Erinnerung und politische Identität in frühen
    Hochkulturen*, 1992).

137 **Cultural vs. Communicative Memory**: Susanne Weigelin-Schwiedrzik makes this point about the Cultural Revolution in her 2006 essay: "In Search of a Master Narrative for 20th-Century Chinese History," *China Quarterly* 188 (December 2006), 1070–1091, https://doi.org/10.1017/S0305741006000555.

138 **"stored" vs. "functional" memory**: Aleida Assmann, "Funktionsgedächtnis und Speichergedächtnis—Zwei Modi der Erinnerung," in *Erinnerungsräume: Formen und Wandlungen des kulturellen Gedächtnisses* (München: C. H. Beck., 2009).

139 **Flooding the media with its version of reality**: See Margaret E. Roberts, *Censored: Distraction and Diversion Inside China's Great Firewall* (Princeton, NJ: Princeton University Press, 2018). Roberts distinguishes between "friction," that is, government efforts to make information harder to obtain, including outright censorship, and "flooding," which involves overwhelming media space with only one version of events.

139 **Memory boom, the role of World War I, "theaters of memory"**: Jay Winter, *Remembering War: The Great War Between Historical Memory and History in the Twentieth Century* (New Haven, CT: Yale University Press, 2006).

140 **Wang Xiaobo symbolizing China's recovery of speech**: This is a central insight of Sebastian Veg in *Minjian: The Rise of China's Grassroots Intellectuals* (New York: Columbia University Press, 2019). I personally was also drawn to Wang in the 1990s and interviewed him for the Baltimore *Sun* in 1996, a year before his death. Some of the material in this section also appeared in an article I wrote for the *New York Review of Books* in 2017.

143 **"The Silent Majority"**: Wang Xiaobo 王小波, *The Silent Majority*, trans. Eric Abrahamsen, (Paper Republic), https://media.paper-republic.org/files/09/04/The_Silent_Majority_Wang_Xiaobo.pdf.

143 **Wang's decision to speak out**: See Sebastian Veg, "Wang Xiaobo and the No Longer Silent Majority," *The Impact of*

China's 1989 Tiananmen Massacre, ed. Jean-Philippe Béja (New York: Routledge, 2010), 93.

144 **Wang influenced by Russell and Foucault**: see my interview with his former wife, Li Yinhe, cited in Ian Johnson, "Sexual Life in Modern China," *New York Review of Books,* 26 October 2017. I also interviewed Professor Cho-yun Hsu on 15 April 2017.

144 **Veg on Foucault and Chinese grassroots intellectual**: See Veg, *Minjian*, 3.

146 **Articles in the government press encouraging tourism**: See, for example, Zhang Danhua, "Red Memories on the Loess Plateau," *People's Daily,* 23 March 2022, 16.

147 **Ma died of natural causes**: "Yangjiagou "xinyuan" de "jiuzhuren shanganning bianqu zhuming aiguo mingzhu renshi Ma Xingmin Jishi 杨家沟"新院"的"旧主人"——陕甘宁边区著名爱国民主人士马醒民纪事 " [Yangjiagou "Xinyuan"'s Old Owner: Shanganning district famous patriotic democrat Ma Xingmin Memo], accessed 20 May 2022, https://web.arch ive.org/web/20221202184304/http://shx.wenming.cn/xwdt/ 201602/t20160226_3171394.htm.

147 **Kang Sheng on the need for violent land reform**: Li Fangchun 李放春, "Dizhuwo' li de qingsuan fengbo—jiantan beifang tugaizhong de "minzhu" yu "huai ganbu" wenti, '地主窝'里的清算风波——兼谈北方土改中的'民主'与'坏干部'问题," [The Liquidation storm in the "landlord nest": and talks on "democracy" and "bad comrade" questions in the northern land reform] *aisixiang,* last modified 4 February 2009, https://web.archive.org/web/2022120 2185703/https://www.aisixiang.com/data/24580.html.

MEMORY: THE LANDLORD'S MANSION

148 **Guo Yuhua's book**: Guo Yuhua 郭于华, *Jicun lishi yu yizhong wenming de luoji* 受苦人的讲述 : 骥村历史与一种文明的逻辑 [Narratives of the sufferers: The history of Jicun and the logic of civilization] (Hong Kong: Chinese University, 2013). Guo follows

academic convention by anonymizing Yangjiagou as "Ji" Village, using an archaic name for the location. I have used Yangjiagou throughout because this anonymizing is pointless. By explaining the village's history, using the true names of the clan members, and adopting a near synonym for Yangjiagou, Guo makes it impossible not to identify the village. Thus I have decided in the interests of simplicity and accuracy to use its real name, Yangjiagou.

149 **Guo Yuhua's career hampered by her activism**: See Ian Johnson, "Ruling Through Ritual: An Interview with Guo Yuhua," *New York Review of Books*, 18 June 2018, https://www. nybooks.com/daily/2018/06/18/ruling-through-ritual-an-interview-with-guo-yuhua/.

CHAPTER 8

156 **Thomas Chen on the significance of Jia's blank boxes**: Thomas Chen, "Blanks to Be Filled: Public-Making and the Censorship of Jia Pingwa's Decadent Capital," *China Perspectives*, 2015, https://journals.openedition.org/chinaperspectives/6625.

MEMORY: SNOW'S VISIT

165 **The 30-minute film was released in 2016**: It is posted on YouTube: "Laohumiao hukan," zhuixun xinghuo zhi yi: Xiang Chenjian 老虎庙·虎侃, "追寻星火之一：向承鉴," [Tiger Temple: "Pursuing One of the Sparks: Xiang Chenjian"] YouTube Video, 17 April 2016, https://www.youtube.com/watch?v=oDpADWHFCjo&list=PLoon9OuQeeDPMQjCxElkBO1otfgKTugpm&index=16&t=357s.

166 **Hearing it, she wonders**: personal correspondence with author, 20 May 2022.

CHAPTER 9

167 Note on Chapter 9: Unless otherwise noted, biographical details on Ai Xiaoming are taken from the author's interviews

(2016, 2021), Zeng Jinyan 曾金燕. "The Genesis of Citizen Intelligentsia in Digital China: Ai Xiaoming's Practice of Identify and Activist," PhD diss., University of Hong Kong, 2017; and Ai Xiaoming 艾晓明, *Xue Tong* 血統 [Lineage], (Beijing: Huacheng Chubanshe花城出版社, 1994), 59.

168 ***This is the real wartime capital of China:*** W. H. Auden and Christopher Isherwood, *Journey to a War*, cited in Stephen R. MacKinnon, *Wuhan, 1938: War, Refugees, and the Making of Modern China* (Berkeley: University of California Press, 2008), 97–98.

169 **Three separate roles in three separate spaces**: Ai described this to me in our 2016 interview. It is more fully analyzed and described by Zeng, "The Genesis of Citizen Intelligentsia," 59.

170 **Ai Luming business history and wealth**: "Ai Luming" 艾路明, *Baidu Baike,* accessed 2 December 2022, https://baike. baidu.com/item/%E8%89%BE%E8%B7%AF%E6%98%8E/ 10773540#:~:text=%E8%89%BE%E8%B7%AF%E6%98%8E %EF%BC%8C%E6%B9%96%E5%8C%97%E6%AD%A6 %E6%B1%89,%E3%80%81%E9%A2%86%E5%86%9B%E4 %BA%BA%E3%80%81%E8%91%A3%E4%BA%8B%E9%95 %BF%20%E3%80%82.

174 **"My father was very strict with us"**: Ai Xiaoming cited in Mirror Media: Zeng Zhijun曾芷筠"Bei fengzhu de ren fanwaipian: jiangjun de nü'er" 被封住的人番外扁：将军的女儿 [The Isolated Person's Other Story: The General's Daughter] Mirror Media, 17 February 2020, https://www.mirrormedia. mg/premium/20200217pol006.

175 **Details of Ai Renkuan's self-confession and biography**: Ai Xiaoming, *Lineage* (1994), 59.

181 **Tan Zuoren essay on Longmen Mountain**: originally published on 4 April 2009 on his blog, it was subsequently censored. It has been republished on numerous sites, for example, Tan Zuoren 谭作人, "Longmenshan——Qing wei beishan haizi zuozheng," 龙门山——请为北川孩子作证 [Longmen Mountain: please testify for the Beichuan children],

China Weekly Report, accessed 30 June 2022, https://www.
china-week.com/html/4894.htm.

182 **"The severe political pressure unleashed . . ."**: Zeng
Jinyan, "Jiabiangou Elegy," *Made in China Journal* (February
2019):139, https://press-files.anu.edu.au/downloads/press/
n6874/pdf/jiabiangou_elegy.pdf.

183 **To avoid political risk**: Zeng, "The Genesis of Citizen
Intelligentsia in Digital China," 95.

MEMORY: BLOODLINES

184 Yu Luoke biographical details and quotations: Shao Jiang,
Citizen Publications in China Before the Internet (New York:
Palgrave Macmillan, 2015), 76–81.

187 **"To this day, Yu Luoke's name is still banned"**: "Jinwan
ruyou baofengzhouyu—jinian jiaxiong Yu Luoke jiuyi sishi
zhounian 今夜有如暴风骤雨纪念家兄遇罗克就义四十六周
年" [Tonight like a Hurricane: Commemorating the Sixtieth
Anniversary of the Martyrdom of my Brother Yu Luoke],
Wanwei Blog, last modified 15 March 2016, https://blog.creaders.
net/u/5568/201603/250396.html.

CHAPTER 10

189 *Remembrance,* **chapter 10**: Much of this is culled from
interviews conducted by the author in 2012 and 2013, which
were published in the New *York Review of Books,* issues dated 4
and 18 December 2014. It was augmented by further interviews
in 2021 and 2022.

192 Wu Di 吴迪, *Zhongxifeng maniu* 中西风马牛, [*China-West: Things
Completely Unrelated*] (Beijing: World Publishing Corp., 2014).

194 **He published it in an English-language monograph**: W.
Woody [pseud.], "The Cultural Revolution in Inner Mongolia:
Extracts for an Unpublished History," ed. and trans. Michael

Schoenhals, *Occasional Paper* (Stockholm: Stockholm University, Center for Pacific Asia Studies, 1993).

194 **In 2000, Wu published the book in Hong Kong**: Wu Di 吴迪, *Neimeng wenge shilu: "minzu fenlie" yu "wasu" yundong* 内蒙文革实录: "民族分裂"与"挖肃"运动, *[Record of the Cultural Revolution in Inner Mongolia: "Ethnic Separatism" and the Movement to "Weed out Counterrevolutionaries"]* (Hong Kong: Mirror Books, 2000).

197 **"I cannot forget what I have done wrong"**: Jiang Haofeng 姜浩峰, "Zhang Hongbing wei 'shimu' daoqian beihou" 张红兵为"弑母"道歉背后, [Behind Zhang Hongbing's Matricide Apology], *Xinmin Weekly*, 21 September 2013, https://web.archive.org/web/20150713080414/http://xmzk.xinminweekly.com.cn/News/Content/2835. **Informing on mother**: Jiang Haofeng, Behind Zhang Hongbing's Matricide Apology. **Spitting on peasant**: Wang Keming 王克明, "'Wenge chanhui huiyilu 文革'忏悔回忆录" [Cultural Revolution Confession Memoir] *Huaxiazhiqing*, accessed 11 February 2022, https://web.archive.org/web/20220211091719/http://www.hxzq.net/aspshow/showarticle.asp?id=10201.

197 **Chen Xiaolu interview**: interview with author, 22 November 2013 in Beijing.

199 **Bloomberg investigation into Song Binbin's family**: "U.S. Family of Mao's General Assimilates, Votes for Obama," *Bloomberg News*, 26 December 2012, https://www.bloomberg.com/news/articles/2012-12-26/chinese-in-ann-arbor-voted-obama-in-elite-family-of-mao-s-rulers#xj4y7vzkg.

201 **The magazine also published a piece by her**: Song Binbin 宋彬彬, "Sishi duonian wo yizhi xiangshuo de hua" 四十多年来我一直想说的话 [Words I've Wanted to Speak for Forty Years], *Remembrance*, 31 January 2021, http://prchistory.org/wp-content/uploads/2014/05/REMEMBRANCE_No80.pdf.

203 **Husband rejected apology**: "Wenge shoushang xiaozhang zhangfu jushou daoqian Chize Song Binbin xuwei" 文革受害校长丈夫拒受道歉 斥责宋彬彬虚伪 [Cultural Revolution Victim President's Husband Rejected Apology, Scolded Song Binbin as "hollow"] last modified 1 February 2014, http://news.sina.com.cn/c/p/2014-02-01/142129388421.shtml.

203 **Cartoons parodying Song Binbin**: see "Drawing the News: Apology Not Accepted," *China Digital Times*, accessed 10 July 2022, http://chinadigitaltimes.net/2014/01/drawing-news-apology-accepted/.

204 **Banned discussion of Song Binbin's apology**: See directive from State Council Information Office reprinted in "Red Guard Apologizes for Role in Teacher's Death," *China Digital Times*, accessed 20 June 2014, https://chinadigitaltimes.net/2014/01/red-guard-apologizes-role-teachers-death/. Song's name was also blocked on microblogs. "Collecting Sensitive Words: The Grass-Mud Horse List," *China Digital Times*, accessed 20 June 2014, http://chinadigitaltimes.net/2013/06/grass-mud-horse-list/.

MEMORY: TIE LIU'S CAFE

206 Huang Zerong interviews conducted on 14 and 15 August 2019.

CHAPTER 11

212 **His name is Tan Hecheng**: Interviews for this chapter were conducted by the author in Dao County in November 2016 and in Beijing in October 2019.

213 **Book published in Hong Kong**: The book was published by Tianxingjian Publishing, 天行健出版社, which was founded in 1994 and dissolved in 2022 after passage of the new National Security Law.

215 **Their findings**: Tan Hecheng, *The Killing Wind: A Chinese County's Descent into Madness During the Cultural Revolution*, trans. Stacy Mosher and Guo Jian (New York: Oxford University Press, 2017), 21.

218 "Rubbing the knife marks made everything recede": Tan, *Killing Wind*, 265.

218 **"China's literati"**: Tan, *Killing Wind*, 265.

223 **One survey of local gazetteers**: See Yang Su, *Collective Killings in Rural China During the Cultural Revolution* (Cambridge: Cambridge University Press, 2011).

MEMORY: VIDEOING CHINA'S VILLAGES

230 All interviews and descriptions for this section recorded by the author on April 23 and 24, 2016, at the oral history conference "Starting from Zero" at Communication University of China, Beijing.

230 **The films are held by Duke University**: See https://reposit ory.duke.edu/dc/memoryproject, accessed 22 July 2022.

PART III

233 **"The reason that I have continued to live . . . "**: This is a slightly modified version of the translation found in *Sources of Chinese Tradition*, compiled by William Theodore de Bary and Irene Bloom, 2nd ed., vol. 1 (New York: Columbia University Press, 1999), 370–372.

CHAPTER 12

235 **"The modern disaster regime"**: Chris Courtney, *The Nature of Disaster in China: The 1931 Yangzi River Flood*, Studies in Environment and History (Cambridge: Cambridge University Press, 2018), 17.

237 **On January 16, Ai Xiaoming returned to Wuhan**: Ai Xiaoming's experiences in Wuhan were reconstructed from in-person interviews in 2021 and Ai's "Pandemic Diary," which was published in *The Initium* in Chinese and excerpted in an issue of the *New Left Review*: Ai Xiaoming艾晓明, "Pandemic Diary," *New Left Review* no. 122 (March–April 2022), 15–21, https:// newleftreview.org/issues/ii122/articles/xiaoming-ai-wuhan-diary.

237 **"Unprecedented in public health history"**: **Gauden Galea**: Gabriel Crossley and Alison Williams, "Wuhan Lockdown 'Unprecedented,' Shows Commitment to Contain Virus: WHO Representative in China," *Reuters*, 23 January 2020, https://web. archive.org/web/20200124203401/https://www.reuters.com/ article/us-china-health-who-idUSKBN1ZM1G9.

239 **"Quarantined in the emergency department"**: Details of Li Wenliang's online postings, "As New Coronavirus Spread, China's Old Habits Delayed Fight" by Chris Buckley and Steven Lee Myers, updated 7 February 2020, https://www.nyti mes.com/2020/02/01/world/asia/china-coronavirus.html.

239 **"Preventable and treatable"**: The statement can still be read on the internet archive at "Wuhanshi weijianwei guanyu dangqian woshi feiyan yiqing de qingkuang tongbao" 武汉市卫健委关于当前我市肺炎疫情的情况通报 [Briefing by the Wuhan Municipal Health Commission on the current pneumonia epidemic in the city], Wuhan Municipal Health Commission, 31 December 2019, https://web.archive.org/web/20200430030406/ http://wjw.wuhan.gov.cn/front/web/showDetail/2019123108989.

240 **Chronology of Li Wenliang's illness**: to date, the best reconstruction of his final days is by Muyi Xiao, Isabelle Qian, Tracy Wen Liu, and Chris Buckley, "How a Chinese Doctor Who Warned of Covid-19 Spent His Final Days," *New York Times*, 6 October 2022, https://www.nytimes.com/2022/10/ 06/world/asia/covid-china-doctor-li-wenliang.html?smid=nytc ore-ios-share&referringSource=articleShare.

241 **Comments on Li's Weibo site**: Yvette Tan, "Li Wenliang: 'Wailing Wall' for China's virus whistleblowing doctor," *BBN News*, 23 June 2020, https://www.bbc.com/news/world-asia-china-53077072.

242 **"A healthy society should have more than one voice"**: Joy Dong, "Two Years After His Death, the Chinese Doctor Who Warned of the Virus Is Remembered," *New York Times*, 7 February 2022. https://www.nytimes.com/2022/02/07/world/ asia/chinese-doctor-li-wenliang-covid-warning.html.

243 **"Panic is leading to problems"**: as translated in Ai, *New Left Review*, 19.

245 Chen Qiushi video, "I am afraid": "Ziyuan jingque, yiqing jingji | Chen Qiushi danianchuliu zhongwu jiaolv huizong baodao (Goingmin jizhe Chen Qiushi Wuhan yiqu caifang shilu xilie 10) 資源緊缺，疫情緊急 | 陳秋實大年初六中午焦慮總結報導（"公民記者陳秋實武漢疫區採訪實錄"系列10） [Supplies are short, the pandemic is urgent Chen Qiushi anxiously reports at noon on the sixth day of the New Year ("Citizen Journalist Chen Qiushi Wuhan pandemic district interview record series 10")] YouTube Video, 29 January 2020, https://www.youtube.com/watch?v=iXozpbomAns&t=276s.

246 "It's 12:40 AM": Zhang Zhan, "Wuhan Huozangchang de hongmingsheng 武汉_火葬场深夜的轰鸣声 20200218 004553" [Explosions Sounding in the Middle of the Night from the Wuhan Crematorium 20200218 00455] YouTube Video, 17 February 2020, https://www.youtube.com/watch?v=C09W CmowMDo.

246 **"Keenly aware of the unprecedented nature . . ."** Yang, Wuhan Lockdown, 84.

248 **"prohibiting people from speaking the truth . . . "** Fang, Fang, *Wuhan Diary*, 16.

248 "If I had known it would come to this": *Wuhan Diary*, 135.

248 **"Over the course of this process of resistance . . . ":** *Wuhan Diary*, 221.

249 **"Over the past year and eight months"**: Chen Qiushi (@chenqiushi404), "Ni hao, wo shi Qiushi 你好，我是秋实 [Hello, I am Qiushi], Twitter post, 30 September 2021. The original post has been deleted, but it can be found archived: https://archive.ph/9UNih.

251 *Baidu* **biography of Li Wenliang**: "Li Wenliang," 李文亮 *Baidu Baike*, accessed 2 August 2022, https://web.archive.org/web/20220802163927/https://baike.baidu.com/item/%E6%9D%8E%E6%96%87%E4%BA%AE/24300481.

MEMORY: SOFT BURIAL

253 *Soft Burial* **wins literary prize**: Wang Yu 王渝, "Fang Fang
    <Ruanmai> huo disanjie Lu Yao wenxuejiang 方方《软埋》获第
    三届路遥文学奖" [Fang Fang's Soft Burial won the third Lu Yao
    literature award] China Federation of Literary and Art Circles, 24
    April 2014, https://web.archive.org/web/20221202191926/http://
    www.cflac.org.cn/ys/wx/wxjx/201711/t20171121_385173.html.

253 *Soft Burial* **denounced**: Luo Siling 罗四鸰, "Zao zuopai
    weigong, zuojia Fang Fang tan <Ruanmai> de "Ruanmai" 遭
    左派围攻，作家方方谈《软埋》的'软埋," [Attacked by left
    wing writers: Writer Fang Fang Talks about the "soft burial"
    of <Soft Burial>] *New York Times China*, 27 June 2017, https://
    cn.nytimes.com/china/20170627/cc27fang-fang/.

253 **Chronology of Soft Burial's ban**: "<Ruanmai> tingyin,
    Jingdong, Dangdang ye xiajia: Fang Fang hen 'wu nai'" "《软
    埋》停印，京东、当当也下架：方方很'无奈," [Soft Burial
    stopped printing, Jingdong, Dangdang took it down too: Fang
    Fang feels helpless] *wxhaowen*, 25 May 2, 2017, https://web.arch
    ive.org/web/20180104132526/http://www.wxhaowen.com/
    article_675f687981ef41359ffe313c8b786da5.shtml.

254 **Cyberspace Administration of China's list of 10
    "historically nihilist" rumors**: Alexander Boyd, "The
    Historical Nihil-List: Cyberspace Administration Targets Top
    Ten Deviation from Approved History," *China Digital Times,* 16
    August 2021, https://chinadigitaltimes.net/2021/08/the-histori
    cal-nihil-list-cyberspace-administration-targets-top-ten-deviati
    ons-from-approved-history/.

CHAPTER 13

257 **The Qing was twice the size of the Ming**: At the Qing's
    peak around 1790, it controlled 14 million square kilometers
    of territory compared to 6.5 million for the Ming. Even when
    it collapsed in 1911, the Qing controlled 12 million. The only

other dynasty that could rival the Qing was the Yuan, but this was essentially just a name for Mongolian control of China that included vast stretches of modern-day Siberia. Its lifespan was also short, and so I think it's fair to give the title to the Qing. It certainly bequeathed modern-day China with its borders in a way that the Yuan did not, and for the purposes of this chapter that is the decisive point.

258 **"a great man of the Chinese people"**: the citation is from Guo Wurong, manager of the Genghis Khan memorial in Inner Mongolia. Cited in Graeme Baker, "Outrage as China Lays Claim to Genghis Khan," *The Telegraph*, 30 December 2006, https://www.telegraph.co.uk/news/worldnews/1538174/Outr age-as-China-lays-claim-to-Genghis-Khan.html, accessed 7 August 2022.

258 **Government claims Tibet since "eternal times"**: See 2011 white paper, "Sixty Years Since Peaceful Liberation of Tibet," Permanent Mission of the People's Republic of China to the United Nations Office at Geneva and Other International Organizations in Switzerland, 11 July 2011, https://web.archive. org/web/20220805100316/https://www.fmprc.gov.cn/ce/cegv/ eng/rqrd/jblc/t953962.htm#:~:text=Over%20the%2060%20ye ars%20since,Autonomous%20Region%2C%20socialist%20const ruction%2C%20and.

258 **"a link between territory and sacredness"**: Michael J. Walsh, *Stating the Sacred: Religion, China, and the Formation of the Nation-State* (New York: Columbia University Press, 2020), 17

259 **The website High Peaks Pure Earth**: "Woeser," *High Peaks Pure Earth*, https://highpeakspureearth.com/category/key-voi ces/woeser/.

260 **Note to Chapter 13**: As indicated in the text, many of the direct quotations are taken from a 2014 interview I did with Woeser and Wang Lixiong in their home. That resulted in a two-part interview in the *New York Review of Books Daily* on 7 and 8 August 2014, at Ian Johnson, "Wang Lixiong and Woeser:

A Way Out of China's Ethnic Unrest?" the *New York Review of Books*, 8 August 2014; and Ian Johnson, "Beyond the Dalai Lama: An Interview with Woeser and Wang Lixiong," *New York Review of Books*, 7 August 2014.

263 **"I put my gloves on . . . "** Tsering Woeser, *Forbidden Memory: Tibet During the Cultural Revolution*, trans. Sara T. Chen (Sterling, VA: Potomac, 2010), vii.

263 **Cultural Revolution Database**: Song Yongyi, ed., "The Chinese Cultural Revolution Database (3rd Edition)" 中國文化大革命文庫光碟 (第三版) [Chinese Cultural Revolution Database DVD (Third Edition)], *Chinese University of Hong Kong Press,* https://cup.cuhk.edu.hk/index.php?route=product/product&product_id=3050.

263 **A New Collection of Red Guard Publications**: Zhou Yuan 周原, *Xinbian hongweishi ziliao* 新编红卫兵资料 [A New Collection of Red Guard Publications. Part I, Newspapers] (Oakton, VA: Center for Chinese Research Materials, 1999), https://www.google.com/books/edition/New_collection_of_Red_Guard_publictions/gLwFwgEACAAJ?hl=en.

265 **. . . the only academic studies**: as per Barnett, Woeser, *Forbidden Memory*, xxxvii.

266 **Tibetan woman wielding a hoe**: Woeser, *Forbidden Memory*, 33.

266 "In the photograph, she looks young": Woeser, *Forbidden Memory*, 52.

267 **"But finally he said, choking"**: Woeser, *Forbidden Memories*, xi.

268 **"Postmemory"**: see Robert Barnett, Benno Weiner, and Françoise Robin, eds., *Conflicting Memories: Tibetan History under Mao Retold* (Leiden: Brill, 2020), 400.

269 **"Chinese rule transformed "a shoppers' and capitalists' paradise"**: Ching Kwan Lee, *Hong Kong: Global China's Restive Frontier* (Cambridge University Press, 2022), 1.

270 **One country-two systems a repetition of Tibetan strategy**: See Ho-fung Hung, *City on the Edge: Hong Kong Under Chinese Rule*, (Cambridge: Cambridge University Press, 2022), 105.

270 "racialist nationalism": Hung, *City on the Edge*, 107.

271 **Anson Chan attacked as a traitor**: Chinese state media cited in Hung, *City on the Edge*, 131.

272 **The center's folk history pages**: In 2022, the university announced that it would no longer support this project. "Bianzhe de hua 编者的话" [Editor's Words], 民间历史 [Folk History], accessed 10 August 2022, https://web.archive.org/web/20220811160323/http://mjlsh.usc.cuhk.edu.hk/Default.aspx.

272 **Sima Lu biography**: Taken from "Zhonggong dangshi zhuanjia Sima Lu 102sui niuyue shishi," 中共党史专家司马璐102岁纽约逝世 [Chinese Communist Party Historian Sima Lu dies at 102 in New York], Voice of America, 30 March 2021, https://www.voachinese.com/a/Sima-Lu-expert-ccp-history-passed-away-102/5832909.html. His party history is in Zhonggong dangshiji wenxian xuancui 中共黨史暨文獻選粹 [Selection of Chinese Communist Party history document] (Hong Kong: 自聯出版社, 1973).

273 **By 2010, 36 million mainlanders visiting Hong Kong**: "HK records 36 mln visitor arrivals in 2010, over 60 pct from mainland," China.org.cn, accessed 2 December 2022, https://web.archive.org/web/20110120233724/http://china.org.cn/travel/2011-01/08/content_21698059.htm.

273 **Southern Hill monitoring campaign**: Ian Johnson, "Lawsuit over Banned Memoir," *New York Times*, 25 April 2015, https://www.nytimes.com/2015/04/26/world/asia/china-lawsuit-over-banned-li-rui-memoir-censorship.html.

273 **Local governments reported how they had banned Hong Kong books**: Michael Forsythe and Andrew Jacobs, "In

China, Books That Make Money and Enemies," *New York Times*, 4 February 2016, https://www.nytimes.com/2016/02/07/busin ess/international/in-china-books-that-make-money-and-enem ies.html.

273 **Yiu Mantin**: In pinyin it is Yao Wentian, but I have kept the original Cantonese romanization as this was how it appeared in his publications.

273 **Yiu Mantin disappearance**: Chris Buckley, "Hong Kong Man Seeking to Issue Book About Xi Is Detained," *New York Times,* 28 January 2014, https://www.nytimes.com/2014/01/ 29/world/asia/publisher-of-book-critical-of-chinas-leader-is- arrested.html.

273 **Yiu Mantin sentence**. "Publisher Yao Wentian (aka Yiu Mantin) Sentenced to 10 years in Prison," Pen America, accessed 30 November 2022, https://pen.org/rapid-action/ publisher-yao-wentian-aka-yiu-mantin-sentenced-to-10-years- in-prison/.

273 **Both men pleaded guilty**: Zheping Huang et al., "A Crackdown on Hong Kong Booksellers," *Quartz*, 17 January 2017, https://qz.com/588511/a-crackdown-on-hong-kong- booksellers-reflects-the-deep-divides-in-chinas-communist- party/.

274 **Televised confessions**: "Writing on the Wall: Disappeared Booksellers and Free Expression in Hong Kong," Research & Resources, Pen America, modified 5 November 2016, https:// pen.org/research-resources/writing-on-the-wall-disappeared- booksellers-and-free-expression-in-hong-kong/, accessed 30 November 2022.

274 **Gui sentence**: Austin Ramzy, "China Sentences Hong Kong Bookseller Gui Minhai to 10 Years in Prison," *New York Times*. 25 February 2020. https://www.nytimes.com/2020/02/25/ world/asia/gui-minhai-china-hong-kong-swedish-booksel ler.html.

274 **The store survives by selling trouble**: Dan Renping 单仁平, "Shao shu gangren buying dongzhe zhiyi 少数港人不应动辄质疑'一国两制'," [The minority Hongkongers shouldn't doubt 'one nation two systems'] *Global Times*, last modified 3 January 2016, https://opinion.huanqiu.com/article/9CaKrnJSR5H.

274 **Universities Service Center stopped hosting the Folk History Project**: http://www.usc.cuhk.edu.hk/folk-history. As of 2022 the site was still running and had been largely archived on the internet archive, "USC for China Studies Collection: A-Z collections," *Chinese University of Hong Kong Library*, 2 December 2022, https://www.lib.cuhk.edu.hk/en/collections/spc/usc-collections/.

MEMORY: THE EMPTY WAREHOUSES

275 Note for Warehouses: For more on Bao Pu, see my 22 January 2016 online interview with him: Ian Johnson, "My Personal Vendetta," https://www.nybooks.com/daily/2016/01/22/my-personal-vendetta-interview-hong-kong-publisher-bao-pu/. For a review of one of his most important books, *The Last Secret: The Final Documents from the June Fourth Crackdown*, see my article Ian Johnson, "China's 'Black Week-end,'" *New York Review of Books*, 27 June 2019, https://www.nybooks.com/articles/2019/06/27/tiananmen-chinas-black-week-end/.

278 **Chen Poking**: Spelling is correct even though it is unorthodox pinyin.

CHAPTER 14

282 Note to Chapter 14: Interviews with Jiang Xue in the Zhongnan Mountains were made on 16 September 2018. The interview with the hermit was made the same day.

284 Details of Xi'an lockdown: See Vivian Wang and Joy Dong, "China, Holding to Its 'Zero Covid' Strategy, Keeps a City of

13 Million Locked Down," *New York Times,* 30 December 2021, https://www.nytimes.com/2021/12/30/world/asia/china-xian-lockdown-covid.html.

284 **People began walking**: See Zhaoxiang de Song shifu 照相的宋师傅, "Xi'an zuowei yizhong chidu" 西安作为一种尺度 ["Xi'an Has Become a Yardstick"], WeChat Subscription, 7 January 2022, https://web.archive.org/web/20220820214031/https://mp.weixin.qq.com/s/E74vG_NVodBCBBY2IxzX6A.

284 **Jiang Xue's account**: Jiang Xue 江雪, Chang'an Shir 长安十日 [Jiang Xue: Ten Days in Chang'an]. Mocun gewu 默存格物, WeChat Subscription, accessed 20 August 2022. The original URL has been blocked. Archived as https://web.archive.org/web/20220105001144/https://mp.weixin.qq.com/s/1wEgqbX-vhfx2zOrNc-4lQ.

285 **200,000 readers**: The piece ultimately gained 210,000 views before being pulled, Jiang Xu 20 August 2022 correspondence.

285 **Hu Xijin on Jiang Xue's article**: See a summary of the controversy in Singapore's *Lianhe Zaobao*, 6 January 2022. Hu Xijin 胡锡进, "Hu Xijing ping Jiang Xue fencheng wenjian: buyao ba kangyi chengjiu yu juti wenti duili 胡锡进评江雪封城见闻：不要把抗疫成就与具体问题对立 [Hu Xijing comments on Jiang Xue's lockdown commentary: Don't pit pandemic control achievements against specific problems] Zaobao, 6 January 2022, https://web.archive.org/web/20220108035614/https://www.zaobao.com.sg/realtime/china/story20220106-1230132.

285 **Entry in the Chinese-language edition of Wikipedia**: "Chang'an Shiri 长安十日" [Ten days of Chang'an], Wikipedia, accessed 20 August 2022, https://zh.m.wikipedia.org/zh-hans/%E9%95%BF%E5%AE%89%E5%8D%81%E6%97%A5.

286 **the public account "Silent Observer"**: 默存格物. It was relaunched as 新默存. As of August 2022 it still existed.

286 **The phrase in Liezi**: "左右曰：「王默存耳．」由此穆王自失者三月而復" ("his attendants told him he had been sitting there quietly.") Most dictionaries gloss this with the meaning

that he had been sitting silently while his spirit roamed. See, for example, "Mo Cun 默存," Jiaoyubu chongbian guoyu cidian xiudingban 教育部重编国语辞典修订版, accessed 20 August 2022, https://dict.revised.moe.edu.tw/dictView.jsp?ID= 27944&word=%E9%BB%98%E5%AD%98.

286 **Ye Fu on *jianghu***: 打不垮的江湖, 23 June 2022. Online at "Dabukua de jianghu 打不垮的江湖," 新默存, WeChat Subscription, accessed 20 August 2022, https://mp.weixin. qq.com/s/DgJ5PkPOuG_OWc1vSmAR0A. Archived at https://web.archive.org/web/20220821142458/https://mp.wei xin.qq.com/s/DgJ5PkPOuG_OWc1vSmAR0A.

289 **Bill Porter on hermits**: See *Road to Heaven: Encounters with Chinese Hermits* (Berkeley, CA: Counterpoint Press, 2009). On his status in China and his comment on seclusion being like graduate school, see my piece in Ian Johnson, "Finding Zen and Book Contracts in Beijing," *New York Review of Books* online edition, 29 May 2012, https://www.nybooks.com/daily/2012/ 05/29/zen-book-contracts-bill-porter-beijing/.

CHAPTER 15

293 **Arendt quote in Jiang Xue article**: "yige qizi de zheyinian" 一个妻子的这一年 ["This Year of a Wife"], *Gongmin*, 2 October 2015, https://cmcn.org/archives/22005. It is also noteworthy that Arendt's *The Origins of Totalitarianism* is widely available in translation. Perhaps the Communist Party sees its relevance as specific to Europe.

297 **China's domestic intelligence services budget rivals the national defense budget**: exact figures are impossible to obtain, but various experts and analysts triangulate statements and budgets. According to Statista, for example, the total budget for domestic intelligence is $205 billion: "Expenditure on public security in China from 2011 to 2021, by government level," 15 December 2022, https://www.statista.com/statistics/1049

749/china-public-security-spending-by-government-level/.
This compares with an official military budget of $230 billion:
"China to raise military budget 7.1% this year," *China Daily*, 6
March 2022, https://www.chinadaily.com.cn/a/202203/06/
WS62245064a310cdd39bc8aacb.html).This represents about 10
percent of total government outlays, based on calculations by
Bloomberg: "China's 2022 Budget: A Breakdown of the Key
Numbers," 4 March 2022, https://www.bloomberg.com/news/
articles/2022-03-05/china-s-2022-budget-a-breakdown-of-the-
key-numbers?leadSource=uverify%20wall.

297 **For problems in the Covid policy**, see, for example,
Yanzhong Huang, *The COVID-19 Pandemic and China's Global
Health Leadership* (New York: Council on Foreign Relations,
2022). **On mishandling demographics,** Carl Minzner,
"China's Doomed Fight Against Demographic Decline," *Foreign
Affairs*, 3 May 2022, https://www.foreignaffairs.com/articles/
china/2022-05-03/chinas-doomed-fight-against-demograp
hic-decline. **For aversion to economic reform**, see Nicholas
Lardy, *The State Strikes Back: The End of Economic Reform in
China?* (Washington, DC: Peterson Institute for International
Economics, 2019). **On educational failure**, see Scott Rozelle
and Natalie Hell, *Invisible China: How the Urban-Rural Divide
Threatens China's Future* (Chicago: University of Chicago
Press, 2020).

298 **Saidiya Hartman**: For a profile of Hartman and her impact,
see "How Saidiya Hartman Retells the History of Black Life,"
by Alexis Okeowo, *New Yorker*, 19 October 2020. Hartman's
book *Scenes of Subjugation* describes her theory of critical
fabulation and how it can be used to describe slavery.

299 **Nguyen on "just memory"**: "Just Memory: War and the
Ethics of Remembrance," *American Literary History*, 2013, pp. 1–
20. doi:10.1093/alh/ajs069.

299 **Sebald on "secondhand memories"**: *On the Natural History
of Destruction* (New York: Modern Library, 2004), 88.

299 **Hirsch on postmemory**: *Family Frames: Photography, Narrative, and Postmemory* (Cambridge, MA: Harvard University Press, 1997), 13.

301 **Foreign festivals pulling films due to Chinese pressure**: See James Tager et al., *Made in Hollywood and Censored by Beijing* (New York: Pen America, 2020), 31, https://pen.org/wp-content/uploads/2020/09/Made_in_Hollywood_Censored_by_Beijing_Report_FINAL.pdf. China also reportedly pulled out of the 2022 Cannes Film Festival because it aired a documentary in 2020 about the Hong Kong protests. See Patrick Brzeski, "Inside China's Conspicuous Absence from Cannes," *Hollywood Reporter*, 19 May 2022, https://www.hollywoodreporter.com/movies/movie-news/cannes-2022-china-conspicuous-absence-covid-hong-kong-1235150139/.

Bibliography

"About Colonial Williamsburg: Annual Reports." Accessed April 20, 2022, https://www.colonialwilliamsburg.org/learn/about-colonial-williamsburg/#annual-reports.

"Ai Luming 艾路明." *Baidu Baike.* Accessed January 10, 2023, https://web.archive.org/web/20221128154605/https://baike.baidu.com/item/%E8%89%BE%E8%B7%AF%E6%98%8E/10773540.

Ai, Xiaoming 艾晓明. "Beifengzhu de ren fanwaipian: jiangjun de never" 被封住的人番外篇：将军的女儿 [The isolated person's other story: The general's daughter]. *Mirror Media,* February 17, 2022. https://www.mirrormedia.mg/premium/20200217pol006.

Ai, Xiaoming 艾晓明. "Jiabiangou Elegy." YouTube Video, 36:24, March 6, 2017. https://www.youtube.com/watch?v=MoNN1F_HegY&t=2182s.

Ai, Xiaoming 艾晓明. "Pandemic Diary." *New Left Review* 122 (March–April 2022).

Ai Xiaoming 艾晓明. "Women yiqi zouguo de lu: chentong daonian wode zuopin xiangdao Zhang Suiqing xiansheng" 我们一起走过的路：沉痛悼念我的作品向导张遂卿先生 [The road we walked together: A sorrowful tribute to Mr. Zhang Suiqing, the mentor of my works]. NewCenturyNet, April 15, 2017. https://web.archive.org/web/20190409221906/http://2newcenturynet.blogspot.com:80/2017/04/blog-post_15.html.

Ai, Xiaoming 艾晓明. *Xue Tong* 血统 [Lineage]. Beijing: Huacheng Chubanshe, 1994.

"Answers to the Italian Journalist Oriana Fallaci." Accessed December 20, 2022, https://web.archive.org/web/20220521071225/http://en.people.cn/dengxp/vol2/text/b1470.html.

"Appendix: Resolution on Certain Questions in the History of Our Party." *Selected Works of Mao Tse-Tung,* vol. 3. Beijing: Foreign Language Press, 1965. http://www.marx2mao.com/PDFs/MaoSW3App.pdf.

Assmann, Aleida. "Funktionsgedächtnis und Speichergedächtnis—Zwei Modi der Erinnerung." In *Erinnerungsräume: Formen und Wandlungen des kulturellen Gedächtnisses.* München: C. H. Beck., 2009.

Assmann, Jan. *Cultural Memory and Early Civilization: Writing, Remembrance, and Political Imagination.* Cambridge: Cambridge University Press, 2011.

Auden, W. H., and Christopher Isherwood. *Journey to a War,* cited in Stephen R. MacKinnon. *Wuhan, 1938: War, Refugees, and the Making of Modern China.* Berkeley: University of California Press, 2008.

Baker, Graeme. "Outrage as China Lays Claim to Genghis Khan." *The Telegraph,* December 30, 2006. Accessed August 7, 2022, https://www.telegraph.co.uk/news/worldnews/1538174/Outrage-as-China-lays-claim-to-Genghis-Khan.html.

Barnett, Robert, Benno Weiner, and Françoise Robin, eds. *Conflicting Memories: Tibetan History Under Mao Retold.* Leiden: Brill, 2020.

Beaverstock, J. V., R. G. Smith, and P. J. Taylor. *A Roster of World Cities.* Leicestershire, UK: GaWC, 1999. doi:10.1016/S0264-2751(99)00042-6.

"Bianzhe de hua 编者的话" [Editor's Words]. 民间历史 [Folk History]. Accessed August 10, 2022, https://web.archive.org/web/20220811160323/http://mjlsh.usc.cuhk.edu.hk/Default.aspx.

Boyd, Alexander. "The Historical Nihil-List: Cyberspace Administration Targets Top Ten Deviations from Approved History." *China Digital Times,* August 16, 2021. https://chinadigitaltimes.net/2021/08/the-historical-nihil-list-cyberspace-administration-targets-top-ten-deviations-from-approved-history/.

Brzeski, Patrick. "Inside China's Conspicuous Absence from Cannes." *Hollywood Reporter,* May 19, 2022. https://www.hollywoodreporter.com/movies/movie-news/cannes-2022-china-conspicuous-absence-covid-hong-kong-1235150139/.

Buckley, Chris. "Hong Kong Man Seeking to Issue Book About Xi Is Held in China." *New York Times,* January 28, 2014. https://www.nytimes.com/2014/01/29/world/asia/publisher-of-book-critical-of-chinas-leader-is-arrested.html.

Buckley, Chris. "Liberal Magazine, 'Forced into a Corner' by China, Girds for Battle." *New York Times,* July 27, 2016. https://www.nytimes.com/2016/07/28/world/asia/china-yanhuang-chunqiu.html.

Buckley, Chris. "Revamped Chinese History Journal Welcomes Hard-Line Writers." *New York Times,* August 17, 2016. https://www.nytimes.com/2016/08/18/world/asia/china-yanhuang-chunqiu.html.

Buckley, Chris. "Vows of Change in China Belie Private Warning." *New York Times,* February 14, 2013. https://www.nytimes.com/2013/02/15/world/asia/vowing-reform-chinas-leader-xi-jinping-airs-other-message-in-private.html.

Cao, Yaxin 曹雅欣. "Xi Jinping: Mieren zhi guo, bi xuanqu qishi" 习近平：灭人之国，必先去其史 [Xi Jinping: To destroy a country's people, start with destroying their history]. *China Daily*, August 6, 2015. https://web.archive.org/web/20221201204953/http://china.chinadaily.com.cn/2015-08/06/content_21520950.htm.

"Chang'an Shiri" 长安十日 [Ten days of Chang'an]. *Wikipedia*. Accessed August 20, 2022, https://zh.m.wikipedia.org/zh-hans/%E9%95%BF%E5%AE%89%E5%8D%81%E6%97%A5.

Chen, Qiushi 陈秋实(@chenqiushi404). "你好，我是秋实！好久不见呀！我计划在2021年12月31日跨年夜，组织一场慈善搏击比赛。联络方式：抖音号quanjishou999." Twitter post, September 30, 2021. https://archive.ph/9UNih.

Chen, Qiushi. "Ziyuan jingque, yiqing jingji | Chen Qiushi danianchuliu zhongwu jiaolü huizong baodao (Goingmin jizhe Chen Qiushi Wuhan yiqu caifang shilu xilie 10)" 資源緊缺，疫情緊急 | 陳秋實大年初六中午焦慮總結報導（'公民記者陳秋實武漢疫區採訪實錄' 系列10) [Supplies are short, the pandemic is urgent. Chen Qiushi nervously reports on the 6th day of the lunar new year. Citizen Journalist Chen Qiushi Wuhan pandemic district reporting series 10]. YouTube Video, 26:47, January 29, 2020. https://www.youtube.com/watch?v=iXozpbomAns&t=276s.

Chen, Thomas. "Blanks to Be Filled: Public-Making and the Censorship of Jia Pingwa's Decadent Capital." *China Perspectives,* January 2015.

Chin, Josh. "In China, Xi Jinping's Crackdown Extends to Dissenting Versions of History." *Wall Street Journal,* August 1, 2016. https://www.wsj.com/articles/in-china-xi-jinpings-crackdown-extends-to-dissenting-versions-of-history-1470087445?mod=article_inline.

"China's Yan'an to Be Revamped into 'City of Revolutionary Museums.'" *Xinhua News*. Accessed April 3, 2021, https://web.archive.org/web/20221205204418/http://www.xinhuanet.com/english/2021-04/03/c_139857078.htm.

"China's 2019 'Red Tourism' Revenue Tops 400b Yuan." *State Council*. Accessed January 10, 2023, https://web.archive.org/web/20221205204123/http://english.www.gov.cn/statecouncil/ministries/202105/19/content_WS60a50610c6d0df57f98d9bef.html#:~:text=BEIJING%20%E2%80%94%20The%20revenue%20generated%20by,NCHA)%20said%20on%20May%2019.

Courtney, Chris. *The Nature of Disaster in China: The 1931 Yangzi River Flood*. Studies in Environment and History. Cambridge: Cambridge University Press, 2018. doi:10.1017/9781108278362.

Crossley, Gabriel, and Alison Williams. "Wuhan Lockdown 'Unprecedented,' Shows Commitment to Contain Virus: WHO Representative in China." *Reuters*, January 23, 2020. https://web.archive.org/web/20200124203 401/https://www.reuters.com/article/us-china-health-who-idUSKB N1ZM1G9.

"Dabukua de jianghu 打不垮的江湖." Xin Mocun新默存. WeChat Subscription. Accessed January 10, 2023, https://web.archive.org/web/ 20220821140558/https:/mp.weixin.qq.com/s/DgJ5PkPOuG_OWc1 vSmAR0A.

DeMare, Brian. *Land Wars: The Story of China's Agrarian Revolution*. New York: Oxford University Press, 2019.

Deng, Yongsheng 邓永胜. "Cong shenmi dao kaifang—zoujin Zhonggong Zhongyang dangshiyanjiushi" 从神秘到开放--走近中共中央党史研究室 [From mystery to openness—a closer look at the Party History Research Office of the CPC Central Committee]. *China News*, July 21, 2010. https://web.archive.org/web/20221202205042/https://www.chinanews.com.cn/gn/2010/07-21/2415049.shtml.

Dikötter, Frank. *Mao's Great Famine: The History of China's Most Devastating Catastrophe, 1958–1962*. New York: Bloomsbury, 2011.

"Document 9: A China File Translation: How Much Is a Hardline Party Directive Shaping China's Current Political Climate?" *ChinaFile*, November 8, 2013. https://www.chinafile.com/document-9-chinafile-translation#start.

Dong, Joy. "Two Years After His Death, the Chinese Doctor Who Warned of the Virus Is Remembered." *New York Times*, February 7, 2022. https://www.nytimes.com/2022/02/07/world/asia/chinese-doctor-li-wenliang-covid-warning.html.

"Drawing the News: Apology Not Accepted." *China Digital Times*. Accessed July 10, 2022, http://chinadigitaltimes.net/2014/01/drawing-news-apology-accepted/.

Escherick, Joseph W. *Accidental Holy Land: The Communist Revolution in Northwest China*. Berkeley: University of California Press, 2022.

Fallada, Hans. *Every Man Dies Alone*. Translated by Michael Hofmann. New York: Melville House, 2009.

Fang, Fang. *Wuhan Diary: Dispatches from a Quarantined City*. Translated by Michael Berry. New York: HarperVia, 2020.

Fang, Lizhi. "The Chinese Amnesia." *New York Review of Books*, September 27, 1990. Translated by Perry Link. https://www.nybooks.com/articles/1990/09/27/the-chinese-amnesia/.

Forsythe, Michael, and Andrew Jacobs, "In China, Books That Make Money and Enemies." *New York Times*, February 4, 2016. https://www.nytimes.com/2016/02/07/business/international/in-china-books-that-make-money-and-enemies.html.

"Fuxing zhi lu·xinshidai bufen zhanlan mianxiang gongzhong kaifang" 复兴之路·新时代部分展览面向公众开放 [The road to rejuvenation: New Era portion is open to public]. Central Commission for Discipline Inspection China. https://web.archive.org/web/20221208180116/https://www.ccdi.gov.cn/toutu/201807/t20180705_175124.html.

Gao, Hua. *How the Red Sun Rose*. New York: Columbia University Press, 2019.

Gao, Ertai 高尔泰. *Huangshan xizhao* 荒山夕照 [Sunset over the desolate mountain]. Personal History WeChat subscription channel, April 13, 2020. Accessed November 30, 2022, https://web.archive.org/web/20221205020329/https://mp.weixin.qq.com/s/9GzSZkioYcQ7XrZPgpkXZA.

Gao, Ertai 高尔泰. *Xunzhao Jiayuan* 寻找家园 [In search of my homeland]. Taipei: Yinke Wenxue Zazhi Chuban Youxian Gongsi, 2009.

"Gongchandang dangshi zhuanjia Sima Lu 102sui niuyue shishi" 中共党史专家司马璐102岁纽约逝世 [Expert on Chinese Communist Party Sima Lu died at 102 in New York]. *Voice of America Chinese*, March 30, 2021. https://www.voachinese.com/a/Sima-Lu-expert-ccp-history-passed-away-102/5832909.html.

Guo, Yuhua 郭于华. *Shoukurende jiangshu: Jicun lishi yu yizhong wenming de luoji* 受苦人的讲述：骥村历史与一种文明的逻辑 [Narratives of the sufferers: The history of Jicun and the logic of civilization]. Hong Kong: Chinese University of Hong Kong Press, 2013.

Hartman, Saidiya. *Scenes of Subjection: Terror, Slavery, and Self-Making in Nineteenth Century America*. New York: Norton, 1997.

Hirsch, Marianne. *Family Frames: Photography, Narrative, and Postmemory*. Cambridge, MA: Harvard University Press, 1997.

"HK Records 36 Mln Visitor Arrivals in 2010, over 60 pct from Mainland." China.org.cn. Accessed December 2, 2022, https://web.archive.org/web/20110120233724/http://china.org.cn/travel/2011-01/08/content_21698059.htm.

Hu, Jie 胡杰, dir. *Guoying dongfeng nongchang* 国营东风农场 [The East Wind State Farm]. 2009; New York: Icarus Films, 2009, DVD. https://icarusfilms.com/df-ew.

Hu, Jie 胡杰, dir. *Maidichong de gesheng* 麦地冲的歌声 [Maidichong's singing voice], 2014. https://www.youtube.com/watch?v=oZ90J3M6C3s&t=21s.

Hu, Jie 胡杰, dir. *Spark*. 2019; New York: Icarus Films, 2019, DVD. https://icarusfilms.com/df-spark.

Hu, Jie 胡杰, dir. *Wode muqin Wang Peiying* 我的母亲王佩英 [My mother Wang Peiying], 2011. https://www.youtube.com/watch?v=W2eaFJXxwTQ.

Hu, Jie 胡杰, dir. *Wosui siqu* 我虽死去 [Though I am gone]. 2007; New York: Icarus Films, 2012, DVD. https://icarusfilms.com/df-gone.

Hu, Jie 胡杰, dir. *Xunzhao Lin Zhao de linghun* 寻找林昭的灵魂 [Searching for Lin Zhao's soul]. 2004; New York: Icarus Films, 2012, DVD. https://icarusfilms.com/df-linzha.

Hu, Jie 胡杰, dir. *Zai Haibian* 在海边 [Beside the sea], 2000. https://www.youtube.com/watch?v=x-BVedSlU_I.

"Hu Jintao huijian quanguo dangshigongzuo huiyidaibiao, Xi Jinping jianghua" 胡锦涛会见全国党史工作会议代表，习近平讲话 [Hu Jintao visits representatives of national working meeting on party history, Xi Jinping gives a speech]. *Xinhua News Agency via Sina*, July 21, 2010. https://web.archive.org/web/20221202204512/http://news.sina.com.cn/c/2010-07-21/175220728776.shtml.

Hu, Xijin 胡锡进. "Hu Xijing ping Jiang Xue fencheng wenjian: buyao ba kangyi chengjiu yu juti wenti duiyic胡锡进评江雪封城见闻：不要把抗疫成就与具体问题对立" [Hu Xijing comment on Jiang Xue's lockdown commentary: Don't pit pandemic control achievements against specific problems]. Zaobao, January 6, 2022. https://web.archive.org/web/20220108035614/https://www.zaobao.com.sg/realtime/china/story20220106-1230132.

Huang, Zheping, Echo Huang, and Heather Timmons. "A Crackdown on Hong Kong Booksellers Reflects the Deep Divides in China's Communist Party." *Quartz*, January 17, 2016. https://web.archive.org/web/20230109083717/http://www.news.cn/english/2021-11/16/c_131 0314611.htm .

Huang, Yanzhong. *The COVID-19 Pandemic and China's Global Health Leadership*. New York: Council on Foreign Relations, 2022.

Hua Xia. "Resolution of the CPC Central Committee on the Major Achievements and Historical Experience of the Party over the Past Century." *Xinhua Net*, November 16, 2021. https://web.archive.org/web/20230109083717/http://www.news.cn/english/2021-11/16/c_131 0314611.htm.

Hung, Chang-tai. "The Red Line: Creating a Museum of the Chinese Revolution." *China Quarterly* no. 184, December 2005.

Hung, Ho-fung. *City on the Edge: Hong Kong Under Chinese Rule*. Cambridge: Cambridge University Press, 2022.

Huxtable, Ada Louise. "Dissent at Colonial Williamsburg; Errors of Restoration." *New York Times*, September 22, 1963.

Illegal and Harmful Information Reporting Center中央网信办举报中心. "Reporting Historical Nihilism to '12377.'" Last modified on April 9, 2021. https://web.archive.org/web/20221205184840/https://www.12377.cn/wxxx/2021/fc6eb910_web.html.

Israel, George L. *Doing Good and Ridding Evil in Ming China: The Political Career of Wang Yangming*. Leiden: Brill, 2014.

"Jiabiangou jishi—01 youpai nongchang" 夹边沟祭事—01右派农场 [Jiabiangou Elegy—01 Rightist Farm]. YouTube Video, 1:17:15, September 6, 2019. https://www.youtube.com/watch?v=9bEBG6Hqb6Y&t=11s.

Jiang, Haofeng 姜浩峰. "*Zhang Hongbing wei "shimu" daoqian beihou*" 张红兵为"弑母"道歉背后 [Behind Zhang Hongbing's matricide apology]. Xinmin Weekly, September 21, 2013. https://web.archive.org/web/20150713080414/http://xmzk.xinminweekly.com.cn/News/Content/2835.

Jiang, Xue 江雪. "Jiangxue: changan shiri" 江雪：长安十日 [Jiang Xue: Ten days of Chang'an] Mocun Gewu默存格物. WeChat Subscription, accessed January 10, 2023. https://web.archive.org/web/20220105001144/https://mp.weixin.qq.com/s/1wEgqbX-vhfx2zOrNc-4lQ.

Jiang, Xue 江雪. "'Xinhuo' liaoluo, er wo zai xunzhao" "星火"寥落，而我在寻找 ["Sparks" is few and far between, and I'm looking]. *Jintian* 1 (2019): 211–234. https://www.jintian.net/121.pdf.

Jiang, Xue 江雪. "Xinghuo yusi piaoling: zai 2018 nian yongbie Tan Chanxue," 星火於斯飄零：在2018年永別譚蟬雪 [Spark drifts in the sky: Farewell to Tan Chanxue in 2018]. *The Initium*, January 6, 2019. https://web.archive.org/web/2/https://theinitium.com/article/20190107-china-dissident-history-tanchanshe/.

Jiang, Xue江雪. "Jiang Xue: You Fu Cong xiangqile 'Xinghuo' qianbei Gu Yan." 江雪：由傅聪想起了"星火"前辈顾雁 [Jiang Xue: Fu Cong reminded me of "Spark" predecessor Gu Yan]. *Caixin*, December 31, 2020. https://web.archive.org/web/20230110211630/https://jiangxue.blog.caixin.com/archives/239996.

Jiang, Yu 江宇. "The History Connotations and Practical Significance of 'Two Cannot Be Rejected.'" *CPC News,* October 12, 2013. https://web.archive.org/web/20221208164809/http://cpc.people.com.cn/n/2013/1012/c69120-23179702.html.

"Jinfang 'lishi xuwu zhuyi' liyong hulianwang qinglue zhongguo," 谨防"历史虚无主义"利用互联网侵略中国, [Beware of "historical nihilism" using the Internet to invade China]. *China Daily*. Accessed December

2, 2022, https://web.archive.org/web/20221202211521/http://china.chi nadaily.com.cn/2015-10/28/content_22303537.htm.

Johnson, Ian. "A Revolutionary Discovery in China." *New York Review of Books*, April 21, 2016. https://www.nybooks.com/articles/2016/04/21/ revolutionary-discovery-in-china/.

Johnson, Ian. "At China's New Museum, History Toes Party Line." *New York Times,* April 3, 2011. https://www.nytimes.com/2011/04/04/world/asia/ 04museum.html.

Johnson, Ian. "Beyond the Dalai Lama: An Interview with Woeser and Wang Lixiong." *New York Review of Books*, August 7, 2014. https://www. nybooks.com/online/2014/08/07/interview-tsering-woeser-wang-lixiong/.

Johnson, Ian. "China's Brave Underground Journal." *New York Review of Books,* December 4, 2014. https://www.nybooks.com/articles/2014/12/ 04/chinas-brave-underground-journal/.

Johnson, Ian. "China's Brave Underground Journal II." *New York Review of Books*, December 18, 2014. https://www.nybooks.com/articles/2014/12/ 18/chinas-brave-underground-journal-ii/.

Johnson, Ian. "China's 'Black Week-end,'" review of *The Last Secret: The Final Documents from the June Fourth Crackdown*, by Bao Pu. *New York Review of Books,* June 27, 2019. https://www.nybooks.com/articles/2019/06/27/ tiananmen-chinas-black-week-end/.

Johnson, Ian. "Finding Zen and Book Contracts in Beijing." *New York Review of Books*, May 29, 2012. https://www.nybooks.com/online/2012/05/29/ zen-book-contracts-bill-porter-beijing/.

Johnson, Ian. "Lawsuit over Banned Memoir Asks China to Explain Censorship." *New York Times,* April 25, 2015. https://www.nytimes.com/ 2015/04/26/world/asia/china-lawsuit-over-banned-li-rui-memoir-cen sorship.html.

Johnson, Ian. "'My Personal Vendetta': An Interview with Hong Kong Publisher Bao Pu," *New York Review of Books*, January 22, 2016. https:// www.nybooks.com/online/2016/01/22/my-personal-vendetta-interv iew-hong-kong-publisher-bao-pu/.

Johnson, Ian. "Ruling Through Ritual: An Interview with Guo Yuhua." *New York Review of Books*, June 18, 2018. https://www.nybooks.com/daily/ 2018/06/18/ruling-through-ritual-an-interview-with-guo-yuhua/.

Johnson, Ian. "Sexual Life in Modern China." *New York Review of Books*, October 26, 2017. https://www.nybooks.com/articles/2017/10/26/sex ual-life-in-modern-china/.

Johnson, Ian. "Wang Lixiong and Woeser: A Way Out of China's Ethnic Unrest?" *New York Review of Books*, August 8, 2014. https://www.nybooks.com/online/2014/08/08/wang-lixiong-woeser-chinas-ethnic-unrest/.

Jurong Maoshan Zhi Bangongshi 句容市地方志办公室 [Jurong Municipal Gazetteer Office], *Jurong Maoshan Zhi* 句容茅山志 [Jurong Maoshan Magazine]. Hefei: Huangshashu Chuban, 1998.

Kurzynski, Maciej. "In Defense of Beauty: Gao Ertai's Aesthetic of Resistance." *Philosophy East and West* 69, no. 4 (2009).

Kundera, Milan. *The Art of the Novel*. Translated by Linda Asher. New York: Harper Perennial, 2000.

Lardy, Nicholas. *The State Strikes Back: The End of Economic Reform in China?* Washington, DC: Peterson Institute for International Economics, 2019.

Lee, Ching Kwan, *Hong Kong: Global China's Restive Frontier*. Cambridge: Cambridge University Press, 2022.

Li, Fangchun 李放春. "'Dizhuwo' li de qingsuan fengbo—jiantan beifang tugaizhong de 'minzhu' yu 'huai ganbu' wenti" "地主窝"里的清算风波——兼谈北方土改中的"民主"与"坏干部"问题 [The liquidation storm in the 'landlord nest': and talks on 'democracy' and 'bad comrade' questions in the northern land reform]. *Aisixiang,* February 4, 2009. https://web.archive.org/web/20221202185703/https://www.aisixiang.com/data/24580.html.

"Li Wenliang," 李文亮. *Baidu Baike*. Accessed August 2, 2022, https://web.archive.org/web/20220802163927/https://baike.baidu.com/item/%E6%9D%8E%E6%96%87%E4%BA%AE/24300481.

Lian, Xi. *Blood Letters: The Untold Story of Lin Zhao, a Martyr in Mao's China.* New York: Basic Books, 2018.

Lifton, Robert Jay. *Thought Reform and the Psychology of Totalism: A Study of "Brainwashing" in China.* New York: Norton, 1961.

"Lishi xuwuzhuyi yu sulianjieti," 历史虚无主义与苏联解体 [Historical nihilism and the dissolution of the Soviet Union]. April 23, 2022. Youku Video. https://v.youku.com/v_show/id_XNTgoNDEwNTk2OA==.html.

Liu, Qiong 刘琼. "Xi Jinping: chengqianqihou jiwangkailai jixuchaozhe zhonghuaminzu weidafuxing mubiao fenyongqianjin" 习近平：承前启后 继往开来 继续朝着中华民族伟大复兴目标奋勇前进 [Xi Jinping: Inherit the past and usher in the future, continue to march towards the great rejuvenation of the Chinese nation]. *Xinhua Net*, November 29, 2012. https://web.archive.org/web/20221222113247/http://www.xinhuanet.com/politics/2012-11/29/c_113852724.htm.

Liu, Zongyuan 柳宗元. *Written in Exile: The Poetry of Liu Tsung-yuan.* Translated by Bill Porter. Port Townsend, WA: Copper Canyon Press, 2019.

Luo, Siling 罗四鸰. "Zao zuopai weigong, zuojia Fang Fang tan <Ruanmai> de 'Ruanmai' 遭左派围攻，作家方方谈《软埋》的'软埋," [Attacked by left wing writers: Writer Fang Fang talks about the "soft burial" of <Soft Burial>] *New York Times China,* June 27, 2017. https://cn.nytimes.com/china/20170627/cc27fang-fang/.

MacKinnon, Stephen R. *Wuhan, 1938: War, Refugees, and the Making of Modern China.* Berkeley: University of California Press, 2008.

Mao, Zedong. "Our Study and the Current Situation," *Selected Works of Mao Tse-tung,* April 12, 1944. https://www.marxists.org/reference/archive/mao/selected-works/volume-3/mswv3_18.htm.

"The Memory Project." Duke University Libraries. Accessed July 22, 2022, https://repository.duke.edu/dc/memoryproject.

"Message from the .rector." *National Museum of China.* Accessed January 10, 2023, https://web.archive.org/web/20230110182649/http://en.chnmuseum.cn/about_the_nmc_593/message_from_nmc_director_595/201911/t20191122_173222.html.

Minzner, Carl. "China's Doomed Fight Against Demographic Decline." *Foreign Affairs,* May 3, 2022. https://www.foreignaffairs.com/articles/china/2022-05-03/chinas-doomed-fight-against-demographic-decline.

"Mo Cun" 默存, *Jiaoyubu chongbian guoyu cidian xiudingban* 教育部重编国语辞典修订版. Accessed January 10, 2023, https://web.archive.org/web/20220821021841/https://dict.revised.moe.edu.tw/dictView.jsp?ID=27944&word=%E9%BB%98%E5%AD%98.

"Noteworthy Problems Related to the Current State of the Ideological Sphere." *ChinaFile.* Accessed November 22, 2022, https://www.chinafile.com/document-9-chinafile-translation#start.

Peng, Xiaoling 彭晓玲, and Yu Ziqing 于子青. "Guanyu zhonggongzhongyang guanyu dangde bainianfendou zhongdachengjiu he lishijingyan deshuoming" 关于《中共中央关于党的百年奋斗重大成就和历史经验的决议》的说明 [Explanation of resolution on major achievements and historical experience of CPC over past century]. *CPC News,* December 1, 2021. https://web.archive.org/web/20230110182927/http://cpc.people.com.cn/n1/2021/1201/c64094-32296476.html.

"Publisher Yao Wentian (Aka Yiu Mantin) Sentenced to 10 Years in Prison." Pen America, last modified May 12, 2014. https://pen.org/rapid-action/publisher-yao-wentian-aka-yiu-mantin-sentenced-to-10-years-in-prison/.

Ramzy, Austin. "China Sentences Hong Kong Bookseller Gui Minhai to 10 Years in Prison." *New York Times,* February 25, 2020. https://www.nyti mes.com/2020/02/25/world/asia/gui-minhai-china-hong-kong-swed ish-bookseller.html.

"The Rectification Campaign." *Baidu Baike.* Accessed January 10, 2023, https://web.archive.org/web/2/https://baike.baidu.com/item/ %E5%BB%B6%E5%AE%89%E6%95%B4%E9%A3%8E%E8%BF%90 %E5%8A%A8/4416458.

"Red Guard Apologizes for Role in Teacher's Death," *China Digital Times,* accessed June 20, 2014, https://chinadigitaltimes.net/2014/01/red-guard-apologizes-role-teachers-death/.

"Renmin ribao: yonghao wenwu ziyuan, jianghao hongse gushi" 人民日报：用好文物资源 讲好红色故事 [People's Daily: Make good use of cultural resources, tell good red stories]. *WeChat,* March 29, 2022. https://web.arch ive.org/web/20221205205423/https://mp.weixin.qq.com/s?__biz=MzI 5NzE4MDI4NQ==&mid=2247494880&idx=5&sn=30dec863a79933e0f 685888ccea84109&chksm=ecbba1f2dbcc28e4f4c6623112ffb9bb8950620d-322bda3390a1b63bd5e1751a12aad65f4796&scene=27.

Ringen, Stein. *The Perfect Dictatorship: China in the 21st Century.* Hong Kong: Hong Kong University Press, 2016.

Roberts, Margret E. *Censored: Distraction and Diversion Inside China's Great Firewall.* Princeton, NJ: Princeton University Press, 2018.

"A Roster of World Cities." GaWC Research Bulletin 5. Accessed April 15, 2022, https://web.archive.org/web/20220314234438/https://www. lboro.ac.uk/gawc/rb/rb5.html.

Rozelle, Scott, and Natalie Hell. *Invisible China: How the Urban-Rural Divide Threatens China's Future.* Chicago: University of Chicago Press, 2022.

"<Ruanmai> tingyin, Jingdong, Dangdang ye xiajia: Fang Fang hen 'wu nai' 《软埋》停印，京东、当当也下架：方方很'无奈,'" [Soft Burial stopped printing, Jingdong, Dangdang took it down too: Fang Fang feels helpless]. wxhaowen.com, May 25, 2017. https://web.archive.org/web/ 20180104132526/http://www.wxhaowen.com/article_675f687981ef4 1359ffe313c8b786da5.shtml.

Sebald, W. G. *On the Natural History of Destruction.* New York: Modern Library, 2004.

Shan, Renping 单仁平. "Shao shu gangren buying dongzhe zhiyi 少数港人不应动辄质疑'一国两制'" [The minority Hongkongers shouldn't doubt 'one nation two systems'] Huanqiu, last modified January 3, 2016. https://web.archive.org/web/20230107205552/https://m.huanqiu. com/article/9CaKrnJSR5H.

Shao, Jiang. *Citizen Publications in China Before the Internet*. New York: Palgrave Macmillan, 2015.

Shiraey, Eric, and Zi Yang. "The Gao-Rao Affair: A Case of Character Assassination in Chinese Politics in the 1950s." In *Character Assassination Throughout the Ages*. Edited by Martijn Icks and Eric Shiraey. New York: Palgrave Macmillan, 2014.

Snow, Edgar. *Red Star over China*. New York: Grove Press, 1968.

Silbergeld, Jerome. *Back to the Red Cliff: Reflection on the Narrative Mode in Early Literati Landscape Painting*. Ann Arbor: Regents of the University of Michigan, 1995.

"Sixty Years Since Peaceful Liberation of Tibet." Human Rights Basic Positions, Information Office of the State Council China, July 11, 2011. https://web.archive.org/web/20211015040928/https://www.fmprc. gov.cn/ce/cegv/eng/rqrd/jblc/t953962.htm#:~:text=Over%20the%20 60%20years%20since,Autonomous%20Region%2C%20socialist%20c onstruction%2C%20and.

Song, Binbin 宋彬彬. "Sishi duonian wo yizhi xiangshuo de hua" 四十多年来我一直想说的话 [Words I've wanted to speak for forty years]. *Remembrance*, January 31, 2012, 3–15. http://prchistory.org/wp-content/uploads/2014/05/REMEMBRANCE_No80.pdf.

Song, Yongyi 宋永毅, ed. "The Chinese Cultural Revolution Database (3rd ed.) 中國文化大革命文庫光碟 (第三版)." Chinese University of Hong Kong Press. https://cup.cuhk.edu.hk/index.php?route=product/product&product_id=3050.

Strassberg, Richard E., ed. and trans. *Inscribed Landscapes: Travel Writing from Imperial China*. Berkeley: University of California Press, 1994.

Su, Lin 苏琳. "Yangjiagou 'xinyuan' de 'jiuzhuren'—shanganning bianqu zhuming aiguo mingzhu renshi Ma Xingmin Jishi" 杨家沟"新院"的"旧主人"——陕甘宁边区著名爱国民主人士马醒民纪事 [Yangjiagou 'Xinyuan's' Old Owner: Shanganning district famous patriotic democrat Ma Xingmin Memo]. Shaanxi Wenming, May 24, 2016. https://web.arch ive.org/web/20221202184304/http://shx.wenming.cn/xwdt/201602/t20160226_3171394.htm.

Suettinger, Robert. *Negotiating History: The Chinese Communist Party's 1981*. Arlington, VA: Project 2049, 2017. https://project2049.net/wp-content/uploads/2017/07/P2049_Suettinger_Negotiating-History-CCP_071 717.pdf.

Tager, James. *Made in Hollywood and Censored by Beijing*. New York: Pen America, 2020. https://pen.org/report/made-in-hollywood-censored-by-beijing/.

Tan, Chanxue 谭蝉雪. *bianzhu Qiusuo: lanzhoudaxue "youpai fangeming ji'an" jishi* 求索：兰州大学「右派反革命集团案」纪实 [Seeking: The Rightist Anti-Revolutionary Group Case at Lanzhou University]. Hong Kong: Hong Kong Tianma Publisher, 2017.

Tan, Hecheng. *The Killing Wind: A Chinese County's Descent into Madness During the Cultural Revolution.* Translated by Stacy Mosher and Guo Jian. New York: Oxford University Press, 2017.

Tan, Hecheng 谭合成. *Xue de shen hua: Gongyuan 1967 nian hunan daoxian wenge datusha jishi* 血的神话：公元1967年湖南道县文革大屠杀纪实 [Blood myths: Chronicle of the Cultural Revolution massacre in Dao County, Hunan Province, 19671967年湖南道县文革大屠杀纪实2010.

Tan, Zuoren 谭作人. "Longmenshan—Qing wei beishan haizi zuozheng" 龙门山—请为北川孩子作证 [Longmen Mountain: please testify for the Beichuan children]. *China Weekly Report*, April 4, 2009. https://web.archive.org/web/20220628223343/https://www.china-week.com/html/4894.htm.

Tan, Yvette. "Li Wenliang: 'Wailing Wall' for China's Virus Whistleblowing Doctor." *BBC News,* June 23, 2020. https://www.bbc.com/news/world-asia-china-53077072.

"Testimony, History and Ethics: From the Memory of Jiabiangou Prison Camp to a Reappraisal of the Anti-Rightist Movement in Present-Day China." Translated by Sebastian Veg. *China Quarterly* 218 (June 2014): 514–539. doi:10.1017/S0305741014000368.

"U.S. Family of Mao's General Assimilates, Votes for Obama." *Bloomberg News*, December 26, 2012. https://www.bloomberg.com/news/articles/2012-12-26/chinese-in-ann-arbor-voted-obama-in-elite-family-of-mao-s-rulers#xj4y7vzkg.

Veeck, Gregory, Clifton W. Pannell, Christopher J. Smith, and Youqin Huang. *China's Geography: Globalization and the Dynamics of Political, Economic, and Social Change.* Lanham, MD: Rowman and Littlefield, 2016.

Veg, Sebastian. *Minjian: The Rise of China's Grassroots Intellectuals.* New York: Columbia University Press, 2019.

Veg, Sebastian. "Wang Xiaobo and the No Longer Silent Majority." *The Impact of China's 1989 Tiananmen Massacre.* Edited by Jean-Philippe Béja. London: Routledge, 2010.

Walsh, Michael J. *Stating the Sacred: Religion, China, and the Formation of the Nation-State.* New York: Columbia University Press, 2020.

Wang, Keming 王克明. *"Wenge chanhui huiyilu"* 文革'忏悔回忆录 [Cultural Revolution confession memoir] Huaxiazhiqing. Accessed February 11,

2022, https://web.archive.org/web/20220211091719/http://www.hxzq. net/aspshow/showarticle.asp?id=10201.

Wang, Vivian, and Joy Dong. "China, Holding to Its 'Zero Covid' Strategy, Keeps a city of 13 Million Locked Down." *New York Times*, December 30, 2021. https://www.nytimes.com/2021/12/30/world/asia/china-xian-lockdown-covid.html.

Wang, Xiaobo. Golden Age. Translated by Yan Yan. New York: Penguin Random House, 2022.

Wang, Xiaobo. *The Silent Majority*. Translated by Eric Abrahamsen. Vienna, Austria: Paper Republic, 1997.

Wang, Yu 王渝. "Fang Fang <Ruanmai> huo disanjie Lu Yao wenxuejiang 方方《软埋》获第三届路遥文学奖" [Fang Fang's Soft Burial won the third Lu Yao literature award]. China Federation of Literary and Art Circles, April 24, 2014. https://web.archive.org/web/20221202191926/http://www.cflac.org.cn/ys/wx/wxjx/201711/t20171121_385173.html.

Wee, Sui-Lee, and Elsie Chen. "Red Tourism Flourishes in China Ahead of Party Centennial." *New York Times*, June 25, 2021. https://www.nytimes.com/2021/06/25/business/china-centennial-red-tourism.html.

Weigelin-Schwiedrzik, Susanne. "In Search of a Master Narrative for 20th-Century Chinese History." *China Quarterly* 188 (December 2006): 1070–1091. https://doi.org/10.1017/S0305741006000555.

"Wenge shoushang xiaozhang zhangfu jushou daoqian Chize Song Binbin xuwei" 文革受害校长丈夫拒受道歉 斥责宋彬彬虚伪 [Cultural Revolution victim president's husband rejected apology, scolded Song Binbin as "hollow"]. Last modified February 1, 2014. https://web.archive.org/web/20230110184059/http://news.sina.com.cn/c/p/2014-02-01/142129388421.shtml.

Winter, Jay. *Remembering War: The Great War Between Historical Memory and History in the Twentieth Century*. New Haven, CT: Yale University Press, 2006.

"Writing on the Wall: Disappeared Booksellers and Free Expression in Hong Kong." Research & Resources, Pen America, last modified November 5, 2016. https://pen.org/research-resources/writing-on-the-wall-disappeared-booksellers-and-free-expression-in-hong-kong/.

Woeser, Tsering. *Forbidden Memory: Tibet During the Cultural Revolution*. Translated Sara T. Chen. Sterling, VA: Potomac Books, 2010.

"Wuhanshi weijianwei guanyu dangqian woshi feiyan yiqing de qingkuang tongbao" 武汉市卫健委关于当前我市肺炎疫情的情况通报 [Briefing by the Wuhan Municipal Health Commission on the current pneumonia epidemic in the city]. Wuhan Municipal Health Commission, published December 31, 2019. https://web.archive.org/web/2020043 0030406/http://wjw.wuhan.gov.cn/front/web/showDetail/201912 3108989.

Wu, Di 吴迪. *Neimeng wenge shilu: "minzu fenlie" yu "wasu" yundong* 内蒙文革实录:"民族分裂"与"挖肃"运动 [Record of the Cultural Revolution in Inner Mongolia: "Ethnic Separatism" and the movement to "Weed out Counterrevolutionaries"]. Hong Kong: Mirror Books, 2000.

Wu, Di 吴迪. *Zhongxifeng maniu* 中西风马牛 [China-West: Things completely unrelated]. Beijing: World Publishing, 2014.

Wu, Guoguang. *Anatomy of Political Power in China*. Singapore: National University of Singapore, 2005.

"Wuhanshi weijianwei guanyu dangqian woshi feiyan yiqing de qing-kuang tongbao" 武汉市卫健委关于当前我市肺炎疫情的情况通报 [Briefing by the Wuhan Municipal Health Commission on the current pneumonia epidemic in the city] Wuhan Municipal Health Commission, December 31, 2019. https://web.archive.org/web/20200430030406/ http://wjw.wuhan.gov.cn/front/web/showDetail/2019123108989.

W. Woody [Pseud.] "The Cultural Revolution in Inner Mongolia: Extracts for an unpublished history." Edited and translated by Michael Schoenhals. *Occasional Paper*. Stockholm: Stockholm University, Center for Pacific Asia Studies, 1993.

"Xi'an xuowei yizhong chidu" 西安作为一种尺度 [Xi'an as a scale] Jiuwen Pinglun 旧闻评论, WeChat Subscription. Accessed August 20, 2022, https://web.archive.org/web/20220216095550/https://mp.wei xin.qq.com/s/E74vG_NVodBCBBY2IxzX6A.

Xi, Jinping 习近平. "Full Text: Xi's explanation of resolution on major achievements and historical experience of CPC over past century." *Xinhua Net*, November 16, 2021. https://web.archive.org/web/2022101 6091747/http://www.news.cn/english/2021-11/16/c_1310314613.htm.

Xi, Jinping 习近平. "Xi Jinping: chengqianqihou jiwangkailai jixu chaozhe zhonghuamenzu weidafuxin mubiao fengyongqianjin" 习近平：承前启后 继往开来 继续朝着中华民族伟大复兴目标奋勇前进 [Xi Jinping: Build on the past and open up the future; continue to advance towards the goal of the Great Nation Rejuvenation of China] Xinhua News, November 29, 2012. https://web.archive.org/web/20221205215653/ http://www.xinhuanet.com/politics/2012-11/29/c_113852724.htm.

Xi, Jinping 习近平. "Xi Jinping: Zai fazhan Zhongguo tese shehui zhuyi Shijian Zhong bu duan faxian, chuangzhao, qianjin" 习近平：在发展中国特色社会主义实践中不断发现、创造、前进 [Xi Jinping: Continue to discover, innovate, and progress in the process of developing socialist society with Chinese characteristics.] CPC News. Accessed December 1, 2022, https://web.archive.org/web/20221201210745/http://cpc.people.com.cn/n/2013/0106/c64094-20101215-2.html.

Xiang, Chengjian 向承鉴. "Dajihuang rang women chedi qingxing" 大饥荒让我们彻底清醒 [The Great Famine made us completely sober], *Caixin*, April 8, 2016. https://web.archive.org/web/20230110203621/https://jiangxue.blog.caixin.com/archives/144972.

Xiao, Muyi, Isabelle Qian, Tracy Wen Liu, and Chris Buckley. "How a Chinese Doctor Who Warned of Covid-19 Spent His Final Days." *New York Times*, October 6, 2022. https://www.nytimes.com/2022/10/06/world/asia/covid-china-doctor-li-wenliang.html?smid=nytcore-ios-share&referringSource=articleShare.

Yang, Lina 杨丽娜, and Zhao Jing 赵晶. "Xi Jinping: Zai fazhan zhongguo tese shehui zhuyi shijianzhong buduan faxian, chuangzao, qianjing" 习近平：在发展中国特色社会主义实践中不断发现、创造、前进 [Xi Jinping: Continue to discover, innovate, and progress in the process of developing socialist society with Chinese characteristics]. CPC News, January 6, 2013. https://web.archive.org/web/20221201210745/http://cpc.people.com.cn/n/2013/0106/c64094-20101215-2.html.

"Yangjiagou 'xinyuan' de 'jiuzhuren'—sha'anganning bianqu zhuming aiguo minzhu renshi ma xingmin jishi" 杨家沟"新院"的"旧主人"——陕甘宁边区著名爱国民主人士马醒民纪事 " [Yangjiagou "Xinyuan's" old owner: Shanganning district famous patriotic democrat Ma Xingmin memo], Zhongguo wenmin wang 中国人民网. Accessed May 20, 2022, https://web.archive.org/web/20221202184304/http://shx.wenming.cn/xwdt/201602/t20160226_3171394.htm.

Yang, Su. *Collective Killings in Rural China During the Cultural Revolution*. Cambridge: Cambridge University Press, 2011.

Yang, Xianhui. *The Woman from Shanghai*. New York: Anchor Books, 2010.

"Yan'an zhengfeng yundong" 延安整风运动 [Yan'an rectification campaign], *Baidu Baike*. Accessed January 10, 2023, https://web.archive.org/web/20221125202408/https://baike.baidu.com/item/%E5%BB%B6%E5%AE%89%E6%95%B4%E9%A3%8E%E8%BF%90%E5%8A%A8/4416458.

Yu, Luowen 遇罗文. "Jinwan ruyou baofengzhouyu—jinian jiaxiong Yu Luoke jiuyi sishi zhounian 今夜有如暴风骤雨——纪今夜有如暴风骤雨——纪念家兄遇罗克就义四十六周年" [Tonight like a hurricane: Commemorating the sixtieth anniversary of the martyrdom of my brother Yu Luoke]. Wanwei Blog, last modified March 15, 2016. https://

web.archive.org/web/20220707195956/https://blog.creaders.net/u/5568/201603/250396.html.

Zeng, Jinyan. "Jiabiangou Elegy: A Conversation with Ai Xiaoming." *Made in China Journal* (February 2019): 131–141. Translated by Isabella Zhao. https://press-files.anu.edu.au/downloads/press/n6874/pdf/jiabiangou_elegy.pdf.

Zeng, Jinyan. "The Genesis of Citizen Intelligentsia in Digital China: Ai Xiaoming's Practice of Identify and Activist." PhD diss., University of Hong Kong, 2017.

Zeng, Zhijun 曾芷筠. "Bei fengzhu de ren fanwaipian: jiangjun de nü'er" 被封住的人番外扁：将军的女儿 [The isolated person's other story: The general's daughter] *Mirror Media,* February 17, 2020. https://www.mirrormedia.mg/premium/20200217pol006.

Zhang, Danhua 张丹华. "Huang tudi shang de hongse jiyi" 黄土地上的红色记忆 [Red memories on the Loess Plateau]. *People's Daily*, March 23, 2022. https://web.archive.org/web/20230106212100/http://dangshi.people.com.cn/n1/2022/0323/c436975-32381640.html.

Zhang, Shihe (Laohu Miao). "zhuixun xinghuo zhi yi: Xiang Chenjian" 追寻星火之一：向承鉴 [Pursuing One of the Sparks: Xiang Chenjian]. YouTube Video, 35:29, April 17, 2016. https://www.youtube.com/watch?v=oDpADWHFCjo&list=PLoon9OuQeeDPMQjCxElkBO1otfgKTugpm&index=16&t=357s.

Zhang, Zhan 张展. "Wuhan Huozangchang de hongmingsheng 20200218 00455 武汉_火葬场深夜的轰鸣声 20200218 004553" [Explosions sounding in the middle of the night from the Wuhan Crematorium 20200218 00455]. YouTube Video, 2:23, February 17, 2020. https://www.youtube.com/watch?v=Co9WCmowMDo.

"Zhonggong dangshi zhuanjia Sima Lu 102sui niuyue shishi" 中共党史专家司马璐102岁纽约逝世 [Chinese Communist Party historian Sima Lu dies at 102 in New York]. *Voice of America,* March 30, 2021. https://www.voachinese.com/a/Sima-Lu-expert-ccp-history-passed-away-102/5832909.html.

Zhou Yuan 周原. *Xinbian hongweishi ziliao* 新编红卫兵资料 [A new collection of Red Guard publications. Part I, Newspapers]. Oakton, VA: Center for Chinese Research Materials, 1999. https://www.google.com/books/edition/New_collection_of_Red_Guard_publictions/gLwFwgEACAAJ?hl=enl.

Illustration Credits

Page 6: the Red Cliff (*Chibi*). Phongsaya Limpakhom, "The ancient battlefield of the red cliff", 2018, via Alamy.

Page 21: Ai Xiaoming, Sim Chi Yin, 2016.

Page 28: a still of Si Jicai from *Jiabiangou Elegy*. Ai Xiaoming, "*Jiagbiangou Elegy*," 2017.

Page 30: a still of a woman's back figure from *The Ditch*. Wang Bing, "*The Ditch*," 2010.

Page 32: a still of Zhang Suiqing from *Jiabiangou Elegy*. Ai Xiaoming, "*Jiabiangou Elegy*," 2017.

Page 45: Jiang Xue's grandfather's house. Jiang Xue, 2019.

Page 52: Jiang Xue's father's study. Jiang Xue, 2019.

Page 58: Jiang Xue. Sim Chi Yin, 2018.

Page 66: photo *Spark* magazine member Zhang Chunyuan, 1956.

Page 68: a group picture of four *Spark* magazine members on the campus of Tianshan Ganquan Agricultural School, left to right: Tan Chanxue, Sun Ziyun, Zhou Shanyou, Ding Hengwu, 1959.

Page 73: Lin Zhao, undated.

Page 75: cover page of *Spark* magazine, Issue I, undated.

Page 83: Zhang Chunyuan in jail, undated.

Page 87: Hu Jie's drawing of Lin Zhao. Hu Jie, "Lin Zhao Behind Bars," 2007.

Page 89: Copies of Zhang Chunyuan's hand-written notes Kaiping detention center, undated.

Page 91: Copy of a document titled "Guanyu hai'ou zhepian shi de yixie qingkuang" 关于海鸥这篇诗的一些情况 [Circumstances regarding the poem "Hai'ou"], undated.

Page 93: Black and white woodblock print. Hu Jie, "Let there be light #16," 2015.

Page 94: Hu Jie in his documentary *Searching for Lin Zhao's Soul.* dGenerate Films Collection, "Searching for Lin Zhao's Soul: Xun Zhao Lin Zhao De Ling Hun," 2004.

Page 142: Wang Xiaobo and Li Yinhe. Mark Leong, 1996.

Page 152: Tiger Temple (Zhang Shihe). Sim Chi Yin, 2018.

Page 159: Chen Hongguo at the reading room "Zhiwuzhi." Sim Chi Yin, 2018.

Page 165: Xiang Chengjian in an interview with Jiang Xue. Jiang Xue, 2016.

Page 171: Ai Xiaoming. Sim Chi Yin, 2016.

Page 203: a cartoon of Song Binbin's apology. BADIUCAO, "道歉 SO SORRY," 2014.

Page 217: Widow's Bridge, Sim Chi Yin, 2016.

Page 221: Tan Hecheng, Sim Chi Yin, 2016.

Page 225: Zhou Qun. Sim Chi Yin, 2016.

Page 238: Ai Xiaoming in protective gear. Ai Xiaoming, 2020.

Page 243: Ai Xiaoming in her apartment. Ai Xiaoming, 2020.

Page 264: destruction in Tibet during the Cultural Revolution. Tsering Woeser, "*Forbidden Memory,*" 2020.

Page 265: a woman wielding a hoe. Tsering Woeser, "*Forbidden Memory,*" 2020.

Page 266: Kashopa being struggled against. Tsering Woeser, "*Forbidden Memory,*" 2020.

Page 275: New Century Press book warehouse in Hong Kong. Bao Pu, 2022.

Page 277: Book cover of *My Life in Prison* by Jiang Qisheng, 2012.

Page 281: a river in the Zhongnan Mountains, Shaanxi. Ian Johnson, 2018.

Page 288: two boulders in the Zhongnan Mountains, Shaanxi. Ian Johnson, 2018.

Index

For the benefit of digital users, indexed terms that span two pages (e.g., 52–53) may, on occasion, appear on only one of those pages.

Locators in *italic* refer to photographs and illustrations.

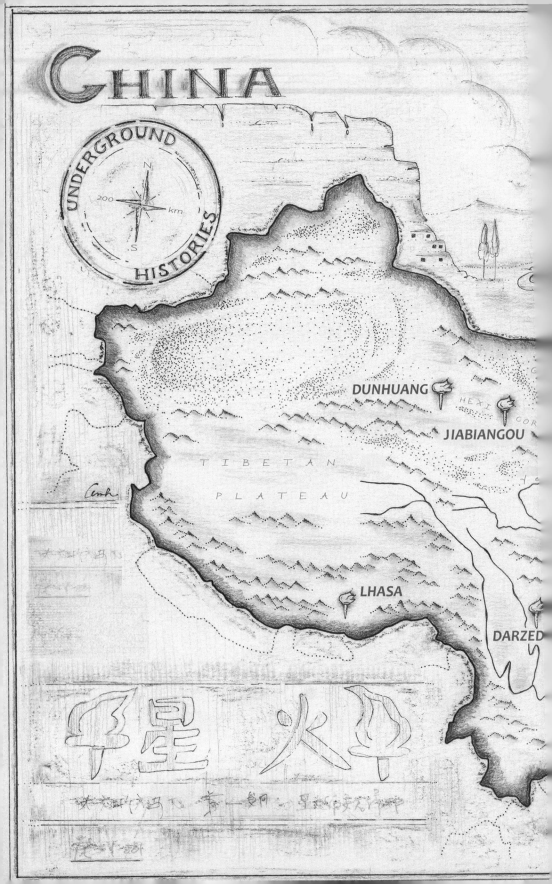